THE KURDISH PREDICAMENT IN IRAQ

A Political Analysis

Michael M. Gunter

St. Martin's Press
New York

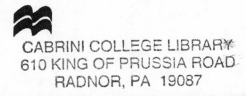

#3987503

ISBN 0-312-21896-6

Library of Congress Cataloging-in-Publication Data

Gunter, Michael M.
    The Kurdish predicament in Iraq : a political analysis / Michael
M. Gunter
        p. cm.
    Includes bibliographical references (p.) and index
    ISBN 0-312-21896-6
    1. Kurds—Iraq—Politics and government. 2. Kurds—Political
activity. 3. Iraq—Ethnic Relations. I. Title.
    DS70.8.K8G86   1999
    956.7'00491597—dc21   98-37355
                                                            CIP

Dedicated to the memory of my father

Dr. Martin J. Gunter

(1919–1993)

Iraqi Sector of Kurdistan

☐ Areas with a Kurdish majority

Km 0   25   50   75
Miles 0   25   50

©1999 Mehrdad Izady

Contents

Acknowledgments

It has been more than 20 years since I spent a year as a Senior Fulbright Lecturer in International Relations at the Middle East Technical University in Ankara, Turkey. The interest first kindled then continues to develop with this my fourth book about the Kurds. I hope my work will have a positive effect by enabling my readers to understand better what is involved in the Kurdish situation. I certainly have learned a great deal along the way and continue to do so daily.

In writing this present analysis, I owe a great debt of gratitude to the more than 50 people—Kurds and others involved with them—whom I have interviewed in the past few years. Most of them are listed in the selected bibliography under "Interviews and Correspondence." I assume fully the responsibility for any errors resulting from my misunderstanding. Hopefully, these mistakes are minimal.

I have also made copious use of various news services on the Internet such as those of the Washington Kurdish Institute and the Turkish Radio Hour (Haywood, California); news clippings such as those of the Institut Kurde de Paris; and the translation service provided by the Foreign Broadcast Information Service (FBIS) that is now online. These were all invaluable tools, but since their reproduction of the original sources sometimes lacked original page numbers, my notes are occasionally inconsistent here. Thus, I have given original page numbers of sources when I could obtain them, but I omitted them when they were not available. Apparently, this minor concession is necessary to use the much greater advantage of the Internet and news clipping services.

I would like to thank Mehrdad Izady for the excellent map of Iraqi Kurdistan he produced for me to use here. He also has been an important source of knowledge. In addition, I would like to thank for their invaluable help and advice Ibrahim Ahmad, Farhad Barzani, Masrour Barzani, Najmaldin Karim, Sheri Laizer, Latif Rashid, and Barham Salih. Michael Flamini, the Senior Editor for the Scholarly and Reference Division at St. Martin's Press, and his many editorial associates have been most helpful and supportive. Both the microcomputer staff and the library staff at Tennessee Technological University in Cookeville, Tennessee— where I have taught political science since 1972—have also been very helpful. In addition, I want to thank the *Middle East Journal, Middle East Quarterly,* and the *Journal of South Asian and Middle Eastern Studies* for permitting me to use some material of mine that appeared there earlier.

To use a consistent transliteration system for the names and terms from Kurdish, Arabic, Turkish, and Persian that appear in this study might have resulted in making some appear needlessly awkward or virtually unrecognizable. Therefore, I have used spellings that seemed most natural to me as an English-speaking reader. Similarly, only Kurdish words in the text not frequently used in English have been italicized. To simplify the text, I also have omitted certain diacritical marks. Although the purist might object, such procedures have not affected the meanings of these terms.

Finally, I want to recognize my wife Judy and our two children—now grown—Michael (and his wife Linda) and Heidi. This book is dedicated to my late father Dr. Martin J. Gunter (1919–1993). It is the sequel to my study *The Kurds of Iraq: Tragedy and Hope* (1992), which I dedicated to my late mother Larissa Kostenko Gunter (1917–1993). I miss them both very much.

Introduction

In May 1992, the Iraqi Kurds held democratic elections that in July of that year led to the formation of a Kurdistan Regional Government (KRG), in which power was equally shared by Massoud Barzani's Kurdistan Democratic Party (KDP) and Jalal Talabani's Patriotic Union of Kurdistan (PUK). During the same summer the Iraqi Kurds also played a major role in the creation of an umbrella Iraqi opposition organization, the Iraqi National Congress (INC). The professed goal of INC was the creation of a democratic and federal post-Saddam Iraq in which the cultural and national destiny of the Kurds at last would be solved.

What an incredible turnabout from Saddam's genocidal Anfal campaign against the Kurds at the end of the Iran-Iraq War in 1988, and, less than three years later, the tragic flight of some 1.5 million Kurdish refugees following the failure of their uprising at the end of the Gulf War in March 1991. Hope blossomed that the long running tragedy of the Kurds in Iraq might finally be ending!

More than six years have passed since those heady days in 1992 when I published my first book on the Kurds of Iraq.[1] Since the positive reception of my work,[2] a new analysis of the tragic descent into civil war and the many other events that have occurred subsequently now seems appropriate. It will serve as a sequel to my earlier study.

I met some of my sources when I traveled to Iraqi Kurdistan in August 1993 at the invitation of both Barzani's KDP and Talabani's PUK. Dr. Najmaldin O. Karim, a prominent Kurdish-

American independent and president of the Kurdish National Congress of North America, served as my guide. He not only seemed to know almost everybody and everything, but he also commanded everybody's respect.

During my trip to Iraqi Kurdistan I was able to meet and interview both Barzani and Talabani, as well as Hoshyar Zebari and Nechirvan Barzani of the KDP politburo and Omar Fatah and the late Rasul Mamand of the PUK politburo, among many others. In addition, I met Fuad Masum, the first prime minister of the KRG; his successor, Kosrat Rasul; and Ahmad Chalabi, the president of the executive council of INC and its effective leader. For three days I also watched as Barzani and Talabani sat together smiling and talking with each other at the KDP's eleventh congress. It appeared that these two old rivals had finally succeeded in bridging their differences for the sake of Kurdish unity. Jawar Namiq Salim, the speaker of the Kurdish parliament, even claimed that a special human rights committee in parliament was not necessary because the entire legislative body would now serve as a human rights committee!

How did everything go so wrong? In December 1997, I was invited by the PUK and the KDP to seek a few answers in London where some of their leaders either now live or frequently visit. I spent an entire day with 84-year-old Ibrahim Ahmad, the legendary rival of Mulla Mustafa Barzani during the 1950s and 60s and Jalal Talabani's father-in-law. I also interviewed Noshirwan Mustafa Amin, a sometime high-ranking member of the PUK politburo and prominent Kurdish scholar; Mahmud Othman (Osman/Uthman), a former close associate and later rival of the Barzanis; Wafiq al-Samarra'i, the former chief of Iraqi military intelligence who defected to the opposition in November 1994; Latif Rashid, a vice president of INC's executive council and brother-in-law of Jalal Talabani; Ahmad Chalabi, the head of INC; Lord Eric Avebury and Frank Baker, two British experts possessing a wealth of practical experience and knowledge in dealing with the Iraqi Kurds; and Muhammad Rasool Hawar, a prominent Kurdish scholar, among others. In March 1998, I had lengthy conversations in the Middle East with Abdullah (Apo) Ocalan, the reclusive leader of the *Partiya Karkaren Kurdistan* (PKK) or Kurdistan Workers Party. Over the past five years I also have had many fruitful conversations with Barham Salih, the representative of the PUK in the United States and a candidate member of its politburo. In addition, I have had opportunities to interview several members of the Barzani family both in the Middle East and the United States.

Since the past often serves as prologue, my present analysis will begin with a look at a study of the Iraqi Kurds written almost a century ago. Several Kurds I met in Kurdistan in 1993 told me I should read it.[3] Next I will look at the two main Kurdish leaders, Barzani and Talabani. Personal details, as distinguished from public facts, are difficult to come by in the traditional Kurdish world and can be very enlightening. Following this I will analyze the rise and fall of the Iraqi opposition that the United States first encouraged and then allowed to be rolled up by Saddam when he briefly entered Irbil at the end of August 1996 as Barzani's ally.

I then will analyze the tragic descent into civil war between the KDP and PUK since May 1994, an on-again, off-again struggle that has destroyed the KRG established with so much hope in July 1992. This will lead into an analysis of the resulting power vacuum that has sucked in such regional powers as Turkey, Iran, Syria, and Baghdad, as well as the United States, among others.

In my concluding chapter I will analyze the applicability of some of the recent general, theoretical writings on nationalism[4] for the Kurdish situation in particular. I will also attempt to draw some modest conclusions and make some recommendations for the future based on the patterns that have emerged from the recent past. My hope is that such an objective analysis will lead to a better understanding of the continuing Kurdish predicament in Iraqi Kurdistan.

1

The Past as Prologue

During my trip through Iraqi Kurdistan in August 1993, I was told, in reply to one of my numerous questions about the country and its inhabitants, to read the Wigrams' *Cradle of Mankind*.[1] Like most students of Kurdish studies, I had heard of this classic but never read it. Thus, my curiosity aroused, I acquired a copy of it upon my return and was, despite its occasional references to obscure events in Scottish history, amply rewarded. Almost a century after it was first written, *Cradle of Mankind* remains a fascinating introduction to the divisions that still haunt the Iraqi Kurds today and are the subject of this study.

Written by a British Christian missionary and his brother who lived and traveled through Kurdistan for ten years during the first decade of the twentieth century, *Cradle of Mankind* is a treasure trove of insights and stories despite the inherent biases its authors inevitably possessed. And although—its subtitle, *Life in Eastern Kurdistan,* notwithstanding—it was written as a paean to the Christian Assyrians who were ultimately decimated by the Muslims during World War I, the Wigrams' study has much to say about the Kurds.

In the preface to the first edition published in 1914, the Wigrams explained the title of their book: "the country . . . is the very *fons et origo* of our Indo-European ancestors. Its traditions connect it with the Garden of Eden, with Noah, and with Abraham" (p. vii). The second edition, which I read, was published in 1922 and simply added two new chapters "to bring the story of the Assyrian nation up to date" (p. vi). One of them was pathetically entitled "Our Smallest Ally."

Early in their narrative, the Wigrams noted that "one of the first impressions which besets a traveller in these parts is the reality of the curse of Babel" (p. 10). They counted "at least six [important languages]. Arabic is dominant on the plains; Syriac and Kurdish in the mountains; Armenian on the plateaus to the northward; and Greek in western Asia Minor. Turkish, except in Anatolia, is only the official language. . . . Naturally each of these main stems branches off into dialects by the score" (p. 10).

"The nationalities are as diverse as the languages, and are interwoven together in the most bewildering entanglement. . . . None of the component races can be trusted to govern the rest, and . . . all are so inextricably intermingled that it is impossible to parcel them out into distinct homogeneous States" (p. 11). Thus, although the Kurds "are a very ancient people" (p. 39n), they "have no national cohesion" (p. 35) and "a 'United Kurdistan' is a . . . Utopian conception" (p. 37).

The Kurds themselves were "uneducated . . . a term of much greater opprobrium than seems quite reasonable in a country where not one man in a hundred is able to read or write" (p. 40). The Wigrams explained that this "lack of education . . . is akin to that 'weakness in arithmetic' which caused the Irishman to be hanged. They [the Kurds] are apt to have more sheep in their villages than they can legitimately account for. They are a pastoral race, leaving agriculture almost exclusively to the Syrians and Yezidis; but we fear that their 'pastoral' ideals are hardly those of Corydon" (p. 40). Although "such doings are hardly criminal according to their own code of morals . . . we fear that yet darker deeds must sometimes be reckoned against them" (p. 40).

The Wigrams then compared the Kurds to various nefarious Scottish outlaws of the past and concluded that "the kindly gallows" would make the state "more gracious" (p. 40), "for if there is one chance in twenty of trouble ensuing, the Kurd does not raid" (p. 316). When the Jewish serf of one Kurdish agha (tribal chieftain or feudal landlord) was robbed by a rival agha, for example, the wronged agha "had a brilliant inspiration. . . . 'I'll go and rob his Jew myself!' That being the way the Kurdish mind works" (p. 318). It was "less risky . . . to raid your opponents' unarmed Christian villages, than his armed Kurdish ones" (p. 318) (Judaism and Christianity were linked in the Kurdish mind.)

Elsewhere, however, the Kurds were referred to as "good respectable brigands" (p. 321) who had "a sport-loving soul" (p. 229). The reader was also admonished that "it is the grossest injustice to judge the modern East by a twentieth-century standard. If you choose to go and live in medieval times (somewhere in the thirteenth century let us say), you must not complain if the people act in fashion reminiscent of that age" (pp. 321–22). "In Kurdistan you are not in the twentieth century, but . . . perhaps in the dark ages outright" (p. 191).

Further unfavorable Kurdish attributes included "their usual insolent confidence" (p. 223) and "a certain ruffianly swagger [that] is the truest hall-mark of a Kurd" (p. 113). Saladin was "the only Kurd whom history is able to mention with esteem" (p. 233). Humorous was "the saying that every Moslem, to be happy, requires at least four wives. A Persian because of her wit, and a Circassian because of her beauty; an Armenian to do the cookery and housework, and a Kurdish woman to thrash, as a wholesome example to the other three" (p. 211n).

The Kurds also had a reputation for toughness and hardiness. "The writer has known an instance of a Kurd, who was shot through the body in a tribal skirmish; after which he walked home, and observed to his wife, 'Beastly nuisance this: here is a brand-new shirt, and two holes in it; and it will want washing too!" (p. 169). A Syrian told the authors that "it is very difficult to poison a Kurd at all" (p. 174). This observation was made in elaboration upon the claim that for a medicine to have any effect it was necessary to "give three times the 'book dose' to an Assyrian, and five times the amount to a Kurd; for then you may produce some sort of effect" (p. 173).

Some individual Kurds, however, came out better in the Wigrams' estimation. Sheikh Abdul Salam of Barzan (c. 1882–c. 1915) was a case in point. The older brother of the legendary Mulla Mustafa Barzani (1903–1979) and thus an uncle of the current Barzani leader Massoud (born 1946), Abdul Salam II was only in his twenties when the Wigrams met him around 1910.

"Like most mountaineers he is of medium height, with a slight and active figure and a grave but pleasant face. . . . By his own immediate followers his commands are obeyed instantly and without question; and we have not the least doubt that had he ordered us to be shot, instead of entertaining us graciously, the sentence would have been executed unhesitatingly, Europeans though we were" (p. 143).

Unfortunately, the Turks executed Abdul Salam II during World War I for reputedly dealing with the Russian enemy. "He had been enticed down to Mosul by the Vali Haidar Beg and there secretly put to death" (p. 369), apparently, according to the Wigrams, in the spring of 1915. (At the end of the twentieth century, Massoud Barzani—the current leader of the Barzanis—continues his family's problematic relations with the Turks.)

The Wigrams used such descriptives for the sheikh as "merciful over-lord" (p. 138) and "tolerant" (p. 369), noting that he was also called " 'the Sheikh of the Christians,' because he treats his Christian vassals so well" (p. 153). They also pointed out that the sheikh "reaped the fruit of his good treatment of his villagers, for not a man, Christian or Moslem, ever dreamt of betraying him to his foes" (p. 139). He was "not only one of the most powerful but one of the most respectable of the mountain chieftains" (p. 136).

Unfortunately for subsequent Barzani-Christian relations, some of the earliest fighting between the Barzanis and the new Iraqi government established from the ruins of the Ottoman Empire after World War I occurred in the early 1930s when the government tried to settle some Assyrians on the hereditary Barzani land. And, of course, the main theme of the Wigrams concerned the often desperate struggles the Christian Assyrian minority had against their inveterate Kurdish foes.

In one place, for example, the authors compared the Assyrian Patriarch to the legendary Prester John, "while a very good imitation of the harpies that tormented Prester John are found in the Kurds that ravage the land" (p. 262). Indeed, most, but not all, of the Christian villages were "little better than serfs to the Kurds near whom they live" (p. 265).

The famous Bedr Khan, often mentioned as a precursor of modern Kurdish nationalists by other scholars,[2] "attacked these Christian tribes in 1845—and perpetrated a massacre so appalling that the years are dated from it to this day" (p. 279). Simko, another noted Kurdish nationalist of the early twentieth century, treacherously murdered his guest, the Assyrian leader Mar Shimun, at the end of World War I.

Foreign residents referred to the process of Kurds quartering themselves in Christian villages and gradually expropriating them as "the hermit crab Act" (p. 177). "If ever one sees a Kurdish village which has good fields, and signs of good cultivation, one can be sure that it was originally Christian, and that it has gone through this process" (p. 178). In this regard the Wigrams related "a weird belief but [one] . . . fully accepted on all hands" that a Kurd "does not himself expect to sleep quiet in his grave unless some Christian places a rag on it in token of forgiveness" (p. 319).

Today the Assyrian nation in Kurdistan has declined to maybe 60,000 people, while the Kurds themselves number well over 3,000,000.[3] Although isolated incidents continue even now, the Assyrian Democratic Movement became a member of the now defunct Iraqi Kurdistan Front in the early 1990s, and five Christians were chosen to sit in the Kurdistan parliament elected in May 1992. Ironically, the population ratio between the Kurds and Assyrians in Iraqi Kurdistan is reversed in the United States, where there are probably more than 200,000 Assyrians but no more than 20,000 Kurds.

Although seasoned travelers, the Wigrams owned to having "some misgiving" when entering "those formidable mountains where he has been promised enlightenment as to what 'real rough travelling' means" (p. 134). "Nothing that runs upon wheels can enter the Kurdistan highlands. And the 'heir of all the ages,' travelling there in A.D. 1900, finds himself no better off than his forerunners of B.C. 1100, whose amazed Great King recorded on slabs of imperishable granite the fact that 'I, Tiglath-Pileser, was obliged to go on foot!' " (p. 111).

The Wigrams found that "Barzan is rather larger than an average Kurdish village, but boasts no distinguishing feature to suggest its importance in the land" (p. 137). While most Kurdish aghas and chiefs were housed apart, "the Sheikh of Barzan 'dwells among his own people,' and his palace is just an agglomeration of several ordinary houses joined in one. It possesses no outer door at all (or none that we have ever discovered), and we entered it by the simple process of stepping on to the roof, and walking across to the summer reception room" (p. 137).

The sheikh "was dressed in a white fez and turban, white shirt and trousers, a black gown trimmed with red, and a green cloak over all. His retinue consisted of between thirty and forty retainers . . . distinguished by their red turbans, and positively festooned with bandoliers. Many of these fellows must have been carrying quite two hundred rounds of ball cartridge" (p. 143). The Wigrams noted that "all showed most obsequious deference towards their young chieftain; and it may give some adequate conception of the reverence which they entertain for him to record the fact that he himself, in his own proper person, is a *ziaret* or place of pilgrimage" (p. 143).

Their meal "consisted of bowls of whey, and of rice with pieces of chicken . . . all helping themselves out of the common dishes with wooden ladles and spoons. . . . To his own men the Sheikh spoke but rarely, though pleasantly and often smilingly; and they never seemed to speak to him unless they had been first addressed" (p. 145). (I myself partook of similar meals with Massoud Barzani and the hereditary leader of the Baradost tribe when I was in Kurdistan in 1993. Jalal Talabani, in comparison, was a more approachable dinner host.)

The Wigrams' conversation with the sheikh was through an interpreter. He "bewailed the universal lawlessness, which, he said . . . was as bad for Kurds as for Christians. . . . 'You have gone to India,' he protested, 'and you stay there, though you are not wanted. Why cannot you come to us who do want you? You would be welcomed everywhere here' " (p. 145). The Wigrams felt that "such feelings are well-nigh universal among all the more reputable chieftains. They would appreciate any strong Government, no matter of what nation or creed" (p. 145). The only ones who would disagree with this desire "are those who have merited hanging," but "we grant that this class would poll strong" (p. 145). Given the breakout of fratricidal fighting among the Iraqi Kurds since 1994, no doubt numerous members of this latter class still prevail.

Before departing, the sheikh of Barzan also consulted the Wigrams about his suffering eyes, a general malady common in those parts due to "dust and want of cleanliness, and aggravated by persistent neglect" (p. 146n). In this particular case, however, the patient turned out to be suffering from trachoma.

The Wigrams noted that "many of course desired medicine, for any Englishman is a doctor by hereditary right; and always carries with him good 'English salt,' which is quinine, as well as other drugs. So, 'distribute medicines manfully' is the rule for the traveller here, whether you chance to know anything about the trade or not. . . . And if you have not the ghost of a notion what the disease is, look doubly wise and administer something harmless and bitter. The nastier the drug, the more it will stimulate the faith of the sufferer, and that, after all, is the essential thing" (p. 173).

In sharp contrast to the sheikh of Barzan, the wandering Heriki Kurds resembled a "horde of human locusts" (p. 127) who "were regarded much in the light of an annual migration of wolves by all the villages on the road" (p. 159). "It is not a good thing for a village to lie in the track of the Heriki, for everything that is not too hot or too heavy they annex and carry away" (p. 127).

Ironically, "those *hostes humani generis* the Heriki Kurds" (p. 149), "if legend tells true . . . were Christians once" (p. 162). According to the "old Nestorian priests," the Herikis still carried the head of "one of the several saints George of Eastern legend. This is the palladium of their tribe, and is borne about in a chest" (p. 163).

Illustrating the lack of an adequate work ethic, the Wigrams told a story about their inability to get a pair of boots repaired in Akra over a period of three days. "Friday (it was explained) had been the Mohammedan Sabbath, and Saturday the Jewish, and Sunday the Christian; and no doubt a Bank Holiday on Monday was only averted by the fact of the boots being prematurely reclaimed. Tuesday, it may be added, is esteemed inauspicious by Christians, because on that day Judas Iscariot made his covenant with the chief priests. Wednesday is the Yezidi Sabbath" (p. 133).

The Wigrams incorrectly considered the Yezidis[4] not to be Kurds and claimed that " 'Devil worshippers' they are indeed" (p. 88). They referred to the Yezidi temple at Sheikh Adi as the "unhallowed Hoodoo House" (p. 106) and "this Domdaniel of Sorcery" (p. 97). The Yezidis, however, are Kurds who still follow an ancient and indigenous, pre-Islamic Kurdish religion. Among the angels they revere is *Malak Tawus* (the Peacock Angel), or Lucifer. Instead of being the prince of evil, however, he is an archangel possessed with extraordinary authority and power over mundane matters. To their credit, the Wigrams did note that the Yezidis had "a religion of Faith, and not of Works. They are under no obligation to make evil their good" (p. 88).

Additional observations regarding ancient Kurdish religions[5] concerned "that oldest faith of the land, the aboriginal tree-worship, [which] still lingers in the villages; and indeed is only despised by the townsfolk when the foreigner is within hearing. . . . A rag from the garments of any sufferer from any disease has only to be tied on to one of its branches to secure relief infallibly" (p. 205).

The Wigrams journeyed through Kurdistan during the final years of the Ottoman Empire, observing that "the Turk has the misfortune to be an anachronism in power. His present methods were those of every European Government some five hundred years ago; but European consciences have developed in the interval, and his has not" (p. 260). Everywhere they saw "that cancer of Ottoman rule—the chronic corruption of the Administration" (p. 38).

Yet even here there was a rationale: "What is an official to do, whose salary, is in the first place, wholly inadequate; and in the second, not paid?" (p. 77). "Reform is anathema to the Turk, for he knows (even if he cannot put the matter into words) that reform means subjection of the Turk to the *rayat* [Christian subjects]" (p. 244). And even the attempted reforms fell short because "the Turk is quite satisfied as soon as he gets veneered" (p. 2).

Although they wrote before the terrible Armenian massacres that occurred during World War I (and that are referred to by many as the "Armenian Genocide"[6]), the Wigrams did devote an entire chapter to earlier, seminal events. Indeed, early in their manuscript, they wrote that the Armenian massacres of 1895 in Diyarbakir were "undoubtedly prompted by the Government of Constantinople; but their agents were the fanatical Kurds . . . who flocked in eagerly from the surrounding villages to take a hand in the work of slaughter and to share in the plunder which followed" (p. 35).

The Armenian question, of course, is beyond the scope of the present study. Interestingly, however, today's PKK (Kurdish guerrillas fighting for independence from Turkey since 1984) have been reported hiding out in the same Tendurek mountain in Turkey once used by the Armenian *Tashnak* revolutionaries.

Changes, of course, have occurred, and it is upon them that hopes have been built for an end to the chaotic divisions that continue to plague the Kurds. Today, for example, there is a cadre of college-educated people, many with degrees from prestigious foreign universities. Two universities—or at least their physical plants—exist in the region's two large cities, Irbil and Sulaymaniya.[7] When I visited them in 1993, both were sorely in need of books and equipment. There also is now a basic infrastructure of roads in many areas, although at one point I had to get out and help push our Land Rover through the then shallow Greater Zab River. What happens along that road when the river rises in the spring is anybody's guess. In addition, there is now electricity available in many areas, when Saddam is not cutting off the power or their own infighting is not sabotaging it.

Less positively in the way of change is the decline or even disappearance of such minorities as the Jews.[8] But probably the most important change—one for the better—is a new awareness of the outside world and the perception among the population, both leaders and followers, that the Kurds both are part of and being influenced by it. Equally important is the increasing "Kurdification" of the local administrations and schools since 1991. Nevertheless, many of the divisions observed by the Wigrams at the dawn of the twentieth century remain at the century's end.

2

Barzani and Talabani

Although long-term economic, political, and social trends
have certainly played their important roles, perhaps more
so than in many other nations, the personalities of Barzani and
Talabani have been absolutely crucial to the development of the
Iraqi Kurdish predicament. For a variety of reasons, however,
there is very little tradition of biographical writing among the
Kurds.[1] This holds true for accounts of the life of Mulla Mustafa
Barzani (1903–1979) himself. David Korn, a well-connected
American ambassador and author, reportedly gave up trying to
write a biography of Mulla Mustafa because he discovered cer-
tain unflattering deeds in the great man's life.[2]

A biographical chapter dealing with the rival partners Massoud Barzani and Jalal Talabani, therefore, should prove especially valuable not only for the personal details not otherwise
available, but, even more important, for better understanding
the context of the Iraqi Kurdish predicament with which their
names at times seem almost synonymous.

SOURCES

In most cases I have gathered my biographical information over
the years from interviewing members of the Barzani and Talabani

families. I also have interviewed close associates and other knowledgeable Kurds and observers. Ayoub Barzani, a scion of the family living in Geneva, Switzerland, gave me a number of details about Mulla Mustafa and his brothers, parents, and ancestors that dovetailed closely with the fascinating details listed by the Wigrams.[3]

Masrour Barzani, the son of the current family head Massoud Barzani, and Farhad Barzani, the son of Loqman Barzani who was a son of Mulla Mustafa, gave me details concerning the present generations. I also spoke with Massoud himself and his heir apparent, Nechirvan Barzani, the son of Massoud's late half-brother Idris Barzani (1944–1987). Hoshyar Zebari, Massoud's young uncle and a high-ranking member of the Barzani-led Kurdistan Democratic Party (KDP), also provided useful family specifics.

For the more traditional Barzanis, these details are not commonly known. Indeed, not even otherwise knowledgeable KDP representatives I interviewed in London had any idea what Massoud's wife's name was, or for that matter how many wives he had. When they checked at my request, they came up with the name "Ruqya," which turned out to be incorrect. Later, Massoud's eldest son, Masrour, assured me that his father had only one wife and that his mother's name was "Jeyra." I believe that this is correct, but it is news to practically every Kurd I have ever asked.

It should be noted at this juncture, incidentally, that—as with other Middle Easterners—Kurds use first names publicly more so than do Westerners. Often, however, Kurds will use the term "Kak" before the first name of a man to render a certain degree of formality and respect, much as Americans will use the term "Mister" before a surname. Thus, among Kurds I often have heard Massoud Barzani referred to as "Kak Massoud." (I am sometimes called "Mr. Michael," instead of "Mr. Gunter.") Jalal Talabani, however, is universally known as "Mam [Uncle] Jalal."

Accordingly, in this chapter particularly I have sometimes used just first names when using surnames would be redundant or even confusing given how many Barzanis there are, for example. By occasionally employing first names I am in no way implying disrespect. Rather I am using speech patterns Kurds themselves have frequently used when speaking to me.

For details about the Talabani family and Mam Jalal himself, I am indebted to a number of his family members. This includes "Mamusta" [my teacher] Ibrahim Ahmad (born 1914)—Mam Jalal's father-in-law and political mentor; Ahmad's wife Galawez (Mam Jalal's mother-in-law); their daughter Shanaz (the younger sister of Mam Jalal's wife, Hero) and Shanaz's husband, Latif Rashid; Sabah Sabir, another Ahmad son-in-law; Sheikh Jengi (born 1928), Mam Jalal's elder half brother; Qubad Talabani (born 1977), Mam Jalal's largely English-raised son; and Dr. Nouri Talabany, a distant cousin. I also have had the opportunity to speak with Mam Jalal himself and his wife, Hero.

In addition, a number of other prominent Kurds who know Mam Jalal well filled in further details. This included Dr. Mahmud Othman (Osman) (born 1938)—once Mulla Mustafa's top lieutenant and personal physician; Noshirwan Mustafa Amin (born 1943), for many years a top assistant of Mam Jalal; Barham Salih, Mam Jalal's current representative in the United States and a candidate member of the PUK politburo; and Dr. Najmaldin O. Karim, the president of the Kurdish National Congress of North America and a physician to Mulla Mustafa Barzani in his later years.

Others included Ahmad Chalabi, the head of the Iraqi opposition Iraqi National Congress (INC); Lord Eric Avebury, a prominent British activist for Kurdish human rights; Frank Baker, an official in the British foreign office; Kamran Karadaghi, a senior Kurdish journalist for the prominent Arabic-language newspaper *Al-Hayat;* Hazhir Teimourian, a prominent Kurdish journalist currently working for *The European;* Sami Shorish, an independent Kurdish journalist; Muhammad Rasool Hawar, an elderly Kurdish scholar presently living in London; Homer Dizeyee, a Kurdish radio broadcaster currently working for the Voice of America in Washington, D.C., and also a well-known singer; and General Wafiq al-Samarra'i, the former Iraqi military intelligence chief who defected to the Iraqi opposition in November 1994. All of these people, of course, knew a great deal about the Barzanis.

Given this list of my biographic sources, I have in most instances dispensed with specific citations in the following analysis. This will make my discussion flow more smoothly and eliminate pedantic and redundant documentation. In all my details, however, I do have a specific reference either on tape and/or in my interview notes. The errors that have inevitably crept into the following analysis should be few, but when they do occur they are my fault for failing to properly understand what I was being told.

THE BARZANIS

Barzan, the eponymous home of the Barzanis, is an old, remote, mountainous, and economically marginal village located on the northern side of the Greater Zab River in the upper regions of Iraqi Kurdistan. The word "Barzan" itself possibly derives from the words for "high place" or "learned brother," but this is simply conjecture. The Wigrams set Barzan amid "the great snow peaks of the Hakkiari Oberland—the *rigidus Niphates* of Horace; the spot where (according to Milton) Satan first planted his feet when he alighted on the new-made world."[4]

Reliable data about the earliest sheikhs of Barzan are obscure and contradictory.[5] Probably sometime in the 1840s, possibly to counter the rapidly rising influence of the Zebari tribe, the Naqshbandi sheikh Seyyid Taha of Nehri (some say the celebrated Naqshbandi mystic Maulana Khalid himself, but this seems highly unlikely given his death c. 1826) reputedly sent his disciple Sheikh Abdul Rehman (also known as Tacedin, an Arabic honorific that means "Crown of religion") to Barzan. Sheikh Abdul Rehman thus became the first Barzani; his arrival set off a lengthy struggle between the Zebaris and the Barzanis that continued well into the twentieth century.[6] Abdul Salam I succeeded Abdul Rehman as sheikh of Barzan for some 30 years, followed by his son Muhammad (died 1902).

Although the Barzanis' power was originally founded on their religious authority as Naqshbandi sheikhs, they also became noted for their fighting abilities and in time developed into the equivalent of a tribe that still wears a distinctive turban with red stripes. Some Barzani sheikhs also gained a reputation for their religious eccentricity. The blind obedience of their followers even earned them a reputation among some as *diwana* (madmen).[7]

Their village Barzan served as a sort of utopian society in which refugees were welcomed. Social anthropologist Martin van Bruinessen even argued that "this contributed to its becoming a centre of Kurdish nationalism."[8] As noted in chapter 1, the

sheikh of Barzan during the early years of the twentieth century
(Abdul Salam II, who was Sheikh Muhammad's son) was also
called the "Sheikh of the Christians" because he treated his
Christian subjects so well.

When the Wigrams visited Barzan early in the twentieth century, they found it "larger than an average Kurdish village, but
boast[ing] no distinguishing feature to suggest its importance in
the land. . . . The Sheikh of Barzan 'dwells among his own people,' and his palace is just an agglomeration of several ordinary
houses joined in one."[9] The Wigrams noted, however, that "all
showed most obsequious deference towards their young chieftain," and "to his own men the Sheikh spoke but rarely, though
pleasantly and often smilingly; and they never seemed to speak
to him unless they had been first addressed."[10] The sheikh's English visitors also noted that his followers "believe in his hereditary sanctity. . . . He himself, in his own proper person, is a *ziaret*
or place of pilgrimage."[11]

Historian David McDowall, however, has pointed out how
Sheikh Abdul Salam II's "ambitions were more than those of a
mere mountain chief and implied association with ethnic nationalists in Istanbul."[12] The sheikh, for example, organized a petition
for the five administrative districts of the Bahdinan area in
which he lived that demanded that Kurdish be adopted for official and educational purposes, that Kurdish-speaking officials be
appointed, and that the Shafite school of Islamic jurisprudence
prevalent among the Kurds (as distinguished from the Hanefite
school prevalent among the Turks) be adopted. When the sheikh
also appeared to be flirting with the Russians, the Ottoman officials finally apprehended and hanged him in 1914.[13]

Abdul Salam II was succeeded by his younger brother,
Sheikh Ahmad Barzani (1884–1969). The last Barzani to bear the
title of "Sheikh of Barzan," Sheikh Ahmad earned a reputation
among some for religious fanaticism. Indeed, historian Stephen
H. Longrigg went so far as to call him a "half-witted Dere Bey" for
reputedly claiming a sort of semidivine status.[14]

The present Barzani generation denies that their forebears
ever claimed any type of semidivine status. Indeed, Masrour
Barzani told me that his great uncle Sheikh Ahmad refused the
government's order to register his followers' land under his
name for tax purposes because it would have made his heirs
believe the land belonged to them, not his followers.

Mulla Mustafa

In time, Ahmad was eclipsed by his younger brother Mulla Mustafa Barzani, who was born on March 14, 1903. (Other brothers apparently included Muhammad Saddiq and Babu Muhammad.) Indeed, Mulla Mustafa became the most famous Kurdish leader of the twentieth century because of his military exploits during his long and fascinating career. Since these events are so well known, however, it will serve no useful purpose to reiterate them here.[15] Suffice it to conclude that, ironically, the most famous Kurdish nationalist of the twentieth century—the Kurdish leader who not only inspired the Kurds of Iraq, but also of Turkey, Iran, and Syria—in some important ways never actually exceeded the bounds of tribal chieftain. Such a situation is only understandable given the stunted development of Kurdish nationalism. It not only symbolizes an important part of the current Kurdish predicament, but it also helps explain why the Kurdish nation remains divided. The present Barzani generation questions this interpretation of Mulla Mustafa, however, asking how he could have brought all the ranks of Kurdish people from different tribes, cities, and regions under his leadership if he had merely been tribal in his outlook.

It appears that Mulla Mustafa had three wives. The first, Mahbob, was a member of the Barzani tribe. She bore him three sons: Ubaidallah (1927–1980), Loqman (1930–1980), and Sabir (1947–1983). All three were apparently executed by Saddam Hussein. Ironically, Ubaidallah, the eldest, had turned against his father and was serving in Saddam's government. He supposedly was killed because of a spontaneous insult he hurled at Saddam concerning Saddam's lowly birth and his questioning of Saddam's war against Iran. Loqman, a leading military lieutenant of his father and living in Baghdad at the time, simply disappeared at the beginning of the Iran-Iraq War in 1980, probably because of his attempt to discover what had happened to his brother, Ubaidallah. Sabir apparently was killed along with some 8,000 other Barzani men whom Saddam, in his own words, sent "to hell"[16] in 1983 in revenge for the Barzanis' support of Iran. Mahbob also had at least one daughter, Aklima.

A second wife named Hafsa was also from the Barzani tribe. She had one son, Idris (1944–1987), and at least two daughters, Kamili and Zekiya. After Mulla Mustafa's defeat in 1975, Idris and

Massoud became co-leaders of the revamped Kurdistan Democratic Party (KDP) until Idris suddenly died of a heart attack,
leaving Massoud as the undisputed leader of the family and
party. Idris's son, Nechirvan Idris, has become an important
member of the KDP politburo and is often considered Massoud's
heir apparent.

Mulla Mustafa's third wife, Hamayl, was the daughter of
Mahmoud Agha, the leader of his hereditary enemy, the Zebari
tribe. He apparently married her for political reasons, a tactic
often used among the Kurds. Members of the present Barzani
generation point out, however, that not all Zebaris were hostile
to the Barzanis and maintain that Mulla Mustafa's marriage to
Hamayl was not for political reasons.

Hamayl, who came to wield considerable power behind the
scenes, bore the senior Barzani six sons: Massoud (born 1946),
the current leader of the family and president of the KDP; Dilshad, the current KDP representative in Germany; Nihad; Sehad;
Sedad; and Wejih, the youngest. The latter four bothers work in
what is termed the KDP's Bureau of the President as Massoud's
assistants. Hamayl also had at least two daughters.

As a result of such plural marriages, generations sometimes
seem mixed up to the Western observer. Uncles and nephews
can be practically the same age, while (half) brothers can be sep-
arated by 20 or even 30 years of age. In addition, arranged marriages between scions of prominent families lead to relations
between prominent rival families.

Reminiscing many years later, Ibrahim Ahmad—who as
leader of the KDP politburo from approximately 1953–1964 was
a long-time rival of Mulla Mustafa—told me that his (Ahmad's)
biggest mistake was helping to bring Barzani back from exile in
the Soviet Union after General Abdul Karim Kassem overthrew
the Iraqi monarchy in July 1958. Ahmad thought that Barzani's
name would be important for the success of the Kurdish revolution. But when Ahmad first saw Barzani again in Prague, he knew
Mulla Mustafa was not the leader Kurdish nationalism needed.

Although an effective military leader, Barzani's ultimate goal
seemed, to Ahmad at least, to be merely furthing his own personal and tribal leadership. The so-called Red Mullah (because
of his long sojourn in the Soviet Union from 1947 until 1958) was
actually a traditional Kurdish tribal leader who only dimly perceived a broader Kurdish nation. Indeed, even Ubaidallah, Mulla

Mustafa's eldest son, charged that his father had not accepted the March Manifesto of 1970 that actually granted the Kurds many of their demands, because "his [Mulla Mustafa's] acceptance of the law (autonomy) will take everything from him, and he wants to remain the absolute ruler."[17]

The present Barzani generation counters that "regardless what he [Ibrahim Ahmad] says, his [Ahmad's] greatest mistake was to underestimate [Mulla Mustafa] Barzani's power and popularity." In reference to Ahmad's helping Mulla Mustafa to return to Iraq in 1958, the Barzanis add that Ahmad "never had the power to send Barzani to or bring him back from somewhere," and they conclude that "Ahmad's hatred still has not vanished, and even on the edge of his grave is incapable of putting his hate aside." As for who was or was not a true Kurdish nationalist, the present Barzani generation faults Ibrahim Ahmad: "Going to Baghdad and Tehran for assistance to weaken Barzani's forces at various times while the Kurdish movement needed unity the most has proven his [Ahmad's] thoughts and beliefs towards Kurdish nationalism a long time ago."

Massoud

Massoud Barzani has clearly been molded by his family's heroic, but at times tragic past. The current leader of the Barzani family and president of the KDP was born in Mahabad, Iran, on August 16, 1946, the same day his father and others founded the KDP. Until his father, Mulla Mustafa, returned from the Soviet Union in 1958, Massoud lived with his wealthy grandfather, a Zebari whom some called a *josh*. (*Josh* means "little donkey" and is a derisive term Kurdish nationalists use for Kurds who support Baghdad. Given their complex vulnerable position, over the years both Barzani and Talabani at times have been accused of being *josh*.)

The political situation forced Massoud to complete his high school studies privately. From 1976–1979, Massoud lived in the United States with his exiled father, Mulla Mustafa. With the fall of the shah of Iran, Massoud returned to Iran, arriving on March 3, 1979, the very day his father died in Washington, D.C. These early years probably predisposed Massoud to take a more cautious position toward the Iraqi government, while assuming that privilege and wealth were his rightful inheritance, as well as burdens that imposed duties toward his people. His early years also contributed to his inherent conservatism.

While Hero Talabani, the wife of Jalal Talabani, is a public personality in her own right, sitting as a member of the parliament of the Kurdistan Regional Government, few even know the name of Massoud's wife. As a member of a traditional, conservative Kurdish family, Massoud's wife does not take any public role. In August 1993, for example, I had dinner with Jalal and Hero Talabani in their Irbil home. Massoud and his wife lived nearby. Hero told me that although Massoud had often visited the Talabani home and, therefore, of course, knew her—she had *never* even met Massoud's wife. I thought this said miles about the differences between the two leaders.

Of course, it is not as simple as traditional versus modern. The present Barzani generation points out—quite correctly concerning Massoud's wife for example—"that it is a personal choice and every person should be given the opportunity to live any life style they chose." Although Massoud clearly inherited his position while Talabani earned his, some of the current Barzani generation and their associates are well educated and move very comfortably in Western circles. Massoud's eldest son, Masrour, for example, is a graduate of American University in Washington, D.C., and speaks excellent English.[18] Masrour's older cousin Ferhad also graduated from an American university and is currently the KDP representative in the United States. Hoshyar Zebari, Massoud's uncle and close political associate, graduated from a British university and also speaks excellent English. As the KDP foreign affairs representative, Zebari is very comfortable moving in cosmopolitan circles.

At times Massoud himself doffs his traditional Kurdish costume for Western garb. Although he uses English translators while Talabani is quite comfortable speaking the language himself, Massoud, unlike his father Mulla Mustafa, clearly understands English. On occasion I have watched Massoud correct his translator while giving an interview. Using a translator gives Massoud more time to think about and craft his replies, while the more voluble Talabani sometimes ends up saying more than he should.

In being more deliberate than Talabani, Massoud is not necessarily less capable. Sometimes being more methodical helps one make fewer mistakes. Talabani has at times acted too precipitously and paid the price. By taking vague U.S. promises of support on their face value, for example, Jalal, to his grief, apparently believed that the United States would not allow Saddam to aid Barzani in August 1996. (See chapter 4.)

Admirers such as Jonathan Randal, the senior foreign correspondent for the *Washington Post,* consider Massoud "that most self-contained and gentlemanly of Kurds."[19] Randal explains Massoud's temporary alliance with Saddam in August-September 1996 by arguing that Massoud had "never forgotten Kissinger's treachery in 1975, had never totally recovered from the humiliation of his years of enforced exile, which he blamed on the United States . . . [and] never stopped worrying about American constancy."[20] Specifically citing the events of 1975 and 1991, Massoud himself recently explained: "We have had bitter experience with the U.S. government. . . . In 1975 . . . it changed its alliances purely in its own interest at the expense of our people's suffering and plight. . . . Their positions during the 1991 uprising were ambiguous and deceitful."[21]

As a result, in 1995, when the opposition Iraqi National Congress (INC) was attempting an offensive against Baghdad, Barzani was more hesitant to join in than Talabani because he simply did not trust that promised U.S. support would be forthcoming. Again Massoud's careful, less trustful attitude toward the U.S. government was probably a product of his and his father's earlier experiences, and was for the most part sound. By its actions over the years the United States has demonstrated that it had no intention of assisting the Kurds except to give humanitarian aid.

One might also speculate that Massoud's more circumspect attitude toward *Kurdayeti* (Kurdish nationalism) was influenced by his long exile in Iran (1975–91), a retreat at times broken by a trip to the United States in the late 1970s to visit his ailing father and, on various other occasions, to make forays into Iraqi Kurdistan to join his forces. Massoud only returned to Iraqi Kurdistan permanently following the Kurdish uprising in March 1991. Talabani, on the other hand, returned to Iraqi Kurdistan in 1977, although he again was forced to flee near the end of the Iran-Iraq War in 1988. Like Massoud, Jalal then returned once more in March 1991.

Massoud, however, has no monopoly on flirting with Baghdad. Indeed, even many of Talabani's friends claim that his biggest mistake was cooperating with the Baathists in the 1960s, while at the same time too uncompromisingly opposing Mulla Mustafa. Talabani's supporters add, however, that today's Baathists are much worse than their predecessors of the 1960s.

Massoud has been described as a defensive man, not an initiative taker. Given the disasters his family encountered in the past and the future's lurking dangers, Massoud looks upon the status quo as good for him and his family. As long as the present situation continues, for example, he will continue to pocket up to what his Kurdish adversaries claim is $1 million per day from the customs collected at the Habur border crossing with Turkey. He sees no reason to change this situation without ironclad guarantees that are, of course, unlikely to be forthcoming.

This has led to accusations of monumental corruption among the Barzanis involving millions being salted away in foreign banks as well as new family mansions being built in the United States. The present Barzani generation denies these corruption charges and argues that "whatever money is collected is well recorded and a team of the Kurdistan Regional Government (KRG) is responsible for collecting and delivering it to the central bank. There are no foreign bank accounts and not even a single apartment is being built or bought." The Barzanis further argue that "current construction in Kurdistan, improvement of the general standard of living, and a relative economic stability in areas controlled by the KDP are substantial proofs of how the money is spent." Finally, the Barzanis ask what the PUK does with the customs it collects from its border crossing with Iran.

The KDP leader has also been criticized for extravagantly traveling around his domain in convoys of more than 25 Toyota Land Cruisers, while his own people are suffering. The Barzanis explain that these so-called convoys are simply necessary security vehicles for Massoud when he travels.

When his enemies denounce him as a tribal, feudal man, they mean that Massoud does not distinguish between his own family's interests and those of the Kurdish people as a whole. Although others conclude that the corruption charges are exaggerated, it is clear that Talabani's attitudes concerning finances are more discrete and that he certainly does not possess as much personal wealth as his rival.

Finally, Massoud lacks the global vision of Jalal. Lord Eric Avebury, for example, related how Talabani asked him about the new French president, Jacques Chirac. Avebury, who also knew Massoud well, added that he could not imagine Barzani inquiring about the same question. Massoud thinks introspectively about only his own region, while Jalal is a man of much wider interests.

TALABANI

Talabani's life is a mirror on Kurdish and Middle Eastern political history over the past 40 years. During his long and eventful career, he has played a major role in everything that has happened to the Kurds. As a young man in 1963, he twice personally negotiated with Egypt's Gamal Abdul Nasser over the future of the Kurds in the Arab world. Since then, Talabani has dealt with virtually every major figure who bestrode the Middle Eastern scene, as well as with the leaders of many of the major world powers. Although he has long held a reputation as being mercurial and too clever for his own good, Talabani's championship of Kurdish nationalism in a world that has given it little, if any, recognition has always been his main guiding principle. As Mahmud Othman, a longtime political rival, concluded in assessing Talabani's seeming lack of ultimate success, "even a genius would not have won for the Kurds given their very negative geopolitical situation."

Jalal Talabani was born in 1933 in Kelkan, a village on the shores of Lake Dokan. Nearby is the middle-sized city of Koy Sanjaq, which is not far from such main cities in the Sorani area as Sulaymaniya and Kirkuk, the latter of which has been described as the main city of the Talabanis. The Talabani family itself goes back at least some 300 years, and there is actually a small village between Sulaymaniya and Kirkuk called Talaban. The origin of the name Talabani is obscure, although Ibrahim Ahmad speculated that it might have originally meant sour hill. Sheikh Jengi, Jalal's older half-brother (they share the same mother) speculated that the family name might have something to do with a word for leaf or tree. It definitely does *not* come from the Arabic word for student, for which the present-day Talabans in Afghanistan are named.

The Talabani sheikhs[22] were known for keeping a *tekiye* or Qadiri lodge where relatives and dependents could meet and hold their rituals. Originally based on their religious authority, in time the Talabanis' power also grew to include military influence. Like the Barzanis, though not a tribe technically, the Talabanis became the functional equivalent of one. Thus, while Jalal rose to prominence as a secular leader, his familial connections no doubt helped in his earlier years.

Jalal's mother Hadija died sometime around 1965, but his father, Sheikh Housan Aldin, lived to see the uprising of 1991. He died in 1993 after being given the wrong medicine when he was ill. In addition to his half-brother—who bears a striking facial resemblance to him but is not as heavy—Jalal also had another brother, Muhammad Salih. This other brother and his two daughters (Hero and Nazdar) were apparently killed by government forces in 1984.

Jalal married Hero Ahmad, the daughter of his political mentor Ibrahim Ahmad, sometime in the late 1960s. As mentioned above, Hero has played an important political role in her own right. Their two sons, Bafel, a physical education instructor, and Qubad, who is studying automotive mechanics, were largely raised by their grandparents in the United Kingdom and have played no political role. (This, of course, is in marked contrast to the Barzani family.) Mukarram Talabani, a distant member of the family, was a former member of the Iraqi Communist Party (ICP), an Iraqi cabinet member, and currently represents Baghdad when it seeks to initiate negotiations with the Kurds. Dr. Nouri Talabany, a distant cousin, is a lawyer and human rights activist living in London.

As indicated above, Jalal Talabani is almost universally known among the Kurds as Mam [Uncle] Jalal. There are at least two stories I was told about the origin of this name. One is that he was given it while young in memory of an admired maternal uncle who had recently died. The other story is that even as a young boy, Jalal took a very serious attitude, spoke well, and was accordingly given a name of distinction. The name "Mam," however, is far from unique in Kurdish society.

Important Events

When he was about five years old, young Jalal moved from Kelkan to Koy Sanjaq where he completed grade and intermediate school. From here he moved on to Irbil and Kirkuk where he finished high school with an impressive 90 percent average. He was not permitted to enter medical school, however, because of his political beliefs and activities.

Indeed, Mam Jalal was apparently born with a passion for politics. To a large extent his public life has always been his private life. In 1946, when he was only 13 years old and still in the sixth grade, he formed a secret student group called the KDP-Education Promotion Society and became its first secretary. The following year he became a formal member of the KDP. In 1948, while in intermediate school, he became the leader of the student society and a member of the first Iraqi student congress held in Baghdad. In 1949, Jalal became a member of the KDP's local committee in Koy Sanjaq. He held a similar position when he moved to Irbil. During the KDP's secret second party congress held in Baghdad in 1951, he was elected to the party's central committee, but he voluntarily resigned in favor of an older lawyer who had just been released from prison.

In 1953, Mam Jalal was admitted into the Baghdad law school, but after three years of study he was forced to drop out and go into hiding because of his political activities. During these years as a law student, Jalal became a member of the local KDP committee in Baghdad and, in January 1953, a member of the party's central committee. (He kept this latter post in the united KDP until 1964 and in the Ahmad-led KDP politburo faction of the KDP until 1970.) In February 1953, he secretly helped to establish the Kurdistan Student Union-Iraq and became its secretary-general.

Following the revolution of July 14, 1958, Talabani was allowed to reenter law school, finally graduating in 1959. Given his active political career, however, he never actually practiced law. He did, however, serve a compulsory term in the Iraqi army reserve upon graduating. In this capacity he was enrolled in the artillery division for three months, trained on Russian T54 tanks, and served as a commander of a garrison tank unit.

Talabani left Iraq for the first time in 1955 to participate in the World Student and Youth Congress held in Poland and from there traveled with an Iraqi youth group to Moscow and China. In the summer of 1957, he again visited Moscow—ostensibly to represent the Kurdish youth in a festival, but actually to meet Mulla Mustafa Barzani for the first time. In 1958, he also became the editor of *Kurdistan,* a Kurdish newspaper that became a standby for the KDP's organ, *Khebat.* For the next three years, in addition to his party activities, he worked as a journalist. He became a member of the administration committee of the Iraqi Journalist Union in 1959 and headed the Iraqi journalists' delegation to Bulgaria in 1960. (Much later in life, Mam Jalal told friends that if he were not a politician he would choose to be a journalist.)

Early in their relationship, Mulla Mustafa (according to both Ibrahim Ahmad and Noshirwan Mustafa Amin) wrote that he loved Mam Jalal as a son. Because of the struggle that began between Mulla Mustafa and the KDP's secretary-general Ibrahim Ahmad after Barzani's return to Iraq in 1958, however, Mam Jalal and Ahmad were suspended from the politburo for a brief time early in 1959, only to be reinstated by the year's end. Thus began Talabani's off-again, on-again struggle against Barzani. During the early 1960s, for example, while in Barzani's good graces, Talabani played a prominent military role in the armed struggle that began against the government in 1961. In time, however, Mulla Mustafa came to characterize Talabani as "an agent for everybody."[23]

In February and again in May 1963, Mam Jalal met Egypt's leader, Gamal Abdul Nasser, in Egypt. Nasser seemed supportive of some of the Kurdish goals, probably because of his fledgling conflict with the Baathists for supremacy in the Arab world. Indeed, Nasser advised Talabani not to return to Iraq because the Baathist regime might imprison and kill him. Talabani also met Algeria's Ahmad Ben Bella on one of the same journeys, and later that same year Jordan's King Hussein. In addition, he traveled to Beirut, Paris, Vienna, Berlin, and Moscow. In 1964, Talabani visited Austria, Britain, France, and Germany. These early international exposures as a Kurdish spokesman apparently drew Mulla Mustafa's jealousy. Talabani's criticism of Barzani's failure to obtain positive negotiating results with the government in Iraq also did not help their relationship.

By 1964, Mulla Mustafa was referring to the KDP politburo headed by Ahmad and Talabani as the "Mawat Empire," in reference to the Kurdish town in which they were headquartered. In July 1964, Mulla Mustafa's son Loqman drove the Ahmad-Talabani group over the border to Iran, and, incidentally, burned Ahmad's library. Mam Jalal and Ahmad rejoined the elder Barzani, however, for a new round of fighting against the government the following April.

Within a year, their intra-Kurdish struggle had broken out again and Talabani began cooperating with Baghdad, a move that even his friends criticized, as mentioned above. In those years, Talabani seemed to be emphasizing his leftist ideology and giving greater stress to defeating feudal and reactionary elements in Kurdistan, rather than securing Kurdish national rights. In 1967, he found time to again visit Algeria to participate in an Arab socialist conference.

When the newly reinstated Baathist government threw its weight fully behind the Ahmad-Talabani group in 1968, Mulla Mustafa began to refer to it as the "new mercenaries."[24] There were repeated clashes between the two Kurdish groups, but eventually Mulla Mustafa won and Baghdad began to negotiate with him. The eventual result was the March Manifesto of 1970 in which Talabani played no role.

Following the adoption of this manifesto, Mam Jalal was allowed to return to the KDP fold, but he was posted as the party's representative in Beirut, an apparent form of exile. In these years, Talabani and his family moved back and forth between Beirut, Cairo, Cyprus, and Damascus. He played no important role in the renewed fighting between the government and Mulla Mustafa that broke out in 1974 and led to the elder Barzani's final defeat in March 1975.

With Kurdish politics now in disarray, Talabani was presented with fresh opportunities. On June 1, 1975, he announced from Damascus the creation of the Patriotic Union of Kurdistan (PUK) made up at the time of two major groups: Komala, a Marxist organization headed by Noshirwan Mustafa Amin;[25] and the Socialist Movement of Kurdistan, led by Ali Askari. The PUK and the newly reconstituted KDP quickly became the two main political parties in Iraqi Kurdistan, a position they continue to hold almost a quarter of a century later.

As mentioned above, Talabani returned to Iraqi Kurdistan in June 1977 and established his headquarters just inside the Iranian border, west of Sardasht at Nawhan. During the succeeding years, however, his PUK seemed to fight against the KDP as much as against the government. Indeed, one of Talabani's top lieutenants, Ali Askari, was captured and executed by the KDP in April 1978. This unfortunate incident still embitters intra-Kurdish relations. Talabani continued to travel abroad, how-

ever, as he took a private trip to the United States in June 1981
and even visited Niagara Falls.

Because of the seeming opportunities offered by the Iran-
Iraq War, beginning in December 1983 Talabani pursued a new
strategy by once again seeking to negotiate with the government
in Baghdad. The KDP, on the other hand, remained firmly opposed to Baghdad in those days, serving as allies to the invading
Iranians. The Baghdad-PUK negotiations came to their pre-
dictable standstill, however, as both sides were pursuing them
merely for tactical reasons, and in January 1985, the PUK resumed its fight against the government.

In November 1986, Talabani traveled to Tehran where he
began to explore a new beginning with Massoud Barzani. This
led to the eventual creation of the Iraqi Kurdistan Front, which
was announced formally in Tehran in June 1988. Also in 1988,
Talabani formally accused Saddam of committing genocide
against the Kurds. For this, Baghdad apparently singled out the
PUK leader as the only Kurd excluded from a government
amnesty offered at the end of the Iran-Iraq War.

In the summer of 1988, Mam Jalal also took another trip to
the United States during which, among numerous other things,
he visited the Human Rights Department at the United Nations
and Jeri Laber, the executive director of Helsinki (now called
Human Rights) Watch. Talabani also spoke with such influential
American Kurds as Najmaldin O. Karim, and he even traveled to
Detroit where he met another important American Kurd, Asad
Khailany. Both Karim and Khailany are important spokespersons
for the miniscule (maybe 20,000 people) Kurdish community in
the United States. In Washington, D.C., Talabani also met several
members of Congress and spoke at the U.S. State Department.
His speech at the Pentagon, however, was canceled at the insis-
tence of Turkish president Kenan Evren.

Shortly after Saddam invaded Kuwait, Talabani paid yet
another visit to Washington but cautioned: "We have been
deceived many times by foreigners. We are determined not to
make the same mistakes again."[26] Queried about whether the
Kurds would join the allies if war broke out, the PUK leader
replied: "We would not," and he even warned that "if the Turkish
Army invades Iraq's Kurdistan, we would stand against it."[27] Talabani hedged his position, however, by noting that "we have

fought Saddam since he assumed power and will continue to fight him until he is toppled." He added that "if the Arab forces liberate Kuwait, we would urge the Kurdish troops to join them," but he asserted that "our fighting would be Kurdish, independent, and separate . . . not . . . as part of foreign armies invading or fighting Iraq."

After Saddam's defeat, the imaginative new Turkish president, Turgut Ozal, broke his country's longstanding policy against negotiating with any Kurdish group and invited Talabani and Mohsin Dizai, a representative of Barzani, to Ankara. Talabani concluded "that a new page had been turned in relations between Turkey and the Kurds of Iraq."[28] For the Kurds of Iraq, "the most significant result . . . was Turkey's lifting its objection to the establishment of direct relations between the Kurdish front in Iraq and the United States." Talabani also explained how "Turkey has for years been putting forth effective and significant obstacles to the struggle we have been waging in northern Iraq" and concluded, "I believe that we were able to convince them that we do not pose a threat to Turkey."[29]

In April 1991, the Iraqi Kurds began a long drawn out set of ultimately unsuccessful negotiations with Baghdad during which the government's television showed Saddam planting a kiss on Talabani's surprised face. Although Saddam also apparently embraced some of the other Kurdish leaders, the ironic kiss with Talabani was the one most people saw, and they were shocked.

As the negotiations progressed, however, it became clear that Barzani was more eager to reach an agreement with Saddam than Talabani was. While Barzani was still negotiating in July 1991, Talabani embarked on a seven-nation tour, only returning to Iraqi Kurdistan in mid-August. With the negotiations at a standstill, Talabani bitterly concluded: "I believe that not even the deadliest enemy of the Arabs has committed treason and crimes against the Arab nation such as the ones committed by the Ba'th Party."[30]

Clearly Barzani and Talabani disagreed on how to proceed. Jalal, on the one hand, thought that the Kurds should not sign any agreement until they were offered a better deal and/or Saddam was eliminated. Massoud, on the other hand, was tempted to take what was being offered because he thought that the Kurds needed protection now and he doubted the West's ability to provide it in the long run.

In May 1992, the Iraqi Kurds held elections that resulted in such a slight edge for Barzani that he and Talabani agreed to split power equally between their two parties. Although both Kurdish leaders claimed that "the elections were a victory for everyone,"[31] in a later interview Talabani admitted, "everyone ended up dissatisfied with the results."[32]

Ever the world traveler, Talabani was again in Ankara during July 1992 where he was quoted as suggesting that the Turks might want to annex northern Iraq. Jalal later explained that what he had really said to Ozal was that the Iraqi Kurds could be part of some sort of broad Middle Eastern federation on an equal basis with the Turks and/or the Arabs.

The following summer (1993) both Talabani and Barzani were part of a larger delegation of the Iraqi opposition INC that journeyed to Washington, France, and Saudi Arabia, among other stops. In the United States, Talabani met Secretary of State Warren Christopher and National Security Advisor Anthony Lake, among others, and proposed that the United States lift the economic sanctions against the Kurds who were considered part of Iraq. For that very reason, however, the United States refused, arguing that to do so would sanction the break up of Iraq. As will be discussed in chapter 3, the United States did promise significant support for INC.

From all accounts both Jalal and Massoud got along quite well on their joint mission. In mid-August 1993, I personally watched for two straight days as they sat next to each other seemingly in close and amicable conversation at the eleventh KDP congress held in Irbil. It might have been the highlight of their cooperation, but even then there were ominous signs that all was not well. When I visited the Talabanis for dinner, for example, one of my KDP guards felt he was treated very rudely by Talabani's guards. By the end of 1993, the KDP and PUK were clearly drifting apart as limited hostilities between the PUK and minor Kurdish opponents led to open disagreements between Talabani and Barzani.

When actual fighting between the two main Kurdish parties finally broke out in May 1994, Talabani was traveling abroad. He had a great deal of trouble returning from Syria through KDP territory. At first Massoud said he would meet Jalal at the border, but he reneged. Then Barzani said that his nephew Nechervan Idris Barzani would meet Talabani and escort him to safety, but this too failed to eventuate. Finally, Talabani was able to return by way of Turkey with the help of the United States.

Three years after the Kurdish infighting had begun, Talabani was again in the United States (August 1997) for a series of calls upon U.S. officials in Washington led by Sandy Berger, President Clinton's national security adviser. They discussed ways to reinvigorate the U.S.-, British-, and Turkish-sponsored "Ankara process" (see chapter 4) to end the KDP-PUK infighting; the state of the Iraqi opposition; the resumption of U.S. humanitarian assistance to Iraqi Kurdistan; the role of Iran and the Kurdistan Workers Party (PKK) in the region; and the implementation of relevant U.N. resolutions. Talabani also met with U.N. Secretary-General Kofi Annan and other U.N. administrators in New York. A similar trip was proposed for Barzani, but it failed to materialize. On his return to Kurdistan, the PUK leader stopped off in Britain, Germany, and Turkey. In May 1998, Talabani returned to Cairo where he spoke at a conference on Arab-Kurdish relations.

Barzani traveled abroad much less frequently, arguing that he had more important things to do in Kurdistan. In September 1998, however, Barzani and Talabani met in Washington, D.C. to sign an accord that would hopefully end their civil war. (See chapter 4.) Traveling separately, both leaders also stopped off for talks in Turkey and various states in Europe.

Personal Notes

The late Turkish president Turgut Ozal (died April 17, 1993) was the only Turkish official Talabani ever really liked. There was good chemistry between the two. Talabani felt that Ozal was the only Turkish leader who ever really understood the Kurdish problem. The others Jalal simply did not like because of what had passed between the two peoples and what he saw as a history of Turkish brutality.

Illustrative of Talabani's negative attitude toward the Turks is a joke he told when he lived in Cairo. While Talabani was shopping for a sheep's head at the market, the butcher asked whether he wanted the ordinary one or the Turkish one. When Jalal inquired about the difference, he was told that the Turkish head was the one with the brain removed. The feeling of animosity was mutual. The conservative Turks probably distrusted

Talabani even more than they did most Kurds because of his socialist background and Kurdish nationalist beliefs.

In contrast, Talabani admires Britain to the extent that he had his two sons raised there. Distinguishing between the British and the Americans, Talabani points favorably to how the British criticized Turkey's intervention against the PUK in October 1997, while the United States remained silent. (See chapter 5 below.) Talabani feels that the United States, unlike the more experienced Britain, often simply does not know what it is doing when it deals with the Kurds. Furthermore, he believes the United States thinks that even when it makes a mistake, the Kurds will have to accept it and return to the fold because they have nowhere else to go.

Talabani's political mentor, Ibrahim Ahmad, in reflecting over his long life, added that one of his great mistakes was his earlier admiration for the Soviet Union and his unwillingness to deal with the United States and Britain. Ahmad explained that the Soviet propaganda was much better. No doubt Talabani, originally a Marxist, suffered from the same handicap.

On the other hand, Talabani ultimately favored the United States over the Soviet Union. His eye was always on the United States. After the Kurdish uprising in 1991, Talabani constantly looked to the United States and the West, while Barzani was much more cautious. Nevertheless, Ahmad Chalabi, the leader of the opposition INC, concluded that one of Talabani's recent strategic errors was antagonizing both Turkey and Iran in 1994. (See chapters 4 and 5 below.) As a result, both of these important neighboring powers worked to strengthen Barzani in his struggle against Talabani.

Although his friends comment on how Talabani has visibly aged in recent years, all still marvel at his continuing energy and health. One friend noted how Mam Jalal cannot stay still for even ten minutes without making another phone call to arrange for yet another meeting.

Others have noted that Talabani actually speaks better Arabic than he does Kurdish. Indeed, Talabani published an analysis of the Kurdish national movement in Arabic in 1971.[33] He also speaks reasonably good Persian, French, English, and a little Turkish. A voracious reader, Talabani particularly enjoys political biographies. He also likes poetry and can read English. When he speaks he often uses Kurdish proverbs and likes good jokes. Despite his family's heritage, religion is not much of a personal influence on him.

By way of criticism, one former close associate asserted that Talabani's two main weaknesses are that he talks and eats too much. Mam Jalal thinks that politics is saying what people like to hear, and, in trying to please everybody, he ends up contradicting himself. To some he comes across as being bombastic and fickle. And although he has acquired great experience in diplomacy, he is too optimistic.

Clearly, in Barzani and Talabani the Iraqi Kurds have been dealt two leaders completely different in their attitudes and their approaches to solving problems. With better foresight, there is still reason to hope that the Kurdish national movement in Iraq can harness the considerable abilities of these two opposing leaders so that their different strengths and skills will complement, rather than continue to degrade, each other.

3

The Iraqi Opposition

The purpose of this chapter is to analyze the Iraqi opposition that arose against Saddam Hussein after the Gulf War. The Kurds, of course, constitute an important component of this opposition and also offer a territorial base for it in the Iraqi homeland. Moreover, the Kurdish future in Iraq will clearly be influenced by the opposition, if and when it ever comes to power. Depending upon how they are counted, as many as 70 opposition groups have existed at one time or another since the Gulf War. Many, of course, are miniscule or even notional. Saddam's vehement pursuit of oppositional figures when Barzani invited his forces into Irbil at the end of August 1996, however, illustrates how he perceived them to be a real threat.

The Iraqi National Congress (INC)—an umbrella formation that at its height included approximately 90 percent of the entire opposition—was (and probably still is) the most important. There are also, however, various Islamic, military officers, and pro-Syrian nationalist groups that have played influential roles.

In writing this chapter, I was able to order and complement my analysis of the documentary evidence with two useful interviews with Ahmad Chalabi, the president of INC's executive council; an interview with General Wafiq al-Samarra'i, the former head of Iraqi military intelligence who defected to the opposition in November 1994; several interviews with Latif Rashid, one of the three INC executive council vice presidents and a Kurd; and interviews with a number of other Kurds who are working closely with the opposition.

EARLIER OPPOSITION GROUPS

Ultimately, of course, an analysis of all the Iraqi groups ever opposed to Saddam's dictatorship is beyond the scope of this chapter. The following, therefore, is only a brief survey of some important historical precedents for the current opposition.

Once the Baathists captured permanent power in 1968, they instituted a police state that effectively controlled any manifestations of successful opposition.[1] What remained was either forced underground or into exile in Syria, Iran, or Europe. Such expatriate groups included the Iraqi Communist Party (ICP); a dissident Baathist group that supported the Syrian Baathists; and the two main Kurdish parties, the Kurdistan Democratic Party (KDP) led by the Barzanis and the Patriotic Union of Kurdistan (PUK) headed by Jalal Talabani.

What is more, unified opposition to the Baathists historically has foundered over ideological or personal matters. The Kurds, for example, still suffer from such divisions as are witnessed by their internal fighting since 1994. Arab opposition groups have also languished from a lack of popular support due to the perception that they acted as fifth columns during the Iran-Iraq War of the 1980s.

The Shiites

Much of the religious opposition to the secular Baathists has been concentrated among the majority Shiites in the south. Indeed, the *Ad Dawa al Islamiyah* (the Dawa or Islamic Call) was originally established by the Shiite clergy in the early 1960s.[2] In 1979, the success of Khomeini's Islamic revolution in Shiite Iran helped transform the Dawa into an organized opposition to Saddam's secular rule.

On November 17, 1982, Iran helped to establish the Supreme Assembly for the Islamic Revolution in Iraq (SAIRI) as an umbrella group for all the Iraqi Shiite parties. Muhammad Baqir al-Hakim—a prominent Shiite religious figure whose father, Muhsin al-Hakim, had been the leading ayatollah of Iraq in the 1960s—became the new organization's chairman. The Shiite organizations formed earlier, however, continued to exist.

In return for Iran's help, SAIRI recognized Khomeini as the supreme commander of the Islamic nation. Nevertheless, or perhaps because of these ties to Iran, the majority of Iraq's Shiites remained loyal to Iraq during the war against Iran. In this case, at least, Arab nationalist bonds proved stronger than Islamic religious ties.

The Kurds

The Kurds in Iraq[3] have been in an almost constant state of revolt ever since Britain artificially created Iraq following World War I. At times they also have been bitterly divided among themselves.

In November 1980, the PUK joined with the ICP, led since 1964 by Aziz Muhammad who himself was a Kurd, and the Socialist Party of Kurdistan in Iraq (SPKI), led by Rasul Mamand and Mahmud Othman, to form the Democratic National and Patriotic Front (DNPF). The KDP was purposely omitted. Thus, the Barzanis' party responded by excluding the PUK when it joined with the partners of the PUK in the Democratic National Front (DNF) a few weeks later.

Yet another front was created in July 1981 by a dissident, former Baathist general Hassan Mustafa Naquib. This organization was known as either the Islamic National Liberation Front or the Iraqi Front of Revolutionary, Islamic, and National Forces. Although considerable publicity was given to these three fronts at the time, they accomplished little. Arguably, however, they did set precedents for the delicate Kurdish unity that was finally achieved in the late 1980s with the creation of the Iraqi Kurdistan Front (IKF) and for the Iraqi oppositional unity itself that was formed in the early 1990s by the Iraqi National Congress.

Upon its creation, the IKF declared that its main goals were to overthrow the Baathist regime of Saddam Hussein, establish a genuinely democratic government in Iraq, and develop a federal status for the Iraqi Kurds. Jalal Talabani and Massoud Barzani became the front's co-presidents.

Although crushed in September 1988 with the end of the Iran-Iraq War and again in April 1991 following the aborted uprising that ensued after Saddam's defeat in the Gulf War, the IKF subsequently came to power when the victorious allies instituted a safe haven and no-fly zone to protect the Kurds. These allied measures were sanctioned by U.N. Security Council Resolution 688 of April 5, 1991, which condemned "the repression of the Iraqi civilian population . . . in Kurdish populated areas" and demanded "that Iraq . . . immediately end this repression." Behind this protection, the Kurds held regional elections in May 1992, established a de facto government in July 1992, and declared a federated state in November 1992.[4]

CREATION OF IRAQI NATIONAL CONGRESS

The immediate roots of the Iraqi National Congress were planted by the agreement of a Joint Action Committee at the end of December 1990 and at a conference held in Beirut, Lebanon, on March 9–11, 1991. At this latter event approximately 300 delegates from some 20 groups—including both secular and Islamic factions as well as the KDP and PUK—formed the Free Iraqi Council chaired by Saad Salih Jabr, a Shiite and son of a former prime minister. By this time Saddam had been defeated in the Gulf War, and the Iraqi opposition was euphoric. The new opposition group announced plans to establish a provisional government to replace the defeated Saddam.

Unity within the opposition proved difficult, however, as "it was consumed by disputes over who represents whom, what percentage and share should each faction have in the organizations, and what each faction's voting rights are."[5] By its own admission, the opposition suffered from "the narcissism of parties that numbered in the dozens, each having no more than 10 or 20 members in most cases." The opposition lacked "a leadership capable of exploiting opportunities, of controlling the means and methods leading to recognizing the rights of the uprising and the opposition, and of representing the opposition before the UN organizations and decision makers."

Even more, of course, the Shiites' and Kurds' sudden defeat, as well as the latter's tragic refugee exodus, their return to the allied-protected safe haven, and their entrance into negotiations with Saddam over their future relations with his government dramatically weakened the opposition. Saad Salih Jabr, the chairman of the Free Iraqi Council, cabled Barzani: "We were surprised and shocked . . . by the Kurdish Front's holding of negotiations with Saddam's regime. We were more shocked by the . . . exchanging [of] kisses and embraces with Saddam at a time when the blood of the . . . Iraqi people in general has not yet dried."[6]

It was not the fervent appeals of their erstwhile allies in the Iraqi opposition that brought the Kurds back to the fold, however, but the failure of their negotiations with Saddam. In late October 1991, the Iraqi dictator also began imposing an economic blockade upon the Kurds, along with withdrawing government officials, in an attempt to break them. These actions instead had the effect of hardening Kurdish resolve and, as mentioned above, helped lead to the creation of a de facto, regional Kurdish government in Iraqi Kurdistan in 1992.

Vienna Conference

Early in 1992, planning was begun for a second opposition conference. The following 25 "influential elements, parties, and personalities"[7] were reported as comprising the preparatory committee: SAIRI, Dawa, IKF, Socialist Arab Baath Party-the Iraqi Command, ICP, Iraqi National Accord, Free Iraqi Council, Independent Organization (Major General Hassan Naquib), Dr. Muhammad Bahr al-Ulum, Islamic Action Organization, Iraqi Democratic Grouping, People's Democratic Party of Kurdistan, Union of Iraqi Democrats-London, United Democratic Party (Ahmad al-Habbubi), National Reform Movement in Iraq, Supreme Council of Iraqi Tribes, Islamic Union of Iraqi Turkomen, Assyrian Democratic Movement, Socialist Party (Mubdir al-Wis), Dr. Abd-al-Ilah al-Nasrawi, Islamic Movement in Kurdistan, Free Officers Movement, Islamic Forces Grouping, Socialist Party of Kurdistan, and Democratic Union in the United States and Canada.

The second Iraqi opposition conference was held in Vienna, Austria, from June 16 to 19, 1992. Some 160 delegates representing numerous different liberal and democratic opposition groups living in London attended, including the Kurds. Despite their reported presence in the preparatory work of the conference, however, important Islamic groups such as the SAIRI and

Dawa only sent observers, apparently because of their suspicions concerning Western influence over the proceedings and traditional reservations over joint actions with secular groups. Pro-Syrian groups were also absent.

Nevertheless, the Vienna conference took a number of steps toward creating INC. It established a national assembly of 87 members in which the Kurds were allocated 22 seats, tentatively broached the idea of federalism for the Kurds, and thus established "a material and human base" that they hoped would be "capable of wrestling power from Saddam."[8] This latter development was said to be "perhaps the most important accomplishment made . . . in Vienna."

The strategy supposedly adopted for removing Saddam relied "on wrestling power from the regime gradually and in phases by letting the leadership of the people and of the armed forces rebel against the regime to topple and destroy it."[9] It was "a new method with which the Iraqis are not familiar, considering that all changes leading to the overthrow of regimes and governments from 1932 to 1968 were made with force by way of the so-called palace and government coup."

The Kurds, however, upset a number of the Arab opposition groups at Vienna by demanding that the conference recognize their right to self-determination and that Iraq's unity was voluntary in return for the Kurds' continued participation within the opposition. Jawad al-Maliki, the chairman of the first opposition conference in Beirut and, as a member of the Dawa party leadership, not present at the Vienna conference, rejected this Kurdish demand "as a step toward secession."[10]

Recognizing that "the factions that did not participate . . . are fundamental forces in the Iraqi opposition,"[11] INC members began to try to correct the situation. Following "contacts and consultations," Barzani visited Damascus in August 1992 where "he gained al-Asad's approval to launch an initiative . . . to expand the scope of [INC] . . . to encompass all the Iraqi opposition and factions and forces." The word "unified" was added to INC's name "to underline this meaning."

Salah al-Din Conference

On October 27, 1992, some 234 delegates representing as many as 90 percent of the Iraqi opposition groups began to gather for the first time on Iraqi soil in the town of Salah al-Din (Salahud-din) just north of the Kurdish regional capital of Irbil. Under the auspices of the Kurds and with the protection of the allied no-fly zone, the opposition was able to create INC's basic institutions.

The national assembly membership was expanded from 87 to 234. Then it created a three-man presidential council that gave equal representation to the Shiites, Kurds, and Sunnis, consisting of: (1) Sayyid Muhammad Bahr al-Ulum, a senior Shiite religious scholar from Najaf who had been exiled by Saddam for his anti-regime activities and was presently based in London, (2) Massoud Barzani, the president of the KDP and one of the two main Iraqi Kurdish leaders, and (3) Major General Hassan Mustafa Naquib, a Sunni Arab and former deputy chief of the Iraqi army general staff who had been purged from the Baathist leadership in October 1970.

Finally, a 26–member executive council was created "to manage the daily operations of the struggle against Saddam."[12] In effect, this organ was a cabinet or council of ministers. Since its membership supposedly "comprises the full spectrum of regional and political groups in the Iraqi opposition," a detailed listing would be useful.

Ahmad Chalabi was chosen as the president of the executive council.[13] As such, he was in effect the prime minister of the opposition's projected government in exile. A Shiite banker and businessman based in London and fluent in English, Chalabi proved to be the most visible and important leader of INC. Hani al-Fekaiki, a Sunni Arab who recently died; Latif Rashid, a member of Talabani's PUK; and Sheikh Humam Hamudi of SAIRI were chosen as vice presidents of the executive council.

Dr. Abd al-Husayn Shaban, an independent democrat, was picked to be the council's secretary. By the summer of 1994, however, he had resigned from the council because of his dual opposition to the U.N.'s continuing embargo against his country and what he saw as undue compulsion for INC to recognize Kuwait's new border with Iraq.

In addition to Rashid, five other Kurds were chosen: Sami Abdurrahman, a respected longtime Kurdish leader who rejoined Barzani's KDP in August 1993; Hoshyar Zebari, a young and capable member of the KDP's politburo, responsible for international affairs; Mohsin Dizai, described as an independent Kurd but in the past identified with Barzani; Kamal Fuad, a senior

PUK leader responsible for foreign relations; and Mulla Ali Abdul Aziz, a leader of the Islamic Movement of Kurdistan.

Various Arab Islamics included Sami al-Askari of Dawa; Nizar Haydar of the Islamic Action Organization; Jasim Hasan and Muhammad Muhammad Ali, who were both described as independent Islamists; Fulayh al-Samarai of the Islamic Bloc; Muhammad Jabbar of the Islamic cadres (but described elsewhere as an independent); Izzat al-Shabandar of the Islamic Forces Grouping or Islamic Assembly; and Talib al-Bayati of SAIRI.

Other Arab leaders included Amir Abdullah, a communist; Riyadh al-Yawar, an Arab nationalist; Ayad Allawi, a former Iraqi intelligence officer who broke with Saddam in 1971 and now headed the Iraqi National Accord; Aziz Ailyan of the Democrats Union; Talib Shabib, a former Iraqi foreign minister currently described as an independent; and Sheikh Sami Azara al-Majoun from the Arab tribes.

Muzafar Arsalan, the leader of the National Turkoman Party of Iraq, and Albert (Arbart) Yelda of the Assyrian Democratic Movement were also appointed to the executive council. Bayar Jabr of SAIRI and Abd al-Sattar al-Duri, an independent, were original members who were no longer serving on the council by late 1994.

The external headquarters of INC was established in London (Trevor House, 100 Brompton Road, London, SW3 1ER. Tel.: 4471-581 3205; Fax: 4471-581-3218)[14] but later moved to a more modest location in the British capital. Its operational or Iraqi base was fixed in Salah al-Din where the conference took place (Tel.: 873-1514503; Fax: 873-1514504),[15] but this location was abandoned after Saddam attacked it in August 1996. (See below.) With the exception of Chalabi, a few of his associates, and the majority of the Kurds, most members of INC chose to remain in London because of the harsh economic conditions and isolation of Iraqi Kurdistan. *Al-Mu'Tamar* became the new organization's weekly newspaper.

Federalism

The question of federalism for the Kurds—which had been discussed previously at the Vienna conference and then declared unilaterally by the Kurds just a few weeks before the gathering at Salah al-Din—was one of the main points of debate. Both

Barzani and Talabani went on record as favoring this option for securing Kurdish rights while still maintaining Iraq's territorial integrity.[16]

Given the relative strength of the Kurds and the weakness of their Arab associates at Salah al-Din, most of those present at the conference came to accept that the Kurds "have special national and ethnic characteristics."[17] Amidst a great deal of discussion, therefore, the conference "approved the right of the Kurds to determine their future without secession and within the framework of the single Iraqi homeland."

GOALS AND STRATEGY

INC maintains that "the rule of Saddam Hussein has been a national tragedy of unprecedented proportions for Iraq and her people . . . [that] has destroyed civil society . . . and brought the country to the brink of destruction."[18] In "uniting all opposition forces to work towards . . . saving the Iraqi people," INC provides "full representation of all groups and communities within the population, including Sunnis, Shias, Kurds, Christians and all other minorities." In so doing, however, "INC does not endorse a particular political program or alignment." Rather, it functions as a type of umbrella organization that "provides an institutional framework so that the popular will of the Iraqi people . . . can be democratically determined and implemented."

"INC's immediate goals are to establish itself as a responsible and credible authority with a base on Iraqi soil, to provide for the humanitarian relief of the Iraqi people . . . and to enlist the support of the international community." In accomplishing the latter, INC "continues to stress the implementation of United Nations Security Council resolution 688 (1991) that demands the end of the repression of the Iraqi people, as well as UNSC resolution 712 (1991) calling for aid to the Iraqi people" from Iraqi oil sales. All of this is to be done while "ensuring the territorial integrity and independence of the nation under a democratic, constitutional, parliamentary and pluralistic structure."

Two "historical actions" or "pillars" have provided "the foundation for INC's mission": the U.N.'s (1) repulsion of Saddam's aggression against Kuwait, and (2) interposition of a no-fly zone in the north and south of Iraq. INC "was formed and is acting in response to the opportunity such international consensus affords." INC itself "is committed to complete compliance with international law as agreed to in the United Nations Charter and as expressed by the United Nations Security Council." Thus, INC "calls for the strict enforcement of all . . . Security Council resolutions . . . including the [territorial integrity] . . . of Kuwait."

Military

The military plays the single most important role in INC's strategy to overthrow Saddam: INC "encourage[s] the truly patriotic elements of the Iraqi military to further isolate Saddam's regime."

Tangible accomplishments in this area, however, have been few. Interviewed in April 1993, General Hassan Naquib, one of the three members of INC's presidential council, conceded: "I do not believe that, in its present condition, the Army is capable of carrying out a successful coup against Saddam because of the private guard . . . the Republican Guard . . . and . . . the infiltration of Saddam's intelligence elements into the ranks of the Iraqi Army and officers."[19]

Muhammad Baqir al-Hakim, the leader of SAIRI, proposed a "political plan" based on five points:[20] (1) creation of a "popular military organization that relies on the Iraqi people," (2) cooperation between this popular military organization and the Iraqi Army, which al-Hakim claimed had responded to such an idea although the Republican Guard had not, (3) unity within the opposition, (4) regional cooperation and coordination, and (5) world public opinion.

Further details concerning the military option emerged in the fall of 1994.[21] INC had established three camps in the Shaqlawah region of Iraqi Kurdistan "to train former militiamen and civilians to become disciplined soldiers." Hammad al-Dulaymi, the chief of one of these camps, claimed: "We have people from all over Iraq, Shiites, Sunnis, Kurds, Turkomans, even Christians," adding that "every month about 80 people flee from the rest of Iraq to northern Iraq, including three or four officers from the Iraqi army."

The soldiers were between 18 and 40 years old. In addition to being trained in the use of light and medium weapons, they also received political instruction on the "abuses of Saddam" and "the meaning of democracy." Unmarried cadets were paid 1,000 Iraqi dinars per month, which was approximately two and a half times as much as a Kurdish civil servant received. Food and medical services were provided without charge and a hospital had been set up in Shaqlawah. Given these benefits and the financial woes of Saddam, many had been attracted for economic reasons. Others joined for ideological ones.

In late 1994, Ahmad Chalabi, the president of INC's executive council, claimed that INC's military force now numbered "about 4,000 Iraqi deserters."[22] They were monitoring troop movements and carrying out "special missions." Chalabi declared that "what is needed in addition to our activities and sanctions is a popular-military push." He seemed to contradict these ideas about using the people in concert with the military to overthrow Saddam, however, when he declared in another interview that "the people cannot destroy Saddam Husayn—they are too hungry, running after food every day."[23] Instead, "if anyone can do so it is the Iraqi army."

This, of course, was similar to the old idea of a coup. However, Hoshyar Zebari, a KDP member of INC's executive council, concluded: "But surely after nearly four years of waiting for this coup, they must know that it is almost impossible to arrange."[24] Zebari suggested that the West continued to support the concept of a coup because it "would leave the country in safe, autocratic, Sunni hands." The West opposed "the democratic solution . . . in which the majority Shi'ites find influence proportionate to their number" because of the "fear . . . that the Shi'ites would fall prey to fundamentalist, expansionist Iran."

In March 1995, Staff Major General Wafiq al-Samarra'i—the former chief of Iraqi military intelligence until his defection to the opposition the previous November—claimed "brilliant success"[25] from a combined INC-PUK mini-offensive that sought to capture Kirkuk and ignite a "rolling coup" against Saddam. The KDP, however, declined to strike at Mosul, and the U.S. Central Intelligence Agency (CIA) withdrew its support. Despite some initial success, the operation soon ground to a halt as the KDP and PUK instead fell into renewed infighting between themselves. (See below.) Following Saddam's intervention in August 1996 and his resulting strike against INC agents in northern Iraq, INC ceased to maintain any military force. It remains today militarily impotent in the face of Saddam.

Finances

Although it is clear that INC has been able to obtain some financing, details were for a long time murky and contradictory. A number of sources claim that the United States had contributed between $30 and $50 million by the end of 1993.[26] After meeting in Washington with U.S. Secretary of State Warren Christopher and Vice President Al Gore in the spring of 1993 as part of an INC delegation, Muhammad Bahr al-Ulum, one of the three members of INC's presidential council, added to these uncertainties when he first declared: "Neither I nor any member of the INC leadership has any knowledge of any U.S. funds paid to the INC to this day."[27] He then claimed, however, that the United States had already matched the $50 million contributed by "some Arab states and some Iraqi financiers." The perceived need for secrecy and al-Ulum's inexperience in dealing with covert U.S. support probably explain his incoherence on this matter.

Further remarks by al-Ulum indicated that before the spring of 1993, certain Iraqis in opposition to Saddam had "squandered" more than $40 million given them by the United States.[28] At first he speculated that these Iraqis were "military people" who had failed in their "coup attempts," but he then claimed that "revealing the details of this matter would harm the opposition's reputation. This is not in our interest." He added, however, that "a day will come when everything will be revealed."

Referring to the same meeting al-Ulum had with U.S. officials in the spring of 1993, Jalal Talabani, the leader of the PUK, claimed, "we have not received any economic or military aid."[29] Six months later Talabani added that when he had visited the United States, "we learned that $42 million was allocated for the opposition," but he explained, "I do not know how this money is being spent. We know nothing about specific U.S. aid."[30]

Other INC officials have mentioned the role of Ahmad Chalabi, the president of INC's executive council and a former banker who in the past had been accused of financial irregularities in Jordan. When asked who was presently financing INC, Hassan Naquib, one of the three members of INC's presidential council, asserted: "That question is for . . . al-Jalabi to answer. He has the details."[31] Naquib added, however, "what I know is that some Iraqi financiers make donations to cover part of the expenses of our political activities."

According to Dr. Abd al-Husayn Shaban, the disaffected former executive council secretary of INC, Chalabi himself declared "I am financing the INC" and that "some people deposited some money with him and that he placed the money at the disposal of the INC."[32] Shaban added, "we have not been accustomed to exercising democracy within or outside the INC." When I interviewed him in December 1997, Chalabi told me that at the height of its support, the United States was giving INC about $320,000 per month and complained that this was not very much. Still another report referred to the "refusal to reveal the sources of the congress' [INC's] financing and insistent refusal to form a committee to run the congress' financial affairs."[33] Chalabi attributed the failure to convene INC's National Assembly to the fact that to do so would cost $600,000 and that it would be "more proper" to spend such sums on other matters.[34]

In April 1995, the *New York Times* published what at the time was a much-discussed article revealing that the CIA had begun its present covert program against Iraq in 1991.[35] From a high of $40 million in 1992, the Clinton administration had scaled back its contribution to less than $20 million a year because of lack of results. The CIA proposed to spend $15 million against Iraq during the following year. The Times article specifically identified INC as one of the recipients of the funds. In subsequent years the United States continued to fund INC and other opposition groups, but never with amounts sufficient for their success. (See below.)

NON-PARTICIPANTS

Although approximately 90 percent of the more than 70-odd Iraqi opposition groups were at one time or another reportedly participating in INC, Ahmad Chalabi admitted even at its height, "some major opposition forces are still not in it."[36] Chief among them have been at times the Islamic groups SAIRI, Dawa, and Islamic Action.

Although all three participated in the Salah al-Din conference, they did so with reservations concerning Shiite representation. Specifically, Muhammad Baqir al-Hakim, the leader of SAIRI, turned down membership on INC's presidential council because "Iraqi Shiites make up well over 65 percent of Iraqis.

Why then do they have only one-third representation in the presidency committee?"[37]

Illustrative of the bitter divisions among some members of the opposition, Muzafar Arsalan, the Iraqi Turkoman member of INC's executive council, claimed the Shiites had proposed that the membership of the presidential council be increased to nine, but that the Turkomen not be included.[38] To such a proposal, Arsalan bitterly responded: "If your concept of democracy is this, then may God protect the Iraqi people."

More consistent in their opposition—although less important in their size—have been as many as 16 nationalist groups that tend to take a pro-Syrian position, including the Arab Baath Socialist Party, Iraqi Command; the Independent Group; the Iraqi Socialist Party; the Arab Socialist Movement; the Unionist Nasserite Grouping; the Iraqi Democratic Grouping; the Iraqi Democrats Union; the Democratic Pan-Arab Grouping; and the National Reconciliation Group.

These groups have been referred to by such names as the "National Action Bureau," the "Coordinating Committee for Nationalist and Democratic Action," and the "Pan-Arab Action Coordination Committee," among others. According to Mahdi al-Ubaydi, one of their senior spokesmen, they believed pro-Western elements were in control of INC and trying to partition Iraq.[39] Specifically, federalism for the Kurds and a no-fly zone in the south were seen as policies aimed at partitioning Iraq and thus constituted "a kind of blackmail against the forces defending a unified, free, and independent Iraq." Finally, objections were raised to the representation formula offered at the Salah al-Din conference.

Defections from INC

By the summer of 1995, INC seemed to be falling apart. The supposed Kurdish base in northern Iraq was racked by civil war between Barzani and Talabani's parties, while internal rifts in INC itself over personalities, tactics, and finances were leading to wholesale defections. The *New York Times* article the previous April concerning CIA financing of INC[40] helped to fuel this situation.

Protesting the way INC was making decisions and professing lack of any knowledge of CIA financing, Bahr al-Ulum suspended his membership in May 1995. The following October he chaired a meeting of Iraqi opposition groups in London seeking to form a new political front for those opposing INC. SAIRI and Dawa, however, did not participate in this new venture.

Three months after Bahr al-Ulum's defection, Naquib became the second member of INC's three-man presidential council to quit, declaring that INC "no longer represents Iraqi patriotic forces and has become the company of Ahmad al-Jalabi. We will never work in it."[41] Concluding that INC was "finished,"[42] Naquib even charged that Barzani had raided his home in Salah al-Din and tried to assassinate one of his top aides. Thus he would no longer be living in Iraqi Kurdistan.

Wafiq al-Samarra'i, the former Iraqi military intelligence chief who had defected to the opposition in November 1994 and by the summer of 1995 headed a miniscule group he called the Iraqi National Movement, went even further by accusing Barzani of having actually tried to assassinate him and of acting as "an agent of the Saddam regime."[43] Specifically, Samarra'i accused Barzani of concluding an agreement with Baghdad to prevent the opposition from attacking Mosul the previous March (see above), attacking Talabani when the PUK leader sought to mass his forces against Saddam, and expelling Arab opposition elements from the area under the KDP's control. For good measure, although somewhat incongruously since he too was now opposing Baghdad, Samarra'i also criticized Barzani for having supported Iran during the Iran-Iraq War in the 1980s.

In response, Barzani denied trying to assassinate Samarra'i, questioned his "suspect role" in the opposition, and accused him of being one of the perpetrators of the genocidal Anfal campaign against the Kurds in the late 1980s.[44] Al-Hakim, al-Ulum, and then even Naquib came to Barzani's defense. After Samarra'i accused al-Hakim of acting along a "chauvinist and racist concept,"[45] the SAIRI leader retorted that his accuser was trying to instigate "fanaticism."

As INC began to unravel, Syria started to encourage an alternative emanating from Damascus and made up of nationalists, Islamists, democrats, and Kurds. Mahdi al-Ubaydi, a spokesman for these groups, suggested that they should create an alternative to INC and declared, "among the first tasks of this front will be to initiate field action in coordination with the military and popular leaders inside Iraq which are in sympathy with the opposition forces, to overthrow the regime."[46]

At the end of July 1995, Muhammad Baqir al-Hakim, the leader of SAIRI, met with a number of these Syrian-based opposition leaders in Damascus. Criticizing INC "as not serious and its efficiency as limited,"[47] al-Hakim proposed the formation of a field command to launch a coup or a popular uprising. Despite encouragement from the Syrian leaders, however, the nationalist groups apparently felt that al-Hakim's proposals were premature since no agreement had been reached on creating a new opposition front. In addition, both Naquib and Samarra'i declined to meet with al-Hakim.

At the end of August 1995, some 50 opposition leaders representing 18 Iraqi opposition groups met in London to consider the unfolding events, including the recent defection of Saddam's son-in-law and high-ranking official, Husayn Kamil, earlier that month.[48] Given the recent defections from INC, a detailed listing of those groups present would be useful. They were: SAIRI, Iraqi National Accord, PUK, ICP, Iraqi Socialist Party, Iraqi Democratic National Accord Grouping, Iraqi National Reform Movement, Islamic Cadres Movement, Iraqi Independent Organization, Islamic Movement in Iraqi Kurdistan, Turkomen Democratic Movement, Assyrian Democratic Movement, Iraqi Democratic Grouping, Iraqi Democrats Union, Iraqi Democratic Islamic Grouping, Committee for Coordination Iraqi Democratic Tendency Forces in Britain, Democratic Pan-Arab Grouping, and World Assyrian Union. Prominent individuals reported in attendance included Muhammad Bahr al-Ulum, Mahmud Othman, Shaykh Husayn al-Sha'lan, Nuri Talabany, Abd al-Sattar al-Duri, Rahim Ajinah, Ismail al-Qadiri, Sami Faraj, Sa'd Abd al-Razzaq, Muhammad Hamawandi, Majid al-Hiti, Nabil Yasin, Riyad al-Zuhayri, and Ali Salih. Notably absent were such INC officials as Ahmad Chalabi and representatives of the KDP.

The participants stressed the need "to prevent the regime from escaping its outcome,"[49] a reference to the defection of Saddam's son-in-law, Husayn Kamil. They then emphasized "the need to develop field action inside the homeland until the regime is gotten rid of completely." The future regime "should guarantee pluralism, the peaceful rotation of power, and the judiciary's independence," as well as "the legitimate rights of the other nationalities and minorities." Finally, the participants spoke of "the need to . . . coordinate among themselves" and to leave "the door open to further meetings and consultations."

Husayn Kamil also sought to form his own opposition movement, which he called the Higher Salvation Council.[50] Although this council would not seek to include all the Iraqi opposition factions abroad, it would try to change the current regime in favor of a free parliamentary system based on political pluralism, intellectual and political freedom, and respect for human rights and liberties, mainly by confronting the regime from within. Thus, it would not be feasible to publicly name many of the new organization's members. However, specifically mentioned as having joined were Sabah Salman, Saddam's former press secretary and currently an opposition writer; Hisham Shawi, a former minister and diplomat; Colonel Saddam Kamil, Husayn Kamil's brother and fellow defector; Sadi Abu-Rukbah, the former director general at the Military Industrialization Organization; and Rasim Awwadi, a former official of the Iraqi Federation of Trade Unions. Wafiq Samarra'i, the former head of Iraqi military intelligence, also indicated that he might work with the new council.

Husayn Kamil accused Ahmad Chalabi and Hassan Naquib of planning to divide Iraq and asserted that he wanted to maintain the state's unity while avoiding civil war. He also said that he would establish ties with the United States and the Arab nations, while avoiding interference in the Palestinian question. In the end, however, Husayn Kamil was unable to win acceptance by the opposition. He and his brother returned to Baghdad in February 1996, only to be gunned down by their relatives for their "treason."

In London, Sharif Ali Bin al-Husayn (Prince Ali), the claimant to the Iraqi throne and leader of the Constitutional Monarchy Movement, claimed to have strong relations with all Iraqi opposition factions. His supposed aim was to topple Saddam and establish an alternative acceptable by the Iraqi people through a free referendum.[51]

Nabil Janabi, the leader of the opposition Democratic National Party argued that King Hussein of Jordan was the legitimate heir to the Iraqi throne and should become the head of a federated constitutional monarchy joining Iraq and Jordan.[52] Other sources indicated that, after his earlier support of Saddam followed by aid to Husayn Kamil, King Hussein did indeed broach the idea of moving the Iraqi opposition from London to Amman, from where it could work to establish a Shiite-Sunni-Kurdish federation in Iraq joined in confederation to Jordan.[53]

Vice President Abdal Halim Khaddam of Syria, however, maintained that King Hussein's plan for a tripartite or quadripartite Iraqi federation based on communal and ethnic regions and joined to Jordan was the first step toward partitioning the Arab region and that it served Israel's policy,[54] a criticism also voiced by pro-Syrian Iraqi opposition groups and, in part, by Prince Ali.

SADDAM STRIKES

By the beginning of 1996, the future of INC and the rest of the Iraqi opposition was not bright. Moreover, even if Saddam somehow were to be removed through assassination or a coup, it seemed more likely that groups actually based in Baghdad would come to power. This was because INC remained a weak, divided organization based largely abroad, supported by foreigners, and lacking a strong leader. Furthermore, important defections had begun to marginalize it, while a host of small alternative opposition groups and fronts had so far failed to fill the resulting gap.

Even more important, internal Kurdish fighting since 1994 between the KDP and PUK—the two main pillars of INC—had destroyed much of its very material and population base. If INC had proven unable to help maintain order in the very portion of Iraq where its fiat supposedly ran, how could it continue to offer itself as a viable option to Saddam in the rest of Iraq? The fact that the internecine Kurdish bloodletting was not really INC's fault, but the Kurds' themselves, only illustrated more clearly how secondary a factor INC was in its own supposed Iraqi bailiwick.

Finally, both the revelations concerning financial support from the United States, on the one hand, and the failure of the United States to support INC more strongly, on the other, had called into question the organization's long-term prospects. By 1994, INC leaders had also begun to admit that such U.S. promises as establishing a safe haven in the south and bringing Saddam to trial had not materialized. For these reasons, then, INC had failed to become a viable democratic option for the Iraqi people.

When Saddam helped Barzani capture Irbil at the end of August 1996, his troops dealt still another blow to INC by seizing its computer and files, and executing some 96 Iraqis who had defected to it.[55] A senior INC official claimed, "in two hours, the Iraqi opposition [had] lost its entire infrastructure,"[56] while a U.S. official concluded, "our entire covert program has gone to hell."[57]

Saddam had also successfully struck at the Iraqi National Accord—an opposition group originally formed with Saudi backing in 1990 and then based in Jordan. As INC declined, the CIA (along with the British intelligence service MI-6) began to support this other group with its membership of seemingly well-placed Iraqi military officers who had defected. Equipped with a powerful new radio station and claiming contacts at high levels of the Iraqi military, the Iraqi National Accord was trying to pull off a coup by senior officers close to Saddam. In January 1996, U.S. President Bill Clinton even authorized $6 million in covert aid to support its activities. This amount was similar or larger than the sum provided by Saudi Arabia and several other Arab states.[58] The new CIA director John M. Deutch also thought that by supporting the National Accord he could help revive both the operations directorate of the CIA and the usage of covert action in U.S. foreign policy.

However, Saddam easily infiltrated the National Accord and in June 1996 executed some 100 of its supporters in Iraq. Some even speculated that Saddam had perpetrated an elaborate sting operation by letting the CIA funnel money and Iraqi defectors into the group for some two years before striking at it. One might sarcastically conclude that there were two great realities governing here. First, if the United States knew about it, Saddam did too. Second, if someone came to the United States needing help to mount a coup against Saddam, they were probably incapable of pulling it off.

THE CIA'S ROLE

Saddam's successful strikes against the opposition led to many recriminations and eventually new revelations concerning the CIA's role in supporting the Iraqi opposition.[59] These covert operations spanned both the Bush and Clinton administrations and grew out of the original miscalculation that Saddam would be overthrown by his own military or by a popular uprising at the end of the Gulf War. Indeed, Bush even called upon the Iraqi people to take matters into their own hands and overthrow the dictator upon the war's conclusion. Heavily criticized after he let the popular uprisings be crushed, Bush then signed a "lethal finding" in May 1991 that ordered the CIA to bring about conditions that would lead to Saddam's demise. Despite a U.S. law that prohibits CIA agents from *directly* participating in assassination plots or supporting popular uprisings against established regimes, lethal findings authorize agents to take whatever other action they deem necessary.

In the covert operation against Saddam, Steven Richter was the CIA official with direct departmental responsibility, while John M. Deutch, the agency's director in 1995, was also involved. Other agents who played crucial roles included Warren Marik, who is now retired and "Bob," not otherwise identified because he is still involved in covert operations. At the operation's height from 1994 to 1996, some 50 agents rotated in and out of a fortified compound in the opposition-controlled town of Salahuddin just north of Irbil. Two staff aides from the Senate Intelligence Committee also accompanied CIA agents on evaluation missions into Iraqi Kurdistan and played an important role in pressing for the operation. Marik later explained that while "nobody said we should provide military training and weapons to the force [INC], nobody said stop it, either."[60]

The Bush administration earmarked an initial $40 million, much of which went to expand an international propaganda campaign the Kuwaiti government was already running to denounce Iraqi atrocities during the invasion in 1990. The CIA gave the contract for this expanded effort to the Rendon Group of Washington, a U.S. public relations and political lobbying firm headed by John Rendon, a former campaign consultant for Jimmy Carter during the 1980 campaign.

Rendon ran the operation from his office in Washington and branch offices in Boston and London. His main activity was to write radio scripts calling on Iraqi army officers to defect. These were then broadcast over two radio stations the CIA established called the Iraqi Broadcasting Corporation and Radio Hurrieh (Freedom). Both broadcast from CIA transmitters in Kuwait (with additional facilities in northern Iraq, Cairo, Amman, and

Jeddah) but were terminated after Saddam moved north in September 1996. Rendon also had unmanned aircraft fly over Baghdad and drop leaflets ridiculing Saddam on his birthday and turned out fake Baghdad newspapers, television films, and radio broadcasts.

Soon the Bush administration adopted a sort of shotgun approach, dispensing covert financial aid to anyone it deemed reasonably able to succeed through any of three possible options. These came to be known as the rolling coup, silver bullet, and palace coup. The first involved getting Kurdish groups to trigger a coup in Baghdad by encouraging them to move south from the territory they controlled in the north. The second sought to use economic sanctions to create a crisis atmosphere in Baghdad that might lead a lone Iraqi security official or family member to assassinate Saddam. The third option advocated a coup against Saddam by disgruntled Republican Guards or Iraqi security branches.

A fourth, rejected option was to pursue a more ambitious Afghan-style covert operation that would inflict major losses on Saddam's loyal Republican Guard forces and lead to a split by the remainder of the Iraqi military. This final choice was not pursued because U.S. authorities felt it would risk disrupting the fragile alliance that was forged during the Gulf War or lead to the unwanted fragmentation of Iraq.

All three of the authorized options were minimal efforts intended to supplement the much larger public U.S. campaign to eliminate Saddam economically and diplomatically, or at least keep him boxed through enforcing U.N. sanctions. The United States never seriously contemplated employing direct military force.

Salah Omar Ali Tikriti, a former member of the Iraqi Baath Party and government information minister, was one of the first members of the opposition supported by the CIA. Together with Ayad Allawi, Tikriti had helped establish the Iraqi National Accord (INA) in 1990. With CIA support, the group then set up a radio station called the Voice of Free Iraq. It operated from Saudi territory and called upon the Iraqi people to overthrow Saddam. In 1991, however, the group fragmented and Tikriti and Allawi went their separate ways.

For a brief period in 1996, the INA again ran a radio station from Amman and London called Al-Mustaqbal (The Future), and it was probably behind yet another called Iraqi Army Radio. Both, however, were shut down after Saddam marched north to aid Barzani in September 1996. In 1997, Al-Mustaqbal resumed broadcasting from Kuwait via the CIA transmitter that earlier had broadcast Radio Hurrieh. Their lack of continuity, however, undoubtedly hurt the effectiveness of these covert radio stations.

Next, the CIA turned its attention to INC, which, as mentioned above, was created in June 1992. The CIA believed that by financing INC it could keep peace among the Kurds, deter Iraqi strikes into the north, and incite opposition to Saddam. Ahmad Chalabi told me that during the INC leaders' visit to Washington in 1993, Vice President Al Gore made promises of support that were even stronger than the Balfour Declaration by which the British pledged the Jews a national homeland following World War I. Chalabi went on to argue, however, that since Francis Fukuyama's concept of the "End of History" so heavily influenced U.S. foreign policy, the United States no longer seemed to think it mattered what mistakes it made. In the end people would simply return to the United States because they had nowhere else to go.

Washington was reluctant to supply INC with such sophisticated weaponry as grenade launchers and armored projectiles because of its fear that an INC victory might lead the Shiites to establish an Islamic-style government *a la* Iran. Under pressure from Turkey, the United States also remained adamantly opposed to the possibility of a Kurdish state somehow emerging from INC's activities. Therefore, INC was given just enough support to cause Saddam trouble, but never enough to actually overthrow him. It was all reminiscent of the CIA's support for Mulla Mustafa Barzani in the early 1970s. In this case too the United States "hoped that our clients [the Kurds] would not prevail. They [the United States] preferred instead that the insurgents simply continue a level of hostilities sufficient to sap the resources of . . . [Iraq]."[61] Of course, "this policy was not imparted to our clients [the Kurds], who were encouraged to continue fighting. Even in the context of covert action, ours was a cynical enterprise."

A U.S. official concluded, however, that INC and the Kurds had exaggerated their own power and misinterpreted what had been promised. "They [the Kurds] claimed they had unbelievable contacts in Baghdad and incredible intelligence on low morale in the Iraqi military. They were so naive in regards to Saddam."[62]

As a result, early CIA support for INC was limited to establishing television and radio stations that broadcast anti-Saddam rhetoric to Baghdad, publishing miniaturized versions of anti-Saddam books, and occasionally sending unmanned aerial reconnaissance vehicles over Iraqi cities to drop propaganda leaflets. The KDP and PUK used CIA funds to buy Toyota Land Cruisers and Jeeps to scurry their leaders around the Kurdish countryside. Suspicious of its new ally Chalabi, the CIA periodically carried out clandestine inspections of his accounts to see how he was actually spending the money.

When the Clinton administration assumed office in 1993, it initially tried to cut the funding for INC because it seemed to be leading nowhere. One CIA source concluded that during the Bush administration, "the question we kept getting from the White House then was 'How much do you need?' After Clinton and [national security advisor Anthony] Lake came in, it changed to 'How much can you get along on?'"[63] Kurdish protests and an effective lobbying effort from Congress, however, soon led to the restoration of INC's funding. A U.S. official privy to these funding debates explained, "the predisposition of everybody in policy and on Capitol Hill is to throw money at these things."[64] In 1993, the CIA also began to shift money from the Rendon operation to direct support for INC, and U.S. officials began visiting the Kurdish region.

By the middle of 1994, the CIA decided that it should have some agents on the ground in Iraqi Kurdistan to oversee INC's operations. In September, two Senate Intelligence Committee staff aides accompanied "Bob," who at that time was the deputy director of the Iraqi Operations Group, into the area. Soon afterward, the committee authorized the CIA to set up a clandestine, semipermanent team. In late October 1994, Warren Marik, a veteran of the agency's covert action program in Afghanistan, led the first field team to establish an office in four rented houses in Salahuddin, the mountain resort town just north of Irbil.

Over the next 2 years some 50 agents rotated in and out of the office as teams of 4 to 10 agents lived there for an average stint of 6 weeks. In addition to advising INC and checking up on its activities, the CIA teams collected their own intelligence and interviewed defectors and dissidents who had escaped to the north.

As noted above, one of these defectors was General Wafiq al-Samarra'i, the former head of Iraqi military intelligence. He claimed to have supporters in strategic positions inside the Iraqi military who could help INC and its Kurdish allies attack Iraqi military units on the edge of the Kurdish-held region. These actions would produce a "rolling coup" that would ignite military revolts in Mosul and Kirkuk and gradually roll Saddam's authority back to a position in which he would become hardly more than the mayor of Baghdad.

Named for the blond, blue-eyed, six-foot-tall agent who helped develop it, the "Bob plan" called for some 20,000 KDP and PUK guerrillas to launch a coordinated strike on the Iraqi garrisons of Mosul and Kirkuk. They would be supported by some 1,000 INC fighters and a similar number from the Iraqi Communist Party. (The latter group was certainly an ironic addition given the former animus the United States held for it.) It was hoped that the offensive would demonstrate the opposition's strength, highlight the Iraqi troops' unwillingness to defend Saddam, and encourage disaffected members of the Iraqi military to desert. Samarra'i was to direct the operation.

Another ironic touch was an attempt to use Iran in the plan. "Bob" asked Chalabi to let Iran know that the United States would look with favor on Iran distracting Iraq by moving troops along its border with Iraq as the operation began. To prove his bona fides, "Bob" supposedly stood in the hallway as two Iranian intelligence agents walked into Chalabi's office to be given what they were told was a message from the United States. As the INC leader explained it, the Iranians "had to see an American there or they wouldn't believe it. Their eyes were popping out of their heads."[65]

What followed next seems strange, but apparently the United States decided that the operation would fail and withdrew its backing. Samarra'i told me he thought the United States was really afraid that if the operation was successful, it would facilitate the Iraqi Shiites' assumption of power in Iraq. In addition, "Bob"'s superiors apparently did not approve of the Iranian contact that they discovered through communications intercepted by the U.S. National Security Agency (NSA). Ironically, U.S. officials also concluded that the operation had been penetrated, and that there was a chance for failure.

Shortly afterward, John M. Deutch—who had become the new director of the CIA in May 1995—instead threw his agency's support to the Iraqi National Accord, which, as mentioned above, was indeed thoroughly penetrated. Apparently, the Clinton administration was anxious to stage a quick palace coup that would not risk a Shiite takeover and would eliminate Saddam before the 1996 presidential elections in the United States. The "Bob plan"'s slower, salami-slicing strategy lost favor.

Although INC and the PUK went ahead with the "Bob plan" in March 1995, the U.S. withdrawal also convinced Barzani to pull out. This, of course, crippled any chance for success. As explained above, Barzani had concluded that the United States was not serious and could not be trusted, a belief he already held because of his father's earlier experiences.

The whole affair also contributed to further bad blood between the KDP and PUK as Barzani attacked Talabani while he was attempting to implement the "Bob Plan" with INC. Indeed, during the following year Barzani actually turned to Saddam to rout Talabani (temporarily) and capture Irbil. The price Barzani paid, of course, was to betray some 100 INC agents to Saddam, who rounded them up and executed them as soon as his troops entered the area. Talabani concluded that Kurdistan "has turned into a graveyard for the opposition forces because of Barzani's treachery."[66]

In response to Saddam's brief occupation of Irbil, the United States did little except strike a few Iraqi military targets south of Baghdad and offer asylum to some 7,200 Kurds who had supported the opposition and were now deemed to be in danger. The CIA had spent more than half a decade and $110 million trying to overthrow Saddam Hussein in what might well be one of its most expensive and sustained failures since the Bay of Pigs fiasco in 1961. Sharp bureaucratic factionalism and confusion within the CIA as case officers battled each other to impress superiors and promote different cliques of Iraqi oppositionists undermined any chance for success. As noted above, however, blame also can be assigned to the White House, Congress, the Defense Department, and the State Department.

There was to be even further fallout. In addition to his planned offensive in March 1995, Samarra'i hatched a plot to assassinate Saddam that ironically led to a top-secret U.S.

Federal Bureau of Investigation (FBI) criminal investigation of the CIA agents supposedly involved for attempting to murder Saddam in violation of U.S. law. Although the agents were ultimately exonerated, the FBI probe had a chilling effect on the CIA effort against Saddam and symbolized the confusion and even self-imposed legalistic ignorance imposed on U.S. espionage and covert action in the present era by an ultra-strict interpretation of the United States law banning assassinations.

Even while he was planning the INC offensive for March 1995, Samarra'i told the CIA team in Salahuddin that his associates still in Iraq could ambush Saddam while he was traveling through Samarra'i's home town of Samarra. The plan was to shoot and disable the first and last cars of Saddam's convoy as it passed over a bridge. Then, once the convoy was blocked, Samarra'i's associates would destroy it.

The CIA authorities immediately rejected the plan and ordered their team in Iraqi Kurdistan not to discuss it any more. The plan was never implemented. Soon, however, the NSA intercepts of Iranian communications concerning the assassination plot led to the CIA team in the field being pulled back to the United States, and criminal proceedings against its members were initiated. These charges were only dropped a year later when CIA and FBI officials realized that they were based on misleading information that was spread in the region by Iraqi dissident leaders and Iranian intelligence agents. The former were apparently upset with the reluctance of the United States to more aggressively move against Saddam, while the latter might have been simply baiting their U.S. enemy to shoot itself in the foot.

In December 1996, Baghdad television even mocked U.S. intelligence when the Iraqi authorities reported how they had captured Iraqi agents working for the United States that fall. Sa'd Dahham Awwad, one of those being interrogated by the Iraqis, declared: "Some people place a halo on the CIA. We, those who are here now provide an example of the assurances they used to make. Where are they now to save me?"[67]

Refugees

Shortly after Saddam struck at the INC office in Iraqi Kurdistan in August 1996, the United States began an air lift of the first group of Kurdish asylum seekers from Turkey—to which they had fled—to the distant U.S. territory of Guam in the south Pacific.[68] The first group of 2,100 Kurds were former employees of the U.S. government or were closely connected with it. Many of them had worked for the Office of Foreign Disaster Assistance (OFDA) or the Military Coordination Center (MCC) that helped to facilitate the no-fly zone over Iraqi Kurdistan. The second group of some 600 Kurds had worked for the CIA or various Iraqi opposition groups, while the third group of approximately 4,200 were former employees of European or U.S. non-governmental organizations (NGOs).

The refugees gave a variety of reasons for their flight. Some said they were simply forced to leave by accusations in the Iraqi media against Kurds who had collaborated with the Americans. Others told of Iraqi soldiers seizing computerized lists of Kurds who had worked with U.S. agencies and systematically hunting down those listed for execution. All claimed to be in fear for their lives.

After being processed for some two months on Guam, most of the Kurds were then flown to the United States where they were to begin a new life. Upon arrival they were turned over to one of 11 nonprofit agencies—including the Kurdish-American-run Kurdish Human Rights Watch (KHRW) in Washington, D.C.—the U.S. government paid to help resettle them in various communities around the country. These cities included Nashville, Tennessee; San Diego, California; Fargo, North Dakota; and Washington, D.C. The refugee agencies were given $1,000 per person to cover the first month of housing, food, and other expenses. In addition, most families were eligible for up to five years of Medicaid, food stamps, and cash assistance.

The specific amount of help the Kurds received, however, varied according to the agency aiding them. For most of the refugees everything in their new home was foreign. They found it strange, for example, that they did not know their neighbors and that Muslims were in the minority. They were also perplexed by the cost of housing and other necessities, as well as the reliance on computers and other technology. Women unaccustomed to Western values realized that they would need to find a job. Given the language barrier, something as simple as taking a bus could turn into a day-long trauma. These, of course, were problems that had been faced by generations of earlier immigrants and usually would be eventually solved.

Six of the refugees suspected of being double agents, were detained by the Immigration and Naturalization Service in Los Angeles. They maintained that they had been falsely accused by personal enemies within the Iraqi opposition, but the specific evidence against them at first was kept secret. In an ironic twist of fate, the former director of the CIA, R. James Woolsey, Jr., volunteered to represent them in court in an effort to win their release. When the evidence against them was finally declassified, it appeared weak and unsubstantiated. But the six suspects remain imprisoned as of October 1998. One former CIA official warned that the case was certain to damage the CIA's future ability to recruit foreign agents. He sarcastically concluded, "the lesson of the six is this: if the going gets tough, the friends of the U.S. could well end up in a U.S. jail."[69]

Renewed U.S. Efforts

Given the repeated blows it had suffered, the Iraqi opposition lacked credibility as the 1990s drew to a close. Rend Rahim Francke, the executive director of the Iraq Foundation in Washington, concluded, "there is nothing in place inside Iraq at this time to take advantage of any weakening of Saddam,"[70] while George Jaffe, the deputy director of the Royal Institute of International Affairs in London, added: "They [the opposition] lack credibility. . . . None has shown the ability to organize effectively, maintain popularity inside Iraq or create a viable alternative."

The prevailing view in both the United States and Britain remained that Saddam was unlikely to fall to a popular uprising. Rather, given the nature of his regime, change was more likely to come from the circle around Saddam. Nevertheless, to supplement its public support of ongoing international sanctions against Saddam's government, the United States continued to consider implementing renewed support for the Iraqi opposition in a variety of ways.

In February 1998, the Committee for Peace and Security in the Gulf, a Washington-based organization consisting of such prominent former government officials as Defense Secretaries Donald Rumsfeld and Frank Carlucci, National Security Advisors Richard Allen and William Clark, and former U.S. Representative Stephen Solarz, among numerous others, recommended to the president an initiative that included some of the following elements:

- Recognize a provisional government of Iraq based on the principles and leaders of INC.
- Restore and enhance the safe haven in northern Iraq to allow the provisional government to extend its authority there and establish a zone in southern Iraq from which Saddam's ground forces would also be excluded.
- Lift sanctions in liberated areas. Sanctions are instruments of war against Saddam's regime, but they should be quickly lifted on those who have freed themselves from it. Also, the oil resources and products of the liberated areas should help fund the provisional government's insurrection and humanitarian relief for the people of liberated Iraq.
- Release frozen Iraqi assets—which amount to $1.6 billion in the United States and Britain alone—to the control of the provisional government to fund its insurrection. This could be done gradually as long as the provisional government continues to promote a democratic Iraq.
- Facilitate broadcasts from U.S. transmitters immediately and establish a Radio Free Iraq.
- Help expand liberated areas in Iraq by assisting the provisional government's offensive against Saddam's regime logistically and through other means.
- Remove any vestiges of Saddam's claim to "legitimacy" by, among other things, bringing a war crimes indictment against the dictator and his lieutenants and challenging Saddam's credentials to fill the Iraqi seat at the United Nations.
- Launch a systematic air campaign against the pillars of his power—the Republican Guard divisions which prop him up and the military infrastructure that sustains him.
- Position U.S. ground force equipment in the region so that, as a last resort, we have the capacity to protect and assist the anti-Saddam forces in the northern and southern parts of Iraq.[71]

That same month (February 1998) it was reported that the CIA had drafted a new plan that called for enlisting Kurdish and Shiite agents to destroy or damage key elements of Iraqi economic and political power such as utility plants or government broadcast stations.[72] The new CIA plan also called for increasing political pressure on Baghdad through propaganda programs such as a Radio Free Iraq. The aim was to try to undermine Saddam by showing Iraqi citizens that he was not invincible, strengthening his opponents inside Iraq, and trying to ignite a rebellion within his inner circle. "This is not a propaganda operation. This is a major campaign of sabotage," explained a senior government official.

Other officials claimed that if the president approved a finding to implement the new plan, it could become one of the biggest covert actions since the end of the cold war and cost tens of million of dollars a year. In meetings with U.S. congress members and public policy organizations such as the American Enterprise Institute, Ahmad Chalabi pressed for renewed support and claimed that Iraq was ripe for a broad-based anti-Saddam revolt: "Our abilities and our impact will develop in a very major way if we are sufficiently supported now."[73]

Given the past record of such activities and the divided opposition's inherent weaknesses, it remained unclear how such a new plan could be any more successful than the old ones—even if the president approved a finding for it. Moreover, Secretary of State Madeleine Albright, CIA Director George Tenet, and National Security Advisor Samuel Berger were all reported to be skeptical of what was being proposed. During February 1998, U.S. public opinion also turned strongly against air strikes on Iraq to enforce U.N. weapons inspections of Saddam's so-called presidential sites. Renewed support for covert efforts against Saddam seemed even more unlikely following U.N. Secretary-General Kofi Annan's brokered deal with Saddam over inspecting the presidential sites.

Nevertheless, in May 1988, President Clinton signed a bill giving $5 million more to the Iraqi opposition.[74] According to the new law's provisions, the funds would be spent on training, organizing, and promoting the unity of the democratic Iraqi opposition. The law also specified "that a significant portion of the support for the democratic opposition should go to the Iraqi National Congress, a group that has demonstrated the capacity to effectively challenge the Saddam Hussein regime with representation from Sunni, Shia, and Kurdish elements of Iraq."

Specifically the new U.S. plan aimed to promote as many as 10–15 small conferences per year that would bring together members of the opposition to discuss such diverse topics as human, civil, and minority rights in Iraq, women in Iraqi society, federalism vs. centralism in Iraq, the role of the United Nations in Iraq's economic development, rebuilding the middle class, and the transition from dictatorship to pluralism.[75] The U.S. plan also called for training sessions conducted by organizational management consultants on office administration, fund-raising, grant proposal writing, accounting, data processing, intra- and intergroup communications, desktop publishing, Internet usage, media relations, and other related topics. An additional $1 (later increased to some $5) million were earmarked to establish a Radio Free Iraq that, unlike earlier covert stations, would publicly acknowledge the support of the U.S. government. Finally, the plan provided that funds would be allocated to the campaign to indict Saddam and his associates for genocide, crimes against humanity, and war crimes.

Some criticized the decision to base Radio Free Iraq in Prague where it would be run by the U.S. cold war Radio Free Europe/Radio Liberty, rather than by an Iraqi opposition group. Although Chalabi welcomed the renewed U.S. support and declared, "we look forward to working with the U.S. Congress and the Clinton Administration in our effort to remove Saddam's regime,"[76] critics of the new plan argued that it would only create an Iraqi opposition debating society on the outskirts of London. Benjamin A. Gilman (R-N.Y.), the chairman of the International Relations Committee in the U.S. House of Representatives, called it a "baby step" that might "lead to a slightly higher profile for the Iraqi opposition abroad but [be of] little help in Iraq."[77]

During the summer of 1998, the Clinton administration reportedly sought new authority from Congress to plan and mount further covert operations against Saddam.[78] This new plan supposedly would go further than previous CIA efforts and seek to weaken and potentially oust the dictator by reaching out even to such Iran-based Shiite opposition groups as SAIRI.

Congress, however, seemed frustrated with the administration's lack of results in the recent confrontations with Iraq over weapons inspections and was seeking a more aggressive posture. In April 1998, for example, Senate Majority Leader Trent Lott (R-Miss.) had met with retired army general Wayne

Downing, the former chief of the U.S. Special Operations Command, to analyze possible military options against Saddam including the hiring of a private military training company to work with the Iraqi resistance.

The Clinton administration, however, reacted with annoyance at what it saw as congressional freelancing on military affairs. Assistant Secretary of State for Middle Eastern Affairs Martin Indyk presented a report that argued for uniting the Iraqi opposition but doubted that it would actually oust Saddam.[79] By sending such seemingly contradictory messages, U.S. policy toward the Iraqi opposition continued to appear muddled and hesitant.

In June 1998, Laurie Mylroie, a Washington-based analyst, released a list of 82 Iraqi opposition groups compiled from data obtained at the U.S. State Department. In many places the list was redundant and dated. Mylroie observed that a number of the groups listed appeared "not to be valid recipients of [potential] U.S. assistance. Many . . . are heavily influenced by Tehran or Damascus or they purport to be communists. Some are strongly suspected of having clandestine ties to Baghdad, and many are not opposition groups, or they no longer exist."[80] This profile, of course, summed up some of the main problems the United States had when trying to work with the Iraqi opposition.

For their part the Kurds continued to see the weak and divided opposition as a poor bet. In September 1998, for example, INC in London called on both the KDP and the PUK to rejoin it: "We would like them to take part in our efforts to put an end to Saddam's reign . . . and rejoin us."[81] Although meeting together for the first time in four years under U.S. auspices and grateful to the Americans for their aid and promised protection, both Barzani and Talabani declined. Barzani explained:

> Our view is that any opposition abroad will not achieve anything. . . . Our situation differs from that of the opposition abroad. . . . If we are not sure the alternative will be democratic and achieves a peaceful solution for the Kurdish People on the bases of Federalism, then it will be very difficult for us to be part of any plan. . . . This project is not ripe. . . . [82]

Talabani concurred:

> We are not part of any foreign plan to topple the current
> regime in Baghdad. . . . Regrettably, the INC has been frozen
> and . . . only Dr. Jalabi [Chalabi] and his two deputies . . .
> remain. . . . We do not believe that the opposition abroad
> can carry out any serious actions.[83]

The U.S. Congress, however, was frustrated by the Clinton administration's seeming unwillingness to take stronger action against Saddam, when he again began to block U.N. inspections in August 1998. Scott Ritter's subsequent resignation from the U.N. inspection team and his stinging denunciations of the administration's inaction fueled this frustration. The U.S. legislative body was probably also emboldened by the threat of presidential impeachment over the Monica Lewinsky scandal.

Thus, in October 1998, Congress passed the Iraq Liberation Act. This potentially far-reaching legislation authorized the administration—but did not require it—to provide $97 million in equipment and arms from U.S. military stocks and to train an Iraqi opposition group or groups that could demonstrate broad-based representation and a record of support for democracy. Then, U.S. air power would protect an opposition army that would capture lightly defended areas in southern and western Iraq and thus encourage mass defections from Saddam's military.[84]

Although only time would tell if this newest attempt to stoke the Iraqi opposition against Saddam would succeed, the past history indicated that it would not. In the first place the opposition remained weak and divided. The Kurds, who—with their armed forces and territory in northern Iraq—constitute the most important part of the opposition, remained conspicuously aloof from the new project. Even if the opposition could field troops, there is no chance that any of Iraq's neighbors would agree to house or train them. The United States was certainly not going to send its own troops into Iraq. Thus, any attempt to field opposition troops promised to replicate the fiasco of the Bay of Pigs.

Most important, the United States did not seem to be serious about overthrowing Saddam. Rather, the entire question of the Iraqi opposition and Saddam's future seemed a political football to be used in U.S. domestic politics. To his credit, the president—although threatened by impeachment—seemed to disdain the "wag-the-dog" mentality of starting a foreign war to save himself domestically. Instead, he apparently had decided his best bet for survival was to follow the public opinion polls, and on this particular matter they indicated deep reluctance toward any further Iraqi adventures. In addition, U.S. bombing of Iraq would result in the deaths of innocent civilians, probably not kill Saddam, and thus simply reinforce Saddam's position. Nevertheless, in December 1998, the United States finally did react to Saddam's failure to cooperate with U.N. inspections by launching a short but heavy bombing campaign against Iraq. As 1999 began, the volatile situation kept alive the possibility of eventual U.S. military action that might lead to Saddam's removal. Only time would tell.

4

The KDP-PUK Civil War

Shortly after the end of the 1991 Gulf War, the Kurds who had fled to the borders of Iran and Turkey after their failed uprising against Saddam were able to return to their homes in northern Iraq.[1] There they began to build a fledgling state and government.[2] This was accomplished largely under the aegis of the Allied Operation Provide Comfort and no-fly zone. The unprecedented United Nations Security Council Resolution 688 of April 5, 1991, also played an important symbolic role by condemning "the repression of the Iraqi civilian population . . . in Kurdish populated areas" and demanding "that Iraq . . . immediately end this repression." In addition, limited but important initial Turkish cooperation and protection played a part.

The Kurds also helped themselves by taking impressive strides toward the unity that so often had proven elusive in the past. The Iraqi Kurdistan Front of eventually eight different parties held elections in May 1992 that led to the formation of a parliament in June and a government in July. In October 1992, this young Kurdish government declared its ultimate intention of becoming a federal state within a future democratic, post-Saddam Iraq.

The two main parties—the Kurdistan Democratic Party (KDP) of Massoud Barzani and the Patriotic Union of Kurdistan (PUK) of Jalal Talabani—split power equally between themselves in a coalition. By the end of 1992, Talabani claimed that "cooperation . . . has been strengthened to the extent that opinions have developed within their ranks, even at leadership levels, calling for unifying these two parties."[3] Barzani added, "it pleases me to assert that all affairs are managed now as if the two were a single party."[4]

It was particularly disappointing for those who wished the Kurds well, therefore, that the KDP and PUK fell out between themselves during 1994 in a civil war that threatened the very existence of everything they had achieved. The purpose of this chapter is to analyze the background of the longstanding KDP-PUK rivalry and the relapse into conflict. Not only will such a study help us better understand the causes for the present intra-Kurdish conflict, but it might also enable us to know how to help bring the conflict to an end and avoid similar problems in the future.

BACKGROUND

The preeminent party in modern Iraqi Kurdish history, the KDP was established in 1946 in response to the earlier creation of the Iranian KDP of the Mahabad Republic.[5] At the KDP's first congress in Baghdad on August 16, 1946, Mulla Mustafa Barzani, probably the most famous Kurdish leader in the twentieth century, was elected president or chairman, and Hamza Abdullah secretary-general. Two landlords, Shaikh Latif (son of Shaikh Mahmud Barzinji of Sulaymaniya, an earlier prominent Iraqi Kurdish leader who had battled against the British in the 1920s) and Shaikh Ziad Aghaz, were chosen as vice presidents. It also was decided to publish a clandestine monthly called *Rizgari* (Liberation), renamed *Khebat* (Struggle) at the party's third congress at Kirkuk in January 1953.[6]

The KDP's original program was vague, speaking of the Kurds' national goals and their desire to live in a state of their own choice. It lacked any progressive social or economic substance due to the dominance held by the traditional, tribal leaders. Given Barzani's long exile in the Soviet Union until the fall of the Iraqi monarchy in July 1958 and the relatively quiescent state of Kurdish affairs until that time, the KDP played only a limited role. Its second congress in Baghdad in March 1951 supposedly was devoted to repairing its disintegrating ranks. One observer concluded that the KDP of those days "was more of a social and cultural gathering than a well-defined political party."[7]

During these early years, an intraparty struggle developed between supporters of the party's secretary-general Hamza Abdullah, a leftist supporter of Barzani, and Ibrahim Ahmad, who at first headed the Iraqi branch of the Iranian KDP. In retrospect, this early party division partially heralded the future split between the KDP and PUK.

Born in 1914, Ahmad was a graduate of the faculty of law at the University of Baghdad. He had published his thesis on Arab-Kurdish relations in 1937. Although he flirted with communism—as did most Kurdish intellectuals in those days—and even spent three years in prison for communist activities in the early 1950s, Ahmad could best be characterized as a leftist Kurdish Nationalist.

When Ahmad emerged from prison in 1953, he replaced Abdullah—who himself was then in prison for his political activities—as secretary-general. Barzani, however, did not like the new KDP leader and spoke disparagingly of his "pride and vanity."[8]

With Barzani's support, Abdullah in turn replaced Ahmad as secretary-general briefly in 1959. However, Abdullah grew too close to the Iraqi Communist Party—apparently proposing to transfer various KDP organizations to its control—and later that year he was permanently removed and Ahmad reinstated. The nascent intra-Kurdish split between the more conservative and traditional, tribal wing of the KDP associated with Barzani, and the leftist, intellectual Marxist wing (later called the KDP politburo) led by Ahmad and increasingly by his son-in-law, Jalal Talabani, was set.

As noted in chapter 2, Talabani was born in 1933 in the village of Kelkan near Lake Dokan in Iraqi Kurdistan.[9] He joined the KDP in 1947 and was elected to its central committee in 1951 at the age of 18. Twice denied entry into medical school because of his political activities, he finally was admitted into law school in 1953. Despite interruptions due to his political activities, he eventually graduated in 1959. He then served as commander of a tank unit in the Iraqi army until he joined Barzani's revolt against the Baghdad government in 1961. When not opposing Barzani, Talabani represented him during the 1960s in several diplomatic meetings in Europe and the Middle East in which he met Gamal Abdul Nasser in 1963.

The Barzani wing was associated with the Kurmanji- or Bahdinani-speaking areas in the mountainous north, while the Ahmad-Talabani group came from the more cultured, Sorani-speaking areas of the south. As Martin van Bruinessen, a leading authority on the Kurds, has noted: "the 'Soran' often find the 'Kurmanj' primitive and fanatical in religious affairs, but they acknowledge their fighting prowess; the 'Kurmanj' often see the 'Soran' as unmanly, unreliable and culturally arrogant."[10] The fact that the Barzani and Talabani families were also associated with the two great rival Sufi orders in Iraqi Kurdistan, the Naqshbandi and Qadiri, possibly provided a further impetus to their rivalry.[11]

During Barzani's sojourn in the Soviet Union, the KDP fell under the control of the Ahmad or KDP politburo faction. Barzani's return signaled an intense struggle within the party between him, "the man of the tribes" and the "reformist," "town-bred intellectuals." It was with this background that Barzani skeptically replied, concerning the role of the KDP: "What it can do it does. But according to me, there is no party, only the Kurdish people."[12]

The struggle intensified in 1964 when Barzani signed a cease-fire accord with Baghdad without informing the politburo. Both factions of the KDP supposedly expelled each other from the party, but Barzani won the day by driving the politburo over the Iranian frontier. This incident apparently led Iran to transfer its support from the politburo to Barzani, thus enabling him to increase his control over the movement. Although Talabani rejoined Barzani in 1965, he soon broke away again, branding Barzani "tribal," "feudal," and "reactionary."[13]

This intra-Kurdish rivalry—as well as the similar, radical, social ideas they shared—in time led the Talabani-Ahmad faction to develop ties with the Baathists, who, after they regained power in 1968, were also wary of Barzani's ties with Iran and other foreign powers. Accordingly, Talabani made a deal with Baghdad that allowed him to control the Sulaymaniya-Kirkuk region. On some occasions, Talabani's guerrillas even fought alongside the government's troops against Barzani, a situation that helped lead to Barzani's reputed characterization of Talabani as an "agent for everybody."[14] At this time Ahmad was living in Tehran and then later Baghdad, thus adding further credence to Barzani's accusations.

The split in the Iraqi Kurdish movement was basic and deep. The Ahmad-Talabani group, at times in cooperation with the Baathists, was challenging Barzani's leadership of the KDP and attempting to expand into his northern mountainous homeland.

Nevertheless, during the fighting of the late 1960s, Barzani's peshmergas (guerrillas) grew into more than 20,000 well-equipped fighters armed with anti-aircraft guns, field guns, anti-tank weapons, and increasing Iranian support. As a result, the Baathists finally decided to abandon Talabani and negotiate with Barzani. Both Talabani and Ahmad contritely returned to the KDP, which had become Barzani's virtual fiefdom.

The promise of the March Manifesto of 1970 on Kurdish autonomy, however, was not realized. Renewed fighting between the Kurds and Baghdad led to Barzani's final defeat and surrender in March 1975. The legendary Kurdish leader died in exile in Washington, D.C., four years later.

After Barzani's collapse, his KDP broke into several factions. To trace their respective fates would serve no useful purpose here. The real heirs of Barzani's KDP proved to be his two sons, the half brothers Idris (1944-1987) and Massoud (born 1946). In Iran they joined a former associate of their father, Muhammad Abdurrahman, popularly known as "Sami," to form the KDP/Provisional Command (KDPPC) in November 1975.

At what was considered the ninth congress of the KDP held on the Iraqi-Iranian-Turkish border December 4-12, 1979, the party reassumed its old name, the KDP. Internal conflicts between the relatively progressive Sami and the more traditional Idris led to Sami leaving the party to establish his own Kurdistan Popular Democratic Party (KPDP). Massoud and Idris in effect shared the reconstituted KDP's leadership until Idris died of a sudden heart attack in 1987. Since that date, Massoud has been the unchallenged leader.

At the party's eleventh congress in August 1993, Sami led his new organization—a combination of three recently united smaller parties (one of which was the KPDP) called the Kurdistan Unity Party—back into the KDP fold and once again became a senior member of the KDP's leadership. The KDP later argued that its expansion in 1993 was one of the factors that caused the PUK to launch what the KDP termed a coup in 1994. (See below.)

Jalal Talabani's PUK represented what was to become the other major faction of the old KDP of Mulla Mustafa Barzani. Shortly after the Baathists crushed the old KDP in March 1975, Talabani canvassed Kurds who had been able to escape from Iraq. In June 1975, he announced in Damascus the formation of the PUK. As described above, this new organization was really the heir of the old KDP politburo that had battled against Mulla Mustafa in the earlier years. Although the PUK adopted the same slogan as the KDP—"autonomy for Kurdistan, democracy for Iraq"—it advocated Marxist principles and denounced the Barzanis as "reactionary."

In 1976, the PUK became the first Kurdish party to return peshmergas to Iraqi Kurdistan. The KDP followed and soon the two groups had several hundred highly mobile fighters mounting raids against Iraq. In the fall of 1977, the PUK moved its headquarters from Damascus to the Sorani-speaking areas of the Sulaymaniya region. Arms and supplies, however, had to come from Syria through Turkey by way of the KDP-controlled areas. Early in 1978, therefore, Talabani sent many of his best fighters to facilitate this movement.

The KDP felt threatened and dealt a bitter defeat to the PUK, whose fighters did not know the terrain. Ali Askari, who had been widely respected as one of Mulla Mustafa's most capable commanders and had become a prominent leader of the PUK after 1975, was one of those killed in this intra-Kurdish bloodletting.

Early in 1979, Ayatollah Ruhollah Khomeini overthrew Shah Muhammad Reza Pahlavi and established an Islamic republic in Iran. This new regime either did not want to or could not enforce the provisions of the Algiers Agreement of 1975 between Iraq and Iran on preventing cross-border Kurdish activities. Once again the KDP began to establish bases in Iran to challenge Baghdad, a situation that helped lead to the Iran-Iraq War of 1980–88.

For much of the war, the Iraqi Kurds partially ruled themselves as Saddam fought for his very existence; both sides endeavored to use the other's Kurds as fifth columns. The KDP supported Iran from the start and at times acted almost as advance units for its attacking armies. The PUK, however, at first wavered between the two antagonists. Both the KDP and the PUK formed mutually hostile fronts with smaller Kurdish parties.

By the fall of 1981, the KDP-PUK relationship had degenerated into open conflict. Following an appeal for unity, the two tempered their relations and even managed to carry out a joint operation in the Sulaymaniya area in August 1982. Iran's major Haj Omran offensive into northern Iraq in July 1983, however, led to new misunderstandings and hostilities between the two.

The KDP saw the situation as an opportunity to magnify its armed opposition to Baghdad with Iranian aid. The PUK, on the other hand, believed that in such a moment of weakness, Iraq would be more willing to negotiate a favorable deal. Indeed, the defeats on the front and unrest among the Kurds had already caused Saddam to begin to try to appease the Kurdish people. Baghdad reemphasized the rights already supposedly enjoyed by its Kurds and the threat fundamentalist Iran represented. This point concerning Iran appealed particularly to the PUK's secular emphasis, rather than the more traditionalist KDP. Some Kurds accused of antigovernment activities were pardoned, while Kurdish soldiers who had deserted from the Iraqi army were granted amnesty.

As the combined Iranian-KDP offensive forced the PUK out of its sanctuary and deeper into Iraq, the PUK and Baghdad agreed to a cease-fire in December 1983. With the help of Baghdad's Iranian Kurdish ally, Saddam and the PUK then signed a so-called Comprehensive Political and Security Agreement.

At first Iraq seemingly agreed to alter the autonomy law in favor of the Kurds and to extend it to other areas. Although the PUK came under heavy criticism from its former Kurdish allies as well as the KDP for dealing with Baghdad, it replied that the cease-fire offered it necessary breathing space and the chance to achieve longstanding Kurdish goals.

In retrospect, however, neither Baghdad nor the PUK viewed their negotiations as anything more than a way to gain time. Although they continued to talk until October 1984, the PUK finally terminated the dialogue at the beginning of the following year and began to reconcile itself with the KDP. By 1986, a KDP official declared: "We are not enemies anymore, but we cannot be considered loyal friends either. So far as we know [Talabani] fights against the Iraqi government."[15]

This understanding was broadened into the Iraqi Kurdistan Front (IKF) that was announced in principle in July 1987 and formally in May 1988, with the addition, over the next few years, of several smaller Kurdish groups plus the Assyrian Democratic Movement. The Islamic Movement of Kurdistan (IMK) led by Sheikh Osman Abdul Aziz, various other Islamic groups, and the Turkomen groups, however, remained aloof.

Upon its creation, the IKF declared that its main goals were to overthrow the Baathist regime of Saddam Hussein, establish a genuinely democratic government in Iraq, and develop a federal status for the Kurds.[16] Jalal Talabani and Massoud Barzani became its two co-presidents. Together they shared the tragedies and hopes of their people during the next several years.

RELAPSE INTO CONFLICT

Based on the above analysis of previous KDP-PUK conflicts, the relapse into intra-Kurdish fighting that occurred following December 1993 and May 1994 is no surprise. Old divisions can be very difficult to overcome. Fighting that began as minor disputes escalated into a renewal of what was essentially the old dispute for ultimate power between the KDP and the PUK. Furthermore, as Danielle Mitterrand, the wife of the French president, observed:

> One wonders how a democracy can flourish in a country abandoned to the bombing of their Iranian and Turkish neighbors and to the destructive intrusions of the Iraqi army with all the exactions, the withdrawal of the currency, power cuts, deportation of the population living in the unprotected part of Kurdistan, the double embargo imposed by the Iraqi government, a complete lack of energy supplies, the burning of the crops, and the daily tragedy of anti-personnel mines.[17]

The Kurdistan Regional Government (KRG) had been weakened from its inception by Barzani's and Talabani's decision not
to participate. This denied the government valuable credibility
and left it in the hands of mere lieutenants. By 1993, the 50/50
principle that split power equally between the KDP and the PUK
in each ministry had further paralyzed the KRG's initiative while
fueling partisanship. Then, in March 1993, there was an important shift in government positions as the PUK introduced some
of its senior leaders into the cabinet. Kosrat Rasul, a leading
member of the PUK politburo, replaced Fuad Masum, who was
more of a technocrat, as the prime minister. Tensions began to
rise as the government became even more partisan.

In the summer of 1993, Sami Abdurrahman's Kurdistan Unity
Party—a recent alignment of three smaller parties that had
previously all been members of the Iraqi Kurdistan Front—
joined the KDP. (See above.) According to the KDP, this unification "changed the balance of Kurdish politics in favor of the
KDP, sending shock-waves through the PUK camp."[18] Thus,
argued the KDP, the PUK felt that it could not win the elections
scheduled for May 1995, and instead opted for a military
coup.

The first fighting occurred in December 1993, when an
apparently pro-Iranian but supposedly socialist group headed
by Hama Haji Mahmoud—who had ostensibly joined the KDP the
previous summer—attacked a KDP base in Sulaymaniya. This
action resulted in several deaths, but even more seriously it
began dividing the KDP and PUK over how to respond.

Then on December 20, 1993, the very day that a strategic
agreement establishing a presidential council including both
Barzani and Talabani had been declared, long-simmering ani-
mosities broke out into more serious fighting between the PUK
and the pro-Iranian Islamic Movement of Kurdistan (IMK).[19] Jabbar Farman, a member of the PUK leadership and minister for
peshmerga affairs in the KRG, refused to implement Barzani's
orders—given as a member of the newly created presidential
council—to calm the situation, and he instead launched strong
attacks against the IMK. A least 200 people were killed in the
fighting that raged for more than a month throughout much of
eastern Iraqi Kurdistan.

The affair caused an open break to begin between the KDP
and the PUK as Barzani accused the PUK of responding too

strongly and unilaterally,[20] adding, "the fighting harms every-body and undermines the credibility of the burgeoning Kur-dish administration and erodes the world's understanding of our cause."[21] As a result, the presidential council, which was to have offered strong executive leadership for the government by bringing in Barzani and Talabani as major participants, proved stillborn, as did the idea of a united peshmerga army.

On May 1, 1994, a local squabble over a piece of land in Qala Diza, northeast of Sulaymaniya, between a junior official of the KDP and tenants belonging to the PUK quickly escalated into major fighting between the two parties. Each side even resorted to executing some of their captured prisoners in cold blood. On one occasion a local cleric actually sanctioned such an execu-tion by issuing a *fatwa* (religious decree).

By the beginning of June more than 600 civilian and military deaths had occurred in fighting throughout much of Iraqi Kur-distan including the cities. In late May PUK forces seized the Kurd-ish parliament building in Irbil. Each side also accused the other of making secret deals with Iran, Turkey, and Baghdad. What is more, the fighting threatened the continuation of much-needed international aid.

Several attempts to arrange a cease-fire failed. On May 21, 1994, a so-called operations room was formed to attempt to supervise a cease-fire, disengage the forces, and normalize the situation. Its members included Massoud Barzani, Kosrat Rasul, Ahmad Chalabi and Hassan Naquib of the opposition Iraqi National Congress (INC), and Abdul Khaleq Zangana of the Iraqi Kurdistan Front. In the coming months all parties gave credit to INC's role in attempting to normalize the situation, but a perma-nent end to the fighting remained elusive.

The warring parties also met at the invitation of the Turks in Silopi, Turkey, on May 30, 1994. Turkey feared that the KDP-PUK conflict would create a power vacuum in northern Iraq that would facilitate the Kurdish Workers Party (PKK) attacks on Turkey that had been continuing since August 1984. The Turks flew the KDP delegation in while the PUK negotiators arrived from Syria. Talabani himself was abroad until June 2, a situation that led to much speculation about what meaning to attribute to his absence. Finally, on June 5, Barzani and Talabani met in Irbil for the first time since the fighting began. Eight days later the two Kurdish leaders met again, this time in Silopi, Turkey. They conferred yet again in Irbil on June 27. Nevertheless, sporadic clashes continued.

THE PARIS AGREEMENT AND EFFORTS TO END THE FIGHTING

From July 16 to 22, 1994, representatives of the two belligerents met in Paris under the auspices of the French government and the Paris-based Kurdish Institute headed by Kendal Nezan, a Turkish Kurd living in exile. Observers from the American and British embassies in Paris were also present, as well as Dr. Najmaldin O. Karim, the president of the Kurdish National Congress of North America.[22] A tentative settlement that amounted to a draft constitution for the KRG was hammered out and signed on July 22.

The Paris Agreement declared, "Iraqi Kurdistan shall be administered by a democratic system that will guarantee pluralism, respect for the Universal Declaration of Human Rights and the rights of the national and religious minorities."[23] More specifically, it listed measures to enhance the authority of the KRG and to eliminate party intervention in governmental affairs: "The governmental decisions shall be taken within the government and within every ministry without interference from political parties." It also reached agreement on wide-ranging reforms for the administration and financial management of the region, as well as a series of measures on how to reorganize and restructure the armed forces.

In addition, the two sides agreed to take a population census and then hold elections by May 1995 when the term of the present parliament would expire. They also promised to pursue a common foreign policy and to establish KRG bureaus in New York and Brussels. Another provision looked forward to the election of "the President of the Iraqi Kurdistan Region . . . by direct universal ballot for a period of 4 years." A closing article declared, "the Kurdish administration should offer political asylum to persecuted Kurds provided they do not have military bases inside Iraqi Kurdistan and do not launch cross-border attacks." The Paris meeting then closed with two appeals addressed to the international community to ease U.N. sanctions on the Kurdish region and to extend Operation Provide Comfort until a democratic Kurdistan had been firmly established.

Although sporadic but at times heavy clashes between the two sides continued in August and early September, 1994,[24] arrangements were set in place to have Barzani and Talabani journey to Paris and sign the agreement under the auspices of French president François Mitterrand. This scenario failed to materialize, however, because Turkey objected that it would be tantamount to establishing a Kurdish state. Ankara feared the demonstration effect such a state would have on its own large and restless Kurdish population.

Accordingly, the new ultranationalist Turkish foreign minister, Professor Mumtaz Soysal, refused to grant transit visas to the Kurdish leaders and practically closed the Turkish border that had been the Kurds' lifeline to the outside world. He also held another tripartite meeting with Iran and Syria in Damascus on August 21, 1994, on how to prevent the creation of a Kurdish state in northern Iraq; made an opening to Baghdad regarding the lifting of U.N. sanctions and the reopening of the oil pipeline between Kirkuk in Iraq and Yumurtalik in Turkey; and encouraged the Iraqi Kurds to make a deal with Baghdad. Turkey had already stopped supplying electricity to Iraqi Kurdistan on June 22, 1994.

Before blaming Turkey for the failure to implement the Paris Agreement, however, it should be noted that based on what had already occurred and that which would subsequently occur, one can guess that even if Barzani and Talabani had signed the accord, their fratricidal clashes would have continued. What is more, Turkey clearly recognized that it had a vested interest in peace among the Iraqi Kurds, as witnessed by its hosting meetings for the Kurds at Silopi in May and June. Similarly, Turkey attempted to bring the KDP and PUK together again following the conclusion of its large military incursion into northern Iraq from March 20 to May 10, 1995. Turkey saw harmony among the Iraqi Kurds as a way to prevent the Kurdistan Workers Party (PKK) from raiding Turkey from Iraqi Kurdish territory. Civil war between the KDP and PUK, however, created opportunities for the PKK to establish camps in northern Iraq. Obviously the Iraqi Kurds must share the blame for seeming to have ignored the Turks at Paris, not to mention for their mindless pursuit of civil war.

The lull in the KDP-PUK fighting during the autumn of 1994 was capped by their "Strategic Agreement" of November 21,

1994, which basically ratified the Paris Agreement of the previous July. This new agreement once again prohibited the use of violence and arms to resolve disputes and stressed the need for dialogue and peaceful means to settle conflicts. It also reiterated the need to conduct a population census to prepare for an electoral register before May 19, 1995, so that a subsequent election could be held. In a moving preamble, the agreement declared:

> The experience of our people, and the latest sad events, [have] provided an important fact, which should be comprehended and learned . . . that the fighting between PUK and KDP is a suicide act for both parties and the annihilation of [the] Kurdistan liberation movement as well as a waste of our people's achievement. It discredits the reputation of the two parties and the Kurdish movement regionally and internationally.[25]

RENEWED FIGHTING

None of these worthy ideals were implemented, however, since the basic, underlying power struggle and the host of other problems remained. In December 1994, these issues once more led to overt fighting even more unrestrained than the previous summer.

The renewed fighting apparently began as a land dispute between the Barzanis and the Harki tribe, who were allied to the PUK. On December 20 and 24, 1994, large scale fighting erupted in Shaqlawa just north of the Kurdish capital in Irbil. The KDP forces looted Talabani's home. Hundreds of fighters and civilians were reported killed within the first ten days of the renewed hostilities, which quickly spread to central and eastern Kurdistan. Fighting was described as being "major and fierce."[26] Citizens staged angry demonstrations against it in Irbil and Sulaymaniya, the two main cities of Iraqi Kurdistan, while 17 other Kurdistani parties also were reported to have issued a statement condemning the violence.[27]

In an attempt to halt the internecine conflict, INC once again entered the picture, this time by forming a so-called follow-up committee consisting of the head of INC, Ahmad Chalabi; Jawhar

Namiq Salim of the KDP; and Kamal Fuad of the PUK. Turkey, Iran, and, ironically, even Baghdad also offered to mediate, while the United States sent a letter appealing for a halt to the madness. But the logic of violence prevailed.

This time the PUK not only seized the Kurdish parliament building, but the entire city of Irbil. Both sides accused each other of imposing economic blockades, stealing millions of dollars from the KRG, sabotaging electrical installations, cultivating narcotics, and conniving with Baghdad and various foreign powers, among other misdeeds. The KDP also accused the PUK of having planted the terrorist bomb that killed some 76 people and injured another 141 in its stronghold of Zakho in northwestern Kurdistan at the end of February 1995. The PUK blamed Baghdad for the bombing and speculated that Barzani's nephew Nechirvan, the head of the KDP's intelligence agency, "was pushing for control" and that Massoud "was not totally in control of the situation."[28]

In reference to Mulla Mustafa Barzani's surrender to Baghdad in March 1975 and his son's reputed current dealings with Turkey and Saddam's regime, the PUK began increasingly to refer to the KDP as "defeatist"[29] and "agents."[30] Talabani also specifically called Barzani a "liar."[31] For its part, the KDP referred to the PUK's actions as "treason"[32] and its fighters as "Jalali jackasses,"[33] an allusion to Talabani's earlier alliance with Baghdad in the 1960s.

Amnesty International reported that "hundreds of people have been unlawfully and deliberately killed in Iraqi Kurdistan. . . . Scores of combatants captured during military clashes are reported to have been deliberately killed, either immediately after surrender or later after being taken into custody. Other killings . . . include . . . unarmed civilian demonstrators and the assassination of political activists."[34]

The human rights organization also detailed "gross irregularities before the Supreme Kurdistan court" involving torture to obtain confessions, as well as torture by police and security personnel involving "beatings all over the body with fists, sticks, rifle butts, cables and hosepipes; kickings, *falaqa* (beatings on the soles of the feet); suspension from the ceiling or against the wall by the hands, . . . burning of the skin with cigarettes . . . [and] electric shock treatment."[35]

RENEWED PEACE EFFORTS

In late January 1995, U.S. President Bill Clinton sent a message to both Barzani and Talabani in which he warned: "We will no longer cooperate with the other countries to maintain security in the region if the clashes continue."[36] The U.S. delegation to Iraqi Kurdistan that delivered Clinton's letter also declared that it supported an INC peace proposal to demilitarize Irbil completely, declare a cease-fire, and establish a provisional administration composed of technocrats and respected individuals to prepare for elections in 6 to 12 months.

At the invitation of the Kurdish National Congress of North America (KNC), a group of Kurdish leaders from North America and Europe met at a conference in Washington, D.C., on March 23–24, 1995. Representatives of the KDP, PUK, and IMK were also present. "The conference expressed its utmost displeasure and outrage over the initiation and continuation of fratricide and suppression of human rights by the major political parties in Kurdistan."[37]

Following extensive discussions, the conference drew up a set of proposals to submit to the warring parties. These proposals were specifically made "to normalize the situation"[38] so that the Paris Agreement of July 1994 and the Strategic Agreement of November 1994 could be implemented. Since they were made by an important group of neutral Kurds and thus offered an objective set of recommendations for ending the fighting, it seems appropriate to cite the KNC proposals in some detail.

1. An immediate cease-fire in all parts of the Kurdistan region to be announced by the leaderships of the two major political parties, along with an immediate end to the propaganda war both at home and abroad.
2. Respecting human rights and releasing all prisoners who have been held by the political parties due to the fighting.
3. Establishment of a transitional government made up of experienced and capable people from political parties and independents. The main responsibilities of this government will be the following:

A. Supervising the withdrawal of armed men and political party militias from Hawler and its environs [Irbil] and all cities and towns of Kurdistan.

B. Receipt of all revenues of the Region, especially customs revenues, by the appropriate legitimate governmental authorities and depositing them in the treasury of the Regional government.

C. Returning all authority to the (Kurdistan) regional government, especially political, financial and military authority.

D. Establishing a commission of experts to investigate what has happened to the customs revenues and the money in the banks, which have caused Kurdistan's current problems.

E. An immediate lifting of all restrictions and obstacles in the way of the free movement of individuals and the free flow of food items and other necessities of life throughout Kurdistan.

F. Conducting a general and complete census with the help of expert international organizations which have expressed the willingness to help in this regard.

G. Making preparations for a free and fair general election in the future leading to a transfer of power in a peaceful and democratic manner.[39]

Although a temporary cease-fire was finally put in place early in April 1995, the KNC proposals themselves fell on deaf ears. One report indicated that "more than 3,000 people have died"[40] since the clashes had begun in December 1993. Although the Kurdish parliament, which was scheduled to expire on June 4, 1995, did have its mandate extended for another year at a special session held on May 27, 1995, this action proved purely symbolic.

Early in June 1995, both the KDP and the PUK put forward detailed peace proposals. However, even though a U.S. State Department delegation also arrived in the region to get peace talks started, the rival plans proved irreconcilable because the PUK tied withdrawal from Irbil to an immediate accord on the some $150,000 per day of customs revenue the KDP was collecting from the Ibrahim al-Khalil [Habur] border crossing with Turkey, while the KDP left the issue of the revenues to be determined by a new government.

In early July, 1995, heavy fighting once again resumed, and by the end of the month, "hundreds of people" were reported killed.[41] The PUK claimed that "the fighting was initiated by the KDP to divert attention from this illegal seizure of funds,"[42] while Barzani maintained that the PUK evacuation of Irbil had to "be the first clause of any agreement. Without that, there will be no agreement."[43]

At this point, the United States attempted to play a mediatory role similar to the one carried out by the French a year earlier in Paris. Robert Deutsch, the director of the Office of Northern Gulf Affairs in the State Department, persuaded the warring parties to meet in Drogheda, a suburb of Dublin, Ireland, from August 9 to 11, 1995, in the presence of senior U.S. officials. INC also participated, while Turkey sent observers. As in Paris the previous year, a solution initially seemed possible, capped once again by a proposal to have Barzani and Talabani ratify the final settlement, this time by journeying to Washington at the end of September 1995. Once again, however, success proved illusory.

At Drogheda, the KDP and the PUK did pledge to maintain a cease-fire, cease media attacks, respect the rights of one another's followers, and release all detainees.[44] They also agreed to hold further talks aimed at finalizing a peace agreement along the following principles: demilitarization of the city of Irbil; formation of a neutral commission under INC auspices; reduction of forces in areas surrounding Irbil; deposit in bank accounts under the supervision of a neutral commission for the regional authority of customs and all revenues collected by the parties no later than 48 hours following the certified demilitarization of Irbil; a return of legitimacy of the regional authority by the reconvening of the elected regional parliament within 48 hours of the certified demilitarization of Irbil; formation of a new wide-based administration for the Kurdish region; respect for the territorial integrity of Iraq; and consideration of Turkey's legitimate security concerns regarding the Kurdistan Workers Party (PKK), which had been carrying on a guerrilla war against Turkey since August 1984.

The question of Turkey's security interests now served to further complicate the issue, because late in August 1995 the PKK launched attacks against the KDP. This latest facet of internal Kurdish bloodletting resulted from the PKK having enjoyed safehouses in Iraqi Kurdistan due to the anarchy prevailing there as a result of the on-again, off-again fighting between the KDP and PUK. When the U.S.-brokered Drogheda talks in early August 1995 appeared to be leading to a settlement of the KDP-PUK infighting, as well as to security guarantees for Turkey in the form of the KDP policing the border, the PKK struck out at the KDP in an attempt to derail a truce that would constrain its freedom to maneuver in Iraqi Kurdistan, as well as to punish the KDP for acting as Turkish "collaborators." The PKK also sought to build on its "pilot regions" in Iraqi Kurdistan by establishing some type of government-in-exile or Kurdish federation.

For their own ulterior motives such regional powers as Syria and Iran, as well as the PUK, apparently encouraged the PKK. The former two states acted because they did not want to see their U.S. enemy successfully broker an end to the KDP-PUK strife and possibly go on from there to sponsor an Iraqi Kurdish state, while Talabani sought in effect to open a second front against Barzani.

Given these added problems, the second round of the Dublin talks from September 12 to 15, 1995, failed. Once again the KDP and PUK were unable to reach agreement on the demilitarization of Irbil and the collection of the customs revenues. An anonymous attempt to assassinate the PUK's Kosrat Rasul in Irbil on September 7, 1995, did not help matters.

Another reason for the failure of the talks, according to Talabani, was "the intransigent position of [the] head of the Turkish delegation who wanted to impose the issue of the PKK, which is not an Iraqi issue and not for discussion."[45] Talabani also accused Turkey of arming his KDP enemy: "Turkey has and is supplying arms to the KDP. This cannot be accepted because Turkey promised us it would not do anything to harm the balance of arms in northern Iraq."[46]

The Turks, for their part, blamed Syria, who resented the U.S. role in the peace process and held "the PUK and the PKK cards . . . to effectively sabotage the Kurdish peace process."[47] Speaking of the failure of the Dublin talks, Muhammad Baqir al-Hakim, the leader of the Iraqi Shiite opposition party, Supreme Assembly of the Islamic Revolution in Iraq (SAIRI), declared, "the talks failed because they were conducted with the aims of the U.S. and Turkey behind them and were against the policies of Iran, Syria and other neighboring countries."[48]

From October 5 to 9, 1995, Iran tried its hand at hosting talks between the two Iraqi Kurdish parties. Although the sides managed again to arrive at a list of the problems that needed to be solved, no actual implementation proved possible. Further mediation by Iran was promised. For its part the Islamic Republic "expressed concern over the meddling of outsiders [the United States] in the region which has led to tension and instability."[49]

In mid-November 1995, a U.S. delegation again headed by Robert Deutsch arrived in Salah al-Din in the Kurdish region of Iraq and opened the third round of the U.S.-brokered peace talks with the KDP. A representative of the Turkish foreign ministry and Ahmad Chalabi of INC were also present. Several days later, the U.S. delegation held separate talks with the PUK. Both sets of talks, however, failed to break the deadlock.

FURTHER FIGHTING

In the summer of 1996, Iran launched assaults in cooperation with the PUK deep into Iraqi Kurdistan against Iranian Kurds sheltering there. Upon withdrawing, the Iranians left equipment for the PUK. As with the repeated Turkish incursions into Iraqi Kurdistan in seeming violation of the no-fly zone, the United States did nothing to respond because to do so was not deemed to be in its national interest. The situation drifted further from a possible peaceful resolution when the United States apparently refused either to try harder to effect a cease-fire among the Iraqi Kurds or to contribute a mere $2 million to an international mediation force that might have forestalled the next round of fighting.[50]

In August 1996, a sudden renewal of the civil war in Iraqi Kurdistan quickly led to its apparent conclusion by mid-September in a KDP victory, only to be followed by a PUK counter-offensive in October that just as quickly retook most of the ground lost the previous month.

These events began with a PUK offensive that Barzani claimed was supported by Iran,[51] a charge Talabani denied.[52] When low-key efforts by the United States failed to stop the fighting, an increasingly desperate Barzani did the unthinkable and turned to Saddam for help. The KDP leader rationalized this action as necessary to preserve Iraqi territorial integrity being threatened by Iran: "After the United States and the West refused to listen to us and help us, we agreed with the central government to end this foreign threat."[53] The attempt by Necmettin Erbakan's new Islamist government in Turkey to reach a broad anti-Kurdish front with Iran, Syria, and Iraq also probably influenced Barzani's actions. The primary reason for his alliance with Saddam, however, was sheer necessity; he had no one else to turn to. For Saddam, of course, it was a god-sent opportunity to reinject himself into Iraqi Kurdistan at the invitation of one of the two main Kurdish groups, despite the opposition of the United States.

On August 31, 1996, a joint Iraqi-KDP strike quickly forced the PUK out of Irbil. Saddam's forces used the few hours they had in the city before they were withdrawn to execute some 96 Iraqis who had defected to the U.S.-financed Iraqi opposition (INC) and to capture sensitive computer equipment and files belonging to it.[54] The United States responded by bombing Iraqi military targets in the south and expanding the no-fly zone there up to the outskirts of Baghdad. Further response was called off, however, when it became clear that Saddam had withdrawn his forces. Amid PUK claims of further Iraqi aid in the form of heavy weapons and soldiers dressed as KDP peshmergas,[55] the KDP took Sulaymaniya a week later. Barzani himself attributed his apparent victory to the fear generated among Talabani's supporters when the PUK radio and television announced that the Iraqi army was pouring into Kurdistan. One KDP peshmerga explained, "they [the PUK] were defeated in their hearts, in their souls. They were throwing away their weapons."[56]

Seemingly routed, Talabani's forces retreated to isolated mountain strongholds in the north along the Iranian border. Barzani proclaimed victory and established a new Kurdish government, with Dr. Roj Nuri Shawyess, an engineer by profession and member of the KDP politburo, as the region's new prime minister. Nechirvan Barzani, Massoud's nephew, was named deputy prime minister. The new government was composed of the KDP, the Islamic Movement, the Kurdistan Communist Party, the Kurdistan Islamic Union, the Turkomen, and the Assyrians, as well as independent figures.[57]

Barzani's victory proved short lived. During the second week of October 1996, Talabani's forces launched a successful counteroffensive that retook Sulaymaniya on October 13, plus much of the territory they had lost the previous month. The KDP accused Iran of supporting the PUK with troops, artillery, and rockets,[58] a charge that mirrored PUK accusations concerning Iraqi support for the KDP the previous month. The PUK now retorted that Barzani had lost everything he had gained so quickly because of the disillusionment within his ranks caused by his deal with Saddam and the lack of Iraqi tank support this time.[59]

ANKARA PEACE PROCESS

By late October 1996, the line separating the two combatants had returned to virtually the status quo before August 1996, with the exception that the KDP now held Irbil. This time, however, it also appeared that the intra-Kurdish violence could spark a renewal of the Iran-Iraq War of the 1980s, with Iraq supporting the KDP while Iran aided the PUK. What is more, the instability in Iraqi Kurdistan also served to draw the Turks in with talk of establishing a security zone ten miles inside the border to prevent the PKK from striking Turkey from its bases in northern Iraq. Finally, the immediate implications for Operation Provide Comfort and its offer of protection by the United States remained uncertain.

The so-called Ankara peace process initiated by the United States, Britain, and Turkey at the end of October 1996 sought to extend the tenuous cease-fire of exhaustion into a renewed search for peace by hosting a new series of talks based on a joint statement of 22 articles. These articles dealt with 4 main issues: (1) formation of an interim coalition government from the KDP and the PUK, other Kurdish parties, and representatives from the Turkomen and the Assyrians; (2) normalization (neutralization) of the city of Irbil, now held by the KDP; (3) transfer of the Kurdistan region's revenues, including those from the Habur border crossing, to the Kurdistan central bank; and (4) setting of a date for general elections.

One new tactic tried was to create a Peace Monitoring Force (PMF) of some supposedly neutral 200 Turkomen and Assyrians to monitor the cease-fire line. Given the unresolved Kurdish power struggle and suspicion that Turkey was actually seeking to use the PMF to further interfere in the region's affairs and possibly even to establish a Turkomen client state there, the

Ankara peace process proved no more successful than the earlier Paris Agreement of 1994 and Dublin negotiations of 1995. Following four fruitless meetings, the process reached an impasse by the summer of 1997, and no date could even be agreed upon for a fifth meeting.

Moreover, as a result of the fighting from August to October, 1996, over 70,000 Kurds had been forcibly deported from their homes in what NGOs characterized as "political cleansing."[60] Apparently, both the KDP and the PUK were deporting their rival's supporters who lived within their territory. Ian Wilderspin, the acting field director for Save the Children in Iraq, asserted: "We've heard of children at gun point being evicted from their homes, houses looted, people forced onto trucks and buses with just the clothes and possessions they carried. Many have lost everything." The deportations appeared to be a way of maintaining the civil war despite the cease-fire and testified to the failure of the Ankara peace process to move the two main antagonists toward any meaningful agreement.

The continuing conflict had further repercussions for life in the region. The KDP's temporary alliance with Baghdad put a strain on all Kurds' relationship with the West and made it more difficult to justify their military defense and continuing need for aid from the West. As mentioned in chapter 3, the United States closed down most of its relief operations and pulled out both foreign and local personnel, leaving those relief operations that remained feeling less secure. However, although France decided to withdraw, the United States and Britain continued to maintain a scaled-down version of OPC after January 1, 1997, renamed Operation Northern Watch. In addition, some NGOs continued to maintain their operations.

On May 14, 1997, some 50,000 Turkish troops entered northern Iraq in an attempt to destroy the PKK units based there and to shore up the KDP forces Turkey hoped would help prevent future PKK attacks upon Turkey from the region. (See chapter 5.) Unlike earlier incursions, this time the Turks did not fully withdraw after completing their mission but maintained a military presence that amounted to an unofficial security zone. Talabani concluded, "Turkey has discarded its neutral role and is now an ally of Barzani."[61]

In September 1997, the KDP and the PUK finally held a fifth meeting of the Ankara peace process in the Turkish capital, but

no breakthrough was made.[62] Early the following month the two
met again in London and at first appeared to be making progress.
The KDP accepted responsibility for paying the salaries of civil
servants working in the PUK zone and ensured both the safe passage of PUK officials through its zone toward Turkey and the free
circulation of trucks to the PUK-controlled zone. The parties also
decided that after these confidence measures were implemented,
there would be further discussions on transition measures before
the organization of elections under international control. Short of
funds, however, the PUK also demanded the immediate sharing
of the customs revenues being collected from the Habur border
crossing by the KDP and the establishment of a coalition government with equal representation from both sides.

OCTOBER 1997 CLASHES

When the KDP failed to agree to these additional points, the
PUK, on October 13, 1997, launched a large-scale offensive Talabani termed Operation Vengeance Storm. Apparently Talabani
launched his attack because he felt increasingly desperate that
the status quo was working against him, and also possibly
because he believed that Barzani had been weakened by the latest round of fighting between the KDP and the PKK that had
been occurring since September 25, 1997. Some of the heaviest
fighting of the entire KDP-PUK civil war ensued as hundreds
were killed and thousands displaced. In an attack on the KDP
headquarters at Sararush just outside of Salahuddin, for example, the PUK fired six GRAD missiles—short-range, Russian-
made, surface-to-surface missiles—that were the most
destructive weapons used yet in the civil war.

After the PUK made significant initial gains, the Turks, who
had been carrying out military operations against the PKK in the
region since the end of September, intervened heavily on the
side of the KDP. Ankara proceeded to bomb the areas controlled
by the PUK along the strategic Hamilton Road northeast of Irbil,
charging that Talabani was now actively cooperating with the
PKK. This accusation apparently was not without some merit.[63]
Turkish tanks also advanced to within a few miles of Irbil.

Barham Salih, the PUK spokesman in the United States,
charged that "the Turks have shifted from being a sponsor of the

[Ankara] peace process to being a party to the conflict."[64] He also claimed that the Turks did not want peace between the KDP and the PUK because it would "help consolidate a viable Kurdish self-government in Iraq, that some in Turkey view with alarm and [as] detrimental to their own Kurdish community." In search of their own outside support, the PUK apparently even asked Baghdad for arms.[65]

By the middle of November 1997, however, the KDP had reasserted control over all the territory it had lost during the PUK offensive the previous month. The crisis between the United States and Iraq over inspection of presidential sites also served to quiet the Kurdish battlefield. The stage was set for yet another attempt at ending the fratricidal Kurdish civil war.

NEW PEACE INITIATIVES

With the conclusion of the latest battles, the KDP still controlled the provinces of Dohuk and Irbil, while the PUK fiat only ran in the province of Sulaymaniya. At the very end of 1997, Talabani sent a letter to Barzani proposing that they make peace. Two weeks later Barzani replied positively. Since their letters represent the most recent, detailed proposals to end the civil war, it would be useful to cite them in full.[66] Talabani's letter appears first.

> Honorable Massoud Barzani President of the Kurdistan Democratic Party (KDP)
>
> Warm Greetings,
>
> Taking into consideration the primary interests of Kurdistan and the Kurdish people, so as to achieve a general reconciliation and to bring about a firm and stable state of peace, mutual esteem and fraternity among all the Kurdistani parties and groups and the Kurdish community, in order to put an end once and for all to the internal war and the Kurdicising of the war in Kurdistan, with the hope of making the new year the year of peace, reconciliation, joy and democracy, the Patriotic Union of Kurdistan in this holy month of Ramadan and in the new year extends both hands to you in

a spirit of fraternity and reconciliation with the intention of achieving a truthful general reconciliation which will result in:

1. Uprooting and eradicating the causes of the internal hostilities.

2. Finding political, just and genuinely proper resolutions for all the predicaments, problems and hostilities in a democratic and peaceful manner.

3. The reunification of the Kurdistan Regional Government and forming a unified government from the representatives of all the Kurdistani parties, which will act as a provisional government, will extend its control over all the regions of Kurdistan, will collect all the revenues and the incomes of all the customs and factories and will ensure peace, stability and all types of democratic freedom for everyone and everywhere in Kurdistan.

4. The preparation for a free general election of the Kurdistan National Assembly, which will undertake the reestablishment of the government, and will get at resolutions regarding the issues and problems with the governments of Iraq and Turkey.

5. The normalization of the situation in the cities of Erbil, Sulaimani and Duhok and all other towns and cities of Kurdistan so that they may become the cities and towns of every Kurd and the centers of political, social and ideological activities for everyone.

6. Indicating a limited period and a deadline for the implementation of all the points that we agree upon.

The Patriotic Union of Kurdistan, as an initiative on its part has decided:

First:

1. To stop all media attacks throughout the Ramadan month with the aspiration that we will mutually make it an everlasting achievement and a firmly settled act, as a means of annihilating the media war forever and returning to objective and scientific analyses in discussing all the issues, problems and predicaments and giving paramount importance to constructive criticism and brotherly alerting and enlightenment and disclosing the realities of events.

2. To return the electric power throughout Erbil in this holy month.

Second:
We put forth the following proposals:

1. The immediate termination of deportation and displacement campaigns of citizens and the formation of a bilateral committee with the participation of some patriotic individuals and Kurdistani party representatives which will undertake the rehabilitation and return of the displaced who are affiliated with all the factions to their former premises.

2. The immediate release of all the prisoners and detainees of all sides.

3. The immediate termination of all pursuing and prosecution campaigns against members and supporters of both sides and their coalescent groups and parties all over Kurdistan.

4. Ensuring the freedom of media and communications and all political, social and ideological activities.

Third:
As soon as possible, the authorized representatives of both the politburos, with the participation of Mr. Aziz Muhammed [the longtime, former first secretary of the Iraqi Communist Party] and the representatives of some Kurdistani parties should meet together to activate a mechanism for the implementation of all the points that we shall decide upon and for the discussion of all the other causes and sources of conflict.

Fourth:
In light of these and on this occasion we render the KDP free:

1. To select any of the agreements and accords that we had mutually accepted and signed, such as the Paris Accord, a bilaterally signed agreement and the resolutions that had been accepted by unanimous voting in the Kurdistan National Congress.

2. To accept the American-British proposals that had formerly been put forward to both sides by Robert Deutsch.

3. To accept the proposals presented by Mr. Aziz Muhammed and Dr. Mahmood Ali Uthman and the National Congress for Peace and Coexistence in Kurdistan.

Fifth:
We have to reach a mutual resolution for the distribution of Kurdistan revenues on all sides, all the Kurdistani officials, all the reconstruction projects, all the martyr families and peshmerga of Kurdistan. Let the representatives of both the two politburos reach a mutual decision on this issue. Together we have to ensure the freedom of trading, traveling and visiting the relatives and acquaintances of each other. Finally, we hope that you would consider our message with patriotic and historic responsibility; we are looking forward to getting a positive reply from you.

Please accept our regards,

Jalal Talabani
Secretary General of the PUK

Barzani replied positively in a letter dated January 14, 1998.

Mr. Jalal Talabani
Secretary General of the Patriotic Union of Kurdistan

Greetings,

Thank you for your letter of December 31, 1997. As Mr. Aziz Mohammed informed you, our response was delayed for a few days due to a series of organizational meetings between the KDP politburo and central committee beginning on the New Year. Undoubtedly, the internal fighting has inflicted enormous hardship to our people both internally and externally. The future of Kurdistan's progress depends upon reconciliation, brotherhood and peace. Kurdish unity and dialogue will pave the way for an honorable and just resolution of the Kurdish people's legitimate aspirations within Iraq's unity and sovereignty.

We believe our proposed peace initiative during the summer and autumn months of 1997 remain[s] viable. We also believe that we could have avoided a great deal of pain and suffering had you presented the positive and welcomed elements in your letter prior to October 13, 1997 [when the last PUK offensive was launched]. In any event, our proposed peace plan aims to end the state of internal fighting and other extraordinary circumstances that have persisted since May 1994.

The proposal aspires to prepare the ground for the restoration of a comprehensive and lasting peace in the interest of our people's security, stability, unity and prosperity. Before detailing the elements of the peace plan, we deem it necessary to emphasize the following principles:

A. The peace plan would be implemented within the Ankara Peace Process. At the same time, we welcome all additional genuine internal and external peace efforts.

B. It is imperative to search for a reasonable and fair alternative to the failed equal power sharing experiment.

C. Due to present circumstances and events, previous agreements and conditions cannot be reinstated. In order to move forward, we cannot retreat to the past and concentrate on blaming one side or the other for failing to implement previous agreements. Because the Paris Agreement and parliamentary decisions were initiated under a joint regional government, we now need to work hard and undertake great efforts to form another joint government.

Phase One:

1. To cease all fighting, adhere to the cease-fire as a basis for building on other positive arrangements and maintain the current military situation.

2. To prohibit the Kurdistan Workers Party's (PKK) military presence in Iraqi Kurdistan and unjustified harmful intervention in the internal affairs of our people.

3. To observe the principles of good neighborly relations with all regional countries within the bounds of international law and Iraq's territorial sovereignty.

4. To condemn terrorism and use of violence to resolve problems in Kurdistan.

5. To end all negative media attacks. Press attacks only aggravate the situation and ultimately undermine confidence building measures.

6. To release all prisoners and people detained for political reasons.

7. To end the deportation of citizens from their homes and towns due to their political affiliations. To form a committee of Kurdish parties together with representatives from the KDP and PUK to supervise the repatriation of all deportees to their original homes, villages and towns, including their safety and security.

8. To refrain from politicizing public services, including electricity, trade and travel. To ensure the continued use of public services for the common good.

9. To refrain from arresting any individual for their political affiliations.

10. To form a joint commission of experts and professionals to monitor the implementation of UNSCR 986 [regarding oil sales by the Iraqi government] for the benefit of our people. To form a second commission to cooperate and coordinate in the fields of health, education and energy.

11. To refrain from any negative actions which lead to undermining confidence building measures.

12. To ensure the safe passage of PUK elements to travel abroad through Zakho by appropriate mechanisms.

13. Revenue distributions were conducted without difficulties in the region from 1991 to May 1994. Although no problems arose, the KDP is prepared to contribute payments to civil servants working in PUK controlled areas, as agreed upon in London on October 6, 1997.

14. To form a Higher Coordinating Committee between the two politburos with the participation of Mr. Aziz Mohammed to follow the implementations of agreed upon measures.

Phase Two:
We believe that genuine efforts in the implementation of measures in Phase One will lead to the establishment of a reasonable degree of mutual confidence. Furthermore, the sponsors of the peace process and people at large would be assured that the process is moving forward and Kurdish consensus was reforming. These developments would enable the implementation of Phase Two, which aims to normalize the situation through the following measures:

1. The return of PUK parliamentarians to fully participate in the Parliament.

2. The formation of an interim government based on the actual results of the 1992 elections.

3. Ensuring the freedom of the two party's political, organizational and media work, including all other legitimate parties throughout Iraqi Kurdistan, without changing the positions of military forces.

4. The new government will collect revenues, ensure the salary payments of civil servants, implement essential projects throughout the region, and monitor the normalization process.

5. The new government will conduct a general census.

Phase Three:

The interim government will hold free and fair general elections under international supervision and guarantee from the three co-sponsor countries of the Ankara Peace Process [the United States, Britain, and Turkey]. These two sides will publicly pledge to respect the outcome of the elections. The Higher Coordinating Committee will set a time-table for each phase to be completed. Each phase of the process must be fully completed before moving on to new measures. The KDP believes that there are a number of common elements between the two plans which would facilitate the peace process. Finally, I hope that the exchange of letters and peace plans during the holy month of Ramadan, and in light of the new year, is the start of a new chapter of goodwill, brotherhood, and lasting peace for our people.

With greetings and respect,
Massoud Barzani

Although a proposed face-to-face meeting between Barzani and Talabani failed to materialize, a flurry of activity began. Early in February 1998, Aziz Muhammed moderated the first of a number of high-level, bilateral meetings between other leaders of the two parties held alternately in Shaqlawa and Koy Sanjak. Upon the conclusion of the first meeting Sami Abdurrahman of the KDP and Kamal Fuad of the PUK announced that they had agreed upon the following confidence-building measures: (1) to continue and enforce the cease-fire, while solving problems between the two sides through dialogue rather than violence; (2) to cease attacking each other through the press and desist from any activities that would jeopardize the peace process; (3) to release prisoners within the coming week, without conditions and according to the procedure determined at the meeting; (4) to end the practice of evacuating regional populations from northern Iraq and give permission for citizens to return to their former homes; a commission was to be established to effect this goal; (5) to forbid the pressure or arrest of citizens on political grounds; (6) to form a joint committee that would commence meetings to ensure the application of U.N. Security Council Resolution 986 of April 14, 1995, on limited Iraqi oil sales for food and other humanitarian needs; (7) to form a coordination and cooperation committee to provide citizens with the necessary health, education, and energy services; (8) to normalize electric, transportation, and trade services in the region, and to form a specialist committee to improve services; and (9) to continue meetings at times and places to be established within the coming days.[67]

By the end of July 1998, 20 meetings had been held, but only minor agreements on technical matters had been reached. The substantive divisions remained, including the attempt to reestablish a united Kurdistan Regional Government.

In addition, both parties continued discreet contacts with Saddam.[68] Talabani himself met with Rafi Dahham al-Tikrit, the director of the Iraqi intelligence service, in Sulaymaniya, while Arslan Bayiz led a delegation from the PUK politburo to the Iraqi capital in September 1997. Barzani also admitted, "the KDP is maintaining a dialogue with the Baghdad administration" and even declared, "in the end our problem will be solved in Baghdad."[69] In April 1998, Nikolai Kalkosov, the Russian ambassador to Iraq, visited Barzani and Talabani and indicated his willingness to mediate between the two, apparently at the behest of Saddam. Early in May 1998, Sami Abdurrahman continued these contacts when he met with the Iraqi deputy prime minister, Tariq Aziz, in Baghdad. Saddam asked that the Kurds expel INC agents from northern Iraq and open negotiations with him on an autonomy agreement.

When asked how relations were going between him and Baghdad, Barzani replied, "our relations are normal, but it would certainly be preferable if there were a third strong party to safe-guard these relations."[70] When then questioned whether the United States might reject the idea of Russian mediation, Barzani declared: "Then let the United States take charge of the task, because it must know that if it neglects the matter, it will create a vacuum which will be exploited and . . . filled by someone other than the Americans." The KDP leader concluded that the Kurdish cause was "greatly neglected by the concerned parties in the region."

Barzani's caution regarding Baghdad apparently resulted from Saddam's recent characterization of him and Talabani as "two small traitors. One of them is in convalescence [apparently Barzani]. But as soon as this emergency situation is over, I know what I will do with them: I will crush them by my boots."[71] Witnesses reported that Saddam then pushed his right foot into the ground.

In July 1998, Fazil Mirani, the interior minister of the KDP regional government, claimed that Saddam had begun allowing PKK fighters to train in the Mahmour camp controlled by Baghdad some 30 miles south of Irbil.[72] Several other PKK camps were also opened in Iraqi territory. The KDP concluded that this was a strong message from Saddam to signal his displeasure at the KDP's continuing cooperation with Turkish incursions into northern Iraq and to put further pressure on the KDP, which was still fighting against the PKK.

In January 1998, a high-level PUK delegation also journeyed to Turkey in an attempt to restore some understanding after their bloody conflict the previous fall. The weakening of the PKK position in northern Iraq—symbolized by the defection of Semdin Sakik, a top PKK military commander, to the KDP and then his actual capture by Turkish commandos—presumably worked toward better PUK relations with Turkey.

Shortly afterward, however, Talabani blamed Turkey for the Kurdish civil war, and he concluded, "the Turkish Government is against any type of Kurdish national identity. . . . They want to finish our experiment with democracy at all costs."[73] Somewhat incongruently, the PUK leader added that the "poor economic situation" was "the main problem of Iraqi Kurdistan."

Actually, by the summer of 1998, the economic situation was improving due to the implementation of U.N. Security Council

Resolution 986, which permitted Iraq to sell oil for food.[74] Several
new buildings, housing complexes, banks, and sports facilities
were constructed in the cities of Irbil, Dohuk, Salahuddin, and
Zakho. In addition, such long-neglected necessities as water and
sewage systems had been installed in all the major settlements.
Engineers were also building several roads in the cities and
resurfacing those that connected the Habur border post with
Dohok and Irbil. Similar progress was occurring in the area controlled by the PUK.

Beginning in June, U.N. security resolution 1153 of February
20, 1998, dramatically increased the permitted amount of oil sales
to $5.256 billion every 6 months, more than twice the annual reg-
ular budget of the United Nations itself. The Kurdistan region was
to receive 13 percent of the funds from the sale of this oil without
undue interference from Baghdad. During the second half of 1998,
this was projected to result in the Kurdish region receiving $155
million worth of food supplies; $46 million toward medicinal sup-
plies and health services; $123 million for restoring electricity
services; $56 million each to agriculture, education, and the
resettlement of displaced persons; and $30 million for water
resources. Some wondered how long Saddam would permit these
large oil sales, since they were eliminating his argument that
sanctions should be lifted for humanitarian reasons. Finally, more
than 30,000 exiled Kurds were helped to return to their former
homes and work. And although much remained to be done, work
also began on the removal of land mines near the Iranian border.

However, the importation of food through the U.N. programs was ironically damaging the agricultural sector in Kurdistan as farmers were unable to sell their substantial crop at a fair
market value. The Kurds also complained that the U.N. agencies
implementing the programs with the oil revenues were corrupt
and inefficient, and were forcing the Kurds to purchase materials
at a much higher price than would be available in Turkey.

Despite an exchange of prisoners and all this flurry of activity, the latest peace initiatives seemed unlikely to lead to a real
settlement. By the end of April 1998, for example, the PUK radio
admitted that the PUK and the KDP "have yet to agree on a new
temporary government or to agree on setting a date for the next
election."[75] Although he was continuing his mediatory efforts,
Aziz Muhammed acknowledged that he had "failed to end the

division which has transformed the regions under their respective control into what resembles two hostile countries," and he blamed "the struggle for power and who would have the upper hand in the Kurdish leadership."[76] Barham Salih, a candidate member of the PUK politburo, also confessed that "peace prospects were not very good."[77]

Dr. Najmaldin O. Karim, the president of the Kurdish National Congress of North America and close observer of Kurdish politics, was also pessimistic: "I wish I could express optimism; however, from what we have seen, I cannot. Most of the issues being discussed presently by the parties are marginal and the real underlying causes of conflict are not being addressed."[78]

BARZANI-TALABANI ACCORD

During the summer of 1998, the United States renewed its attempts to further the peace initiatives. In a letter to Congress on the "Status of Efforts to Obtain Iraq's Compliance with U.N. Resolutions," U.S. President Bill Clinton made the following declaration concerning the situation in Iraqi Kurdistan:

> Both Barzani and Talabani have made positive, forward-looking statements on political reconciliation. We will continue our efforts to reach a permanent reconciliation through mediation in order to help the people of northern Iraq find the permanent, stable settlement which they deserve, and to minimize the opportunities for Baghdad and Tehran to insert themselves into the conflict and threaten Iraqi citizens in this region.[79]

Then, on July 17, 1998, David Welch, the U.S. principal deputy assistant secretary of state for Near Eastern affairs, led a delegation of U.S. state department officials and a Turkish foreign ministry official to Iraqi Kurdistan in an effort to galvanize the new peace initiatives. The Welch delegation met first with Barzani in Salahuddin and then with Talabani in Sulaymaniya. Although no substantive agreement was reached, Welch invited both Kurdish leaders to Washington for talks.

Following a successful high-level meeting at the end of August in Sulaymaniya between KDP officials and Talabani, in early September 1998 first Barzani and then Talabani actually journeyed to Washington; on the way both stopped off for talks in Ankara. After separate individual meetings with U.S. state department officials, the two Kurdish leaders finally met personally for the first time since the summer of 1994 when their fighting had first started. Upon initially seeing each other, Talabani reportedly exclaimed in a Kurdish maxim something to the effect that his eyes were dancing to see Barzani again. The more taciturn KDP leader did not specifically reply.

After two days of lengthy sessions, they reached an accord witnessed by Welch and termed "Final Statement of the Leaders' Meeting September 17, 1998." As the fruit of more than four years of struggle and negotiation, it would be useful to quote the document in full.

Reaffirmation of Previous Achievements

On behalf of the Kurdistan Democratic Party (KDP) and Patriotic Union of Kurdistan (PUK), we thank Secretary Albright and the US government for facilitating a series of amicable and productive meetings here in Washington over the past several days. We appreciate their efforts in helping to bring us back together and to assist us in creating a framework for future cooperation. The meetings have been a major step forward towards a full and lasting reconciliation, which will provide new hope to the Kurds, Turkomen, and Assyrians and Chaldeans of the Iraqi Kurdistan region of Iraq.

Both parties also welcome the continuing engagement of the governments of Turkey and the United Kingdom in the peace and reconciliation process. We wish to recognize the irreplaceable role our separate consultations in Ankara and London played in making these talks a success.

In Washington, we have discussed ways to improve the regional administration of the three northern provinces and to settle longstanding political differences within the context of the Ankara Accords of October 1996. We have reached several important areas of agreement on how to implement those accords.

We affirm the territorial integrity and unity of Iraq. The three northern provinces of Dohuk, Irbil and Sulemaniyah are part of the Iraqi state. Both the KDP and the PUK unequivocally accept the recognized international boundaries of Iraq. Both parties are committed to preventing violations of the borders by terrorists or others.

Both parties will endeavor to create a united, pluralistic, and democratic Iraq that would ensure the political and human rights of Kurdish people in Iraq and of all Iraqis on a political basis decided by all the Iraqi people. Both parties aspire that Iraq be reformed on a federative basis that would maintain the nation's unity and territorial integrity. We understand that the U.S. respects such aspirations for all the Iraqi people.

Both parties condemn internal fighting and pledge to refrain from resorting to violence to settle differences or seeking outside intervention against each other. We will endeavor to bring to justice those who violate the peace, whatever their political affiliation or motivation.

Both parties also agree that Iraq must comply with all relevant UN Security Council resolutions, including the human rights provisions of Resolution 688.

To help ensure a peaceful environment for reconciliation, we will intensify our arrangements to respect the cease fire, facilitate the free movement of citizens and refrain from negative press statements.

Transition Phase

We have agreed to enhance the Higher Coordination Committee (HCC) to ensure that the humanitarian requirements of the people of the Iraqi Kurdistan region are met and their human and political rights are fulfilled. The decisions of the HCC will be by the unanimous consent of its members.

The HCC will prepare for a full reconciliation between the parties, including normalizing the situation in Irbil, Sulemaniyah and Dohuk; re-establishing a unified administration and assembly based on the results of the 1992 elections; providing exclusive control of all revenues to the regional administration; and organizing new regional elections.

The HCC will enhance coordination and cooperation among local public service ministries that serve the needs of the people throughout the Iraqi Kurdistan region. The parties will ensure that these ministries receive adequate revenue for their operation. The KDP acknowledges that, revenue differences will require a steady flow of funds for humanitarian services from the current KDP area to the current PUK area.

The HCC will establish a process to help repatriate everyone who had to leave their homes in the three northern provinces as a result of the prior conflict between the parties, and to restore their property or compensate them for their losses.

The HCC will ensure that both parties cooperate to prevent violations of the Turkish and Iranian borders. It will establish reasonable screening procedures to control the flow of people across these borders and prohibit the movement of terrorists. Both parties, working with the HCC, will deny sanctuary to the Kurdistan Workers Party (PKK) throughout the Iraqi Kurdistan region. They will ensure that there are no PKK bases within this area. They will prevent the PKK from destabilizing and undermining the peace or from violating the Turkish border.

The HCC will endeavor to form an interim joint regional government within the next three months to be ratified by the regional assembly.

Unified Administration

Within three months of its re-formation, the Assembly will meet at its building in Irbil, with subsequent meetings there or in Sulemaniyah or Dohuk. The members of the interim assembly will be those individuals who were elected to the parliament in 1992.

The first meeting of the interim assembly will be within three months. After the assembly is established, it must authorize all subsequent decisions of the HCC and/or the interim regional government.

The interim assembly may decide to add additional functions to the operations of the HCC, including unifying relations with the international community.

To provide a safeguard for regional elections and to help normalize the status of Irbil. Dohuk and Sulemaniyah, the HCC and the assembly may establish a joint PUK-KDP-Turkomen-Assyrian security force. The new regional government may subsequently choose to take further measures to unify peshmerga (militia) command structures.

After the regional elections described below, the interim assembly will be replaced by a new regional assembly. This regional assembly will form a new regional government based on the voting strength of each party in the assembly.

When the regional government has been formed, the HCC will be dissolved automatically. The term of the regional assembly [and] the regional government will be three years.

Revenue Sharing

Until the new interim joint regional government is established, a steady flow of funds for public service ministries will be directed from the current KDP area into the current PUK area, due to revenue differences. The HCC, in consultation with the existing ministries of taxation and finance, is responsible for the apportionment of revenues throughout the region.

When the interim joint government is established, it will become responsible for the collection and distribution of all revenues.

After the election of a new regional assembly, a single Ministry of Revenue and Taxation will have exclusive responsibility for collecting all revenues, including taxes and customs duties. The funds collected will be at the disposal of the regional government for uses authorized by the regional assembly.

Status of Irbil, Dohuk and Sulemaniyah

The interim assembly and the HCC will address the normalization of Irbil, Dohuk, Sulemaniyah and other cities. The HCC may call on international mediation regarding this issue, if it deems it expedient.

The status of these cities must be normalized to a sufficient degree that free and fair elections can be held.

Elections

The interim assembly and the HCC will be responsible for organizing free and fair elections for a new regional assembly, to take place no later than six months after the formation of the interim assembly.

The composition of the new regional assembly will be based on the best available statistical data on the population of the three northern governorates and the distribution of ethnic and religious groups there. Seats will be set aside for the Kurdish, Turkomen, and Assyrian and Chaldean communities.

If possible, the interim assembly and the HCC, working with the international community, will conduct a census of the area in order to establish an electoral register. If international assistance is not available in time, the interim assembly and the HCC will conduct a census on their own, or—making reference to existing data—they will construct a best estimate of the population in consultation with outside experts.

The interim assembly and the HCC will also invite international election monitors to assist both in the election itself and in training local monitors.

Situation in the Iraqi Kurdistan Region

UN Security Council Resolution 688 noted the severe repression of the Iraqi people, particularly the Kurdish people in Iraq. The potential for repression has not eased since 1991, when the resolution was passed. It is worth noting that in the past year the UN Special Rapporteur for Iraq reported finding strong evidence of hundreds of summary executions in Iraqi prisons and a continuation by the regime of the policy of expelling Kurds and Turkomen from Kirkuk and other cities. This policy amounts to ethnic cleansing of Iraqi Kurds and Turkomen, with their lands and property appropriated by the government for disbursement to ethnic Arabs. Many of the new arrivals participate in this scheme only because of government intimidation.

In light of this continued threat, we owe a debt of thanks to the international community for assisting with our humanitarian needs and in preventing a repeat of the tragic events of 1991 and the horrific Anfal campaigns of 1987 and 1988.

The United Nations special program of "oil-for-food" for the Iraqi Kurdistan region has eased the humanitarian condition of the people. We welcome the support of the international community for the continuation of this program, with its specific allotment to the Iraqi Kurdistan region, and hope that, in the near future, a liaison office for the region can be established at ECOSOC headquarters to better coordinate the provision of the aid. We also hope that, in the event that benefits from the "oil-for-food" program are suspended due to unilateral action by the government of Iraq, the UN will address the continuing economic needs of Iraqi Kurdistan and the plight of the people there.

The United States, the Republic of Turkey and the United Kingdom through Operation Northern Watch have helped to protect the area. We call upon them and the rest of the international community to continue to exercise vigilance to protect and secure the Iraqi Kurdish region.

The many non-governmental organizations that operate in the three northern provinces have diminished our isolation and helped us in countless ways.

Future Leader-to-Leader Meetings

The President of the KDP and the Secretary General of the PUK will meet at least every two months inside or outside Iraqi Kurdistan at mutually acceptable sites.

Pending the agreement of governments, we hope to hold the first such meeting in Ankara and a subsequent meeting in London.

The Ankara meeting would include discussions on our joint resolve to eliminate terrorism by establishing stronger safeguards for Iraq's borders. The London meeting may explore further details concerning the status of Irbil, Dohuk and Sulemaniyah, and help establish a mechanism for the conduct of free and fair elections.

Timetable:

On or before:

October 1: The KDP begins to extend appropriate financial assistance on a monthly basis to the public service ministries in the PUK areas.

October 15: Timeline for repatriation of persons displaced by the former conflict. Agreement on restoration of property or compensation by responsible parties.

Beginning

November: Joint consultation with the Government of Turkey.

November 1: Coordination and Cooperation of humanitarian ministries complete. Revenues contributed by KDP to the ministries flowing from KDP areas to PUK areas.

November 15: Progress report on repatriation, unification of ministries and revenue sharing.

January 1: First meeting of the interim assembly.

March 1: Interim Joint Government establishes a plan to normalize Irbil, Dohuk and Sulemaniyah.

April 1: Interim Joint Government establishes a plan for the organization of elections.

July 1: Regional elections.[80]

Flanked by Barzani and Talabani, U.S. Secretary of State Madeleine Albright publicly announced their new accord before some 40 guests gathered in the Treaty Room of the U.S. State Department. Albright also made general promises of U.S. support for the Kurds—contingent upon their continuing unity—by declaring:

The renewed spirit of reconciliation between Mr. Barzani and Mr. Talabani, exemplified by their joint meeting and joint statement today, will make it easier for the United States and others to help their people. They have set a timetable for resolving their differences fully consistent with the principles laid down in the 1996 Ankara Accords. We encourage them and will help where we can to see that this agenda is met. Without unity, the road ahead will remain very difficult. With unity, there is every reason for the Iraqi Kurds to look forward with hope. . . . The United

States will decide how and when to respond to Baghdad's
actions based on the threat they pose to Iraq's neighbors, to
regional security, to vital U.S. interests and to the Iraqi people, including those in the north.[81]

Although Albright's pronouncement did not constitute an iron-
clad agreement of protection, it was—in contrast to Nixon's and
Kissinger's covert and unkept promises of a quarter of a century
earlier—a public declaration. Thus, it could not be so cavalierly
ignored. In addition, both Kurdish leaders claimed that Albright
made even stronger promises of protection to them verbally.[82]
Finally, the United States made it clear it would continue to
enforce the no-fly zone through Operation Northern Watch and
also continue to seek the implementation of U.N. Security Council Resolution 688 which condemned the repression of the Iraqi
civilian population in Kurdish populated areas. The secretary of
state's specific mention for the first time of the phrase "and to
the Iraqi people, including those in the north" reinforced this
continuing commitment. In return, both Kurdish parties agreed
that the United States was the only power that could have brokered such an accord and that consequently its role had been
instrumental.

On the other hand, Albright's circumspect attitude was
appropriate because the accord—like others before—was really
just an ambitious agreement to agree. It set forth a timetable for
re-establishing a unified regional administration, contained provisions for regional elections by the summer of 1999 and for revenue sharing based on the needs of the population, and, in a
gesture toward Turkish fears concerning the PKK, provided for
the security of the Iraqi Kurdish borders. What if the Kurds failed
to implement these timetables and fulfill their commitments?

Given the longstanding divisions among the Iraqi Kurds, the
opposition of the PKK, whose presence in northern Iraq would
be threatened by the accord, and, of course, the negative attitudes toward Kurdish rights long held by all the surrounding
regional powers, it remained to be seen whether this new accord
would be any more fruitful than earlier ones.

Initial Turkish coolness to the accord was particularly dis-
turbing because the United States claimed it had made special
efforts to involve the Turks in drawing it up. The Turks, however,
apparently felt that they were being presented with a *fait accom-*

pli and were given only the pretense of having been consulted. How could such an agreement between two longtime Kurdish rivals have been reached so quickly if the United States had not been working for some time behind the Turkish back?

Specifically, the Turks objected to the term "federative basis" in the accord, fearing that it could sanction an independent Kurdish state. The Turks also disapproved of the phrase "establishing stronger safeguards for Iraq's borders," since this could prevent them from further military incursions into northern Iraq in pursuit of the PKK.[83] Other Turkish fears possibly included the accord's influence on the Turkish Kurds, the loss of control over profitable smuggling routes, the future of water rights and Turkey's ambitious GAP project to harness the water, and the proposed Baku-Ceyhan oil pipeline. Within days of the accord's signing, the Turks again sent troops into northern Iraq and threatened war against Syria because of its support for the PKK and other hostile acts. As Jalal Talabani tellingly observed concerning Albright's promises of protection for the Iraqi Kurds: "the international protection is . . . against alleged or possible Iraqi oppression and is not for protection against Turkish or Iranian interference. . . . We believe that the Turkish military interference can sometimes be more dangerous than the Iraqi military interference."[84] Finally, in November 1998, after considerable prodding from the United States and renewed assurances from the Iraqi Kurds, the Turks eased their opposition.

As for the Iraqi Kurds, previous experience suggested that mutual exhaustion from fighting leads to initiatives that outline procedures for establishing peace. But the inherent struggle for power between the two parties—fueled by the hostility of the regional powers—prevents the actual implementation of peace, and eventually fighting resumes. Although it was clear that the Barzani-Talabani accord was a significant attempt to break this unfortunate cycle, only time would tell if it would.

5

Power Vacuum

As noted in chapter 4, the de facto Kurdish state that was created in Iraqi (northern) Iraq shortly after the end of the Gulf War has virtually collapsed due to the on-again, off-again civil war between its two main parties, Massoud Barzani's Kurdistan Democratic Party (KDP) and Jalal Talabani's Patriotic Union of Kurdistan (PUK). As a result of their round of fighting from August to October 1996, there are now two separate rump governments in Iraqi Kurdistan: the KDP's in Irbil and the PUK's in Sulaymaniya. Inevitably, the resulting instability and power vacuum have drawn in neighboring Turkey and Iran, among others such as the United States, Syria, and, of course, Iraq.

Beginning in 1992, Turkey and Iran (along with Syria) held semi-regular tripartite conferences on how to prevent this Kurdish state from forming in northern Iraq. They were afraid of the precedent such a state would create for their own restless Kurds. Since 1995, however, no more tripartite conferences have been held, as both Turkey and Iran have each begun increasingly to support opposing factions in the Iraqi Kurdish civil war. Turkey backs Barzani's KDP in order to win its support in preventing the Kurdistan Workers Party (PKK)[1] from raiding Turkey from its safehouses in KDP territory bordering on Turkey, as well as to keep open the oil pipeline from Iraq to Turkey that the United Nations authorized to begin pumping again in 1996. Iran supports the PUK as a way to prevent Turkey—along with its NATO ally and Iran's sworn enemy, the United States—from gaining influence on Iran's western border in oil-rich northern Iraq, as well as a way to intervene in the business of its long-standing enemy, Iraq.

Although both the United States (accompanied often by Turkey and Britain) and Iran have helped to broker separate cease-fires between the warring Iraqi Kurdish factions, each saw the other as working at cross purposes in these efforts and thus sought to sabotage the other's initiatives. Following the failure of the U.S.-Turkish sponsored talks in Drogheda, Ireland, in August–September 1995, for example, Muhammad Baqir al-Hakim—the leader of the Iranian-backed Iraqi Shiite opposition, the Supreme Assembly of the Islamic Revolution in Iraq (SAIRI)—declared, "the talks failed because they were conducted with the aims of the U.S. and Turkey behind them and were against the policies of Iran."[2] When Iran tried its hand at hosting talks between the two Iraqi Kurdish parties from October 5 to 9, 1995, the Islamic Republic "expressed concern over the meddling of outsiders [Turkey's ally, the United States] in the region which has led to tension and instability."[3]

The round of fighting between the KDP and PUK from August to October 1996 involved not only Saddam's forces, which fought on the side of the KDP while Iran (albeit much less blatantly) backed the PUK, but also the United States, which responded by bombing Iraqi targets in the south of Iraq. To complete the confusing picture, the United States' ally Turkey supported the KDP, thus ironically making the United States and Iraq silent partial allies at the same time the United States was bombing Iraq. Indeed, Iran claimed: "Saddam's army moved into the Kurdish area with the U.S. green light."[4]

The large-scale Turkish military interventions into northern Iraq in pursuit of the PKK in March 1995 and again in May and September 1997 predictably drew heavy criticism from Iran. This was not only because of Turkey's connection to the United States, but also because of a series of joint Turkish-Israeli protocols that began in 1996 and that Iran saw as a threat to its own security. As one Iranian report explained: "The Zionists . . . by coming closer to the borders of . . . Iran . . . plan to threaten the national security of our country."[5] The United States, for its part, was one of the very few who supported Turkey's incursions—despite the fact that the United States supposedly was protecting Iraqi Kurdistan from outside (read, Iraqi) intervention.

In July and August 1996, some 2,000 Iranian Revolutionary Guards—with the approval of the PUK—drove about 250 kilometers into Iraqi Kurdistan in pursuit of rebellious Iranian Kurds who were sheltering there. Upon withdrawing, the Iranians left some of their weapons behind for the PUK. This action drew heavy criticism from Turkey and was one of the main catalysts for the renewal of the KDP-PUK civil war from August to October 1996. Despite the no-fly zone, the United States remained silent during the Iranian incursion, not wanting to create any more problems for itself.

The purpose of this chapter is to analyze the dynamics of the power vacuum that has arisen in Iraqi Kurdistan. In so doing, significant light will be thrown not only upon the situation, but also upon the little-known competition between Turkey and Iran over Iraqi Kurdistan that has become an important aspect of their much larger competition in the post–cold war Middle East.

BACKGROUND

As prominent journalist Robert Kaplan recently noted, "The Turkish-Persian relationship is among the most complex of civilizational rivalries."[6] It is made all the more complicated today by the secularist-Islamist divide that separates the two neighbors in addition to their competition over oil and transport routes freed up by the collapse of the Soviet Union. Nevertheless, the two states were long able to maintain surprisingly friendly relations because both had calculated that such a policy would serve their respective interests.[7] Thus, as noted above, Turkey and Iran, along with Syria, held semi-regular tripartite conferences from 1992 to 1995 on how to meet the common threat of a Kurdish state in northern Iraq.

Although Turkey allowed the United States to set up bases in Turkey to enforce the no-fly zone over northern Iraq—an action Iran strongly opposed because it seemingly allowed the United States to threaten Iran as well as succor an unwanted proto-Kurdish state bordering on Iran—overall Iranian-Turkish cooperation continued in the form of a joint security committee established to exchange information and carry out inspections relating to border security. In the spring of 1994, Iran turned over 14 PKK guerrillas to the Turks, and it did not allow the Turkish bombing of the PKK's Zaleh camp in Iraqi Kurdistan near the Iranian border—an attack that killed 20 Iranians—to upset their relations.

For its part, Turkey agreed to crack down on the activities in Turkey of the *Mojahedin-e Khalq,* an Islamic socialist organization violently opposed to the Iranian government. Turkey also did not support U.S. President Bill Clinton's call in May 1995 for his country's allies to join the United States in cutting off all trade and investment with Iran in order to further the U.S. policy of double containment of Iran and Iraq. Despite its longstanding alliance with the United States, Turkey seemed determined to at least follow a policy of critical dialogue with Iran. Necmettin Erbakan's elevation in June 1996 to become modern Turkey's first Islamist prime minister, however, ironically initiated a series of steps that by attempting to draw the two states still closer together threatened instead to end their cooperation. The ongoing civil war in Iraqi Kurdistan proved to be one of the catalysts in this process.

One of Erbakan's first acts as prime minister was to journey to Iran where he negotiated a $23 billion deal for Iranian natural gas and called for talks among Muslim Turkey, Iran, Syria, and Iraq whose goal would be to replace the forces of the U.S.-backed Operation Provide Comfort or Poised Hammer enforcing the no-fly zone over Iraqi Kurdistan. Erbakan also called for a new Islamic trading organization (the so-called Developing Eight or D-8 that prominently included both Turkey and Iran) that would seemingly reorient Turkey away from its Western military and economic partners.

These initiatives upset Turkey's secularist military, whose role as the ultimate defender of Turkey's secular democracy is constitutionally guaranteed through Turkey's National Security Council (MGK).[8] Erbakan's Iranian gas deal also seemingly flew in the face of the new U.S. Iran-Libya Sanctions Act or D'Amato Law sanctioning any state investing more than $40 million in Iran's oil and gas industry, and it thus further troubled Turkish secularists who sought U.S. support for eventual membership in the European Union.

Erbakan's initial moves soon foundered, however, amid fresh Turkish accusations about PKK infiltrations from Iran. The renewal of the Iraqi Kurdish civil war in August 1996—in which Iran supported the PUK, while Turkey sided with the KDP and thus implicitly Iraq—also worked against a Turkish-Iranian agreement on the basis of Islamic unity. Criticizing the Turkish proposal at this time to establish a security belt along its borders with Iraq in order to prevent PKK infiltration into Turkey and the subsequent "impudence"[9] of a Turkish incursion into Iraqi Kurdistan, an adviser to Iranian president Ali Akbar Hashemi-Rafsanjani denounced "the covetous eyes of the Ankara statesmen, which are focused on the oil resources in northern Iraq." The Iranian spokesman charged that Turkey considered its actions justified because of its support for the U.S. forces of Operation Provide Comfort: "This policy has practically led to a buildup of military instability in the region, the intensification of the civil war in northern Iraq, the violation of Iraq's territorial integrity, and the further weakening of the Baghdad government."

In December 1996, Rafsanjani visited Ankara, but Erbakan's proposal that Turkey and Iran cooperate in the defense industry field was greeted with total disdain by the Turkish military, which even refused an Iranian military delegation access to the F-16 and CASA aircraft producer Turkish Aerospace Industry premises frequently visited by foreign delegations in the past. The United States breathed a sigh of relief that its NATO ally would not be sharing defense arrangements with a state it considered to be supportive of terrorist activity aimed at NATO and the West. Israel too was pleased that its incipient defense relations with Turkey would not be nipped in the bud.

In a thinly veiled critical reference to the United States, Israel, and the Turkish military, Rafsanjani declared: "There are centers of power in the world who are not interested in Turkey and Iran maintaining cordial relations and we can see the footprints and traces of ill intentions in some of the incidents occasionally taking place for the purpose of spoiling our relations."[10] Expressing "concern" about northern Iraq, the Iranian president added, "Iran, Turkey, Syria and Iraq should cooperate seriously in order to establish tranquillity and peace in the region and see to it that this region does not serve as a hotbed of crisis or instability for our countries."

In February 1997, Iran's ambassador to Turkey, Mohammed Reza Bagheri, attended a controversial "Jerusalem night" in the Ankara suburb of Sincan—a stronghold of Erbakan's Refah (Welfare) Party—where he publicly expressed support for efforts to introduce *Sharia* or Islamic law to Turkey. A few days later the Turkish military drove dozens of tanks through the streets of Sincan in an apparent demonstration of strength against the Islamists. Mutual diplomatic expulsions between Turkey and Iran followed.

Later that same month, General Cevik Bir (whose name literally means "vigorous one")—the deputy chief of staff and known in the West for earlier commanding the United Nations forces in Somalia—journeyed to Washington along with Abdullah Gul, an important Erbakan deputy. There Bir (who strikes a rather impressive physical appearance, speaks good English, and even expresses somewhat progressive positions on the Kurdish issue) stole the Islamist Gul's thunder by condemning the rise of religious power in Turkey and directly accusing Iran of sponsoring anti-Turkish terrorism as well as trying to destroy the secular Turkish state: "The fact that the PKK organization carries out terrorist activities against Turkey, through Iran, constitutes an important problem in our relations with this country."[11]

Shortly afterward, the military continued its campaign against the Erbakan government by presenting a list of some 18 demands in the National Security Council to halt the creeping Islamization in Turkish society it accused Erbakan of fomenting. These directives included a ban on pro-*Sharia* propaganda, tighter restrictions on religious dress, measures to prevent Islamist militants from entering the state administration and military, the limitation of the *Imam Hatip* religious secondary schools, and curbs on the sale of pump-action shotguns reputedly being bought by Islamists. An unpublicized tenth demand dealt with the prevention of alleged Iranian attempts to destabilize Turkey:

> In order to protect our nation from a backward regime, and from an exploitation of religion, which would lead in all likelihood to conflict, the activities, attitude, and conduct of the Iranian Islamic Republic against our country's regime must be obstructed; to this aim, but without destroying our neighborly and economic relations with Iran, a package of precautionary measures to prevent detrimental and injuri-

ous activities must both be prepared and put into application.[12]

In addition to this anti-Iranian directive, a report by the Turkish
National Intelligence Organization (MIT) declared that there
were five major militant Islamist groups active in Turkey whose
members received training in heavy arms in Iran and financial
support from that country.[13] The Turkish parliamentary border
security research committee added its report concerning the
location of PKK training and logistic support camps in Iranian
territory.[14] This report detailed increasing numbers of incidents
of border violations, attacks, and mine-laying activities by PKK
guerrillas infiltrating from Iran, despite the agreement signed
between Iran, Turkey, and Iraq on September 15, 1993, to prevent
illegal crossings. The report also criticized Erbakan for telling
the Iranians while he had been in Tehran the previous summer
that he did not believe MIT intelligence reports concerning these
Iranian actions. A few weeks after the report had been released
General Kenan Deniz, the chief of the domestic security department of the general staff, declared, "Iran is using terrorism for its
political ends [and] giving logistical support to the PKK and also
supports fundamentalist Islamic organizations . . . to harm the
established order in Turkey."[15]

In the middle of March 1997, Iranian foreign minister Ali
Akbar Velayeti arrived in Ankara in an attempt to soothe matters. Erbakan offered apologies for any misunderstandings,
which he blamed on the press, but Turkish president Demirel
informed Velayeti that Iranian officials should not interfere in
Turkey's internal affairs. In Tehran, Defense Minister Mohammed
Furuzande blasted Turkey for its "cooperation with the Zionist
regime, which is threatening the Islamic world."[16] Furuzande also
asserted that Turkey had "lost much world prestige" because of
its cooperation with Israel and added that Iran was counting on
Erbakan to obstruct the implementation of any agreements with
the Jewish state. A commentary appearing in a pro-regime daily
supervised by Iran's spiritual leader Ayatollah Ali Khamenei
added that Turkey "had bid farewell to Islamic traditions."[17]

At the beginning of April 1997, Bir pushed the Turkish military's anti-Islamist campaign further when he declared that com-
bating anti-secular Islamist forces had become the military's top
priority, more pressing even than the on-going struggle against

Kurdish separatism that had been occupying the military for more than a decade.[18] General Deniz added that "allowing free rein to religious extremism . . . would be tantamount to the State committing suicide."[19]

TURKISH INCURSIONS INTO IRAQI KURDISTAN

On May 14, 1997, Turkey sent a reported 50,000 troops into northern Iraq in an attempt to destroy the PKK's so-called Zap Republic and other PKK units sheltering there. Although the largest to date, this intervention was simply the latest in a long series of such actions taken against the backdrop of an involved history. Moreover, this time the Turks also left some 8,000 troops inside the Iraqi Kurdish border after finishing their original mission in June 1997. The growing Turkish-Iranian struggle in the power vacuum of Iraqi Kurdistan was coming to the forefront as it had never before.

The Republic of Turkey had only given up its territorial claim to northern Iraq (Mosul) in 1925 after a protracted dispute with Britain, which held the area as a mandate from the League of Nations. Although recognizing the new situation, Turkey has continued to view the situation as having been forced upon it in a moment of weakness. In May 1995, Turkish president Suleyman Demirel even proposed that the border should be rectified in favor of Turkey. He only withdrew his suggestion after it received a quick, universal rebuke from the Arab states and Iran.[20]

During the 1980s, the Iraqi government was unable to enforce its fiat in Iraqi Kurdistan due to its terrible struggle against Iran. Accordingly, the Turkish and Iraqi governments had an agreement that allowed the Turkish military to make frequent incursions into northern Iraq in pursuit of PKK units harboring there. Although this agreement lapsed following the end of the Iran-Iraq War in 1988, Turkey began a new series of military incursions into the territory following the end of the Gulf war in 1991. This Turkish action was taken because PKK units once again were using the resulting power vacuum in Iraqi Kurdistan as a base from which to raid Turkey.

These incursions were facilitated by Turkey's association with the United States enforcement of the no-fly zone over Iraqi

Kurdistan following the Gulf War. The Turkish incursions were only begrudgingly accepted by Iraq and the Iraqi Kurds themselves, however, as there was little they could do in practice to prevent them. Despite their frequency and intensity, moreover, they seemed to have little effect. The Turks were unable to eliminate the PKK from northern Iraq as the PKK simply melted away whenever the Turks came after them. Turkey blamed this situation on a variety of factors including aid and sanctuary given the PKK by Syria, Iran, and others.

In October 1992, both Turkey and the Iraqi Kurds supposedly joined forces in an attempt to evict the PKK from its sanctuaries in northern Iraq, but the PKK's surrender to Talabani's PUK turned out to be more of a window dressing to appease the Turks than a defeat of Ocalan's organization. In March 1995, Turkey sent some 35,000 troops into northern Iraq in another futile attempt to wipe out the PKK. By this time the Iraqi Kurds themselves had fallen into the bitter civil war between the KDP and the PUK that was facilitating the PKK's activities. Given their own perceived interests, therefore, the KDP tacitly supported the Turkish intervention since it was helping them to rid their territory of PKK intruders. The PUK—already more sympathetic to the PKK than was the KDP and located to the southeast and thus not troubled as much by PKK units—denounced Turkey's actions, a position shared by Iran, which did not want a NATO ally of its sworn enemy, the United States, approaching its western border in Iraqi Kurdistan.

Similarly, both the PUK and Iran tacitly supported the PKK when it attacked the KDP in the fall of 1995. During this KDP-PKK fighting, the PUK saw the PKK as an ally against its enemy, the KDP, while Iran viewed the PKK as fighting to prevent a pro-Turkish KDP from asserting its influence all through Iraqi Kurdistan. Although Iran had historically supported the more conservative KDP rather than the PUK, Tehran began to switch its backing once the KDP seemed to be coming to an understanding with Turkey.

To further counter the developing Turkish-KDP understanding, Iran—in agreement with the PUK—deployed near Sulaymaniya as many as 5,000 fighters from the SAIRI's Badar Forces in November 1995. These forces were Iraqi Shiites opposed to the Iraqi government and supported by Iran. Despite the assurances of Iran's deputy foreign minister Alaaddin Brujerdi that this deployment would not upset the balances between the KDP and PUK,[21] neither Turkey nor the KDP could have been pleased.

In June 1996 the situation was further inflamed when the KDP killed an important member of the Surchi family (which led the tribally oriented Kurdistan Conservative Party) during a squabble over the Surchis' ultimate allegiances in the KDP-PUK struggle for mastery in Iraqi Kurdistan. What is more, in late July 1996, the PUK allowed some 2,000 to 3,000 Iranian troops to pursue rebellious Iranian Kurds deep into PUK territory in return for Iranian arms. The KDP denounced this action in no uncertain terms: "The leaders of the PUK . . . have perpetrated a treasonous and shameful deed. . . . Through this military coordination, the PUK leaders want to realize material and military gains to use in the internal [Iraqi Kurdish] strife."[22]

Iran's moves clearly strengthened the PUK while weakening the KDP and thus Turkey. Following the outbreak of renewed KDP-PUK fighting in mid-August 1996, and alarmed at the turn of events, the KDP—as noted in chapter 4—reached an agreement with Saddam that allowed Barzani to retake Irbil from Talabani in August 1996, an action in part justified by both Barzani and Saddam in terms of foreign Iranian support for the PUK. Amid PUK accusations of further Iraqi support, the KDP quickly followed up its newly won advantage and chased the PUK to the Iranian frontier.

Seeking to counter its rival's charges of collusion with Saddam, the KDP released documents reputedly written by Talabani indicating the extent of his collaboration with Iran.[23] Although the PUK denied that it had received tangible military support from Iran, while the KDP tried to downplay the extent of support given it by Baghdad, in truth, both Iraqi Kurd-ish parties had upped the ante by soliciting outside aid in their ongoing civil war.

Following the U.S. counterstrikes against Baghdad and given Iraq's pariah status, Saddam was quickly forced to pull back his overt support for the KDP. Turkey, alarmed over the fighting and resulting chaos that were allowing the PKK to strengthen its position in northern Iraq, announced that it too would intervene in Iraqi Kurdistan by establishing a security zone extending several miles into Iraqi territory to interdict PKK raids into Turkey. Iran called on Turkey to "immediately abort the plan"[24] and recalled that "some political observers . . . consider the expansionist power lust of some power factions in Turkey and the multiplicity of its domestic problems . . . as the basis for Ankara's decision to attack northern Iraq."[25]

The reference was to Turkey's former claim to Mosul [Iraqi Kurdistan] and its oil resources, as well as Turkey's incipient domestic struggle between the Islamists and the secularists. Indeed, Tansu Ciller's True Path Party (DYP) wing of the Turkish government coalition was sympathetic to the U.S. position on Iraqi Kurdistan in such matters as the continuation of Operation Provide Comfort, while the Islamist prime minister, Necmettin Erbakan, not only opposed them but sought active cooperation with Iran. Surveying the wreckage of his domain, Iran's new ally, Jalal Talabani, for his part, declared: "In addition to Baghdad, we hold the Turkish Government responsible for everything that has taken place in the area. We do not have friendly relations with the Turkish Government anymore."[26]

Nevertheless, by the end of October 1996, the PUK proceeded to regain practically all the territory it had lost to the KDP the previous month. Once again the KDP blamed Iran: "The Iranian Islamic regime has stepped up its direct intervention in support of Talabani's PUK and has sent several thousand new troops with heavy weapons across the border."[27] Barzani himself declared, "Suleymeniyeh was taken with the help of Iranian guards, Iranian weapons, and Iranian bombs."[28] Sami Abdurrahman, a top aide of Barzani, claimed, "one of the reasons for these [Iranian] attacks is our friendship with Turkey. We call on Turkey to help us."[29]

The so-called Ankara peace process began at the end of October 1996. As noted in chapter 4, it consisted of renewed mediation attempts by the United States, Turkey, and Britain to end the KDP-PUK civil war. Despite continuing efforts into October 1997, however, the Ankara peace process failed to progress beyond achieving anything more than another cease-fire. The opposition of Iran proved a major reason for this state of affairs: "The mediation attempts made by the U.S., Britain, and Turkey are not destined to settle the Kurdish issue. . . . As a matter of fact, none of the above countries has a bright record from the standpoint of the Kurdish people."[30] Alluding to its opposition, Tehran further explained that the United States "lacks the necessary means and instruments to mediate in Iraqi Kurdistan and does not have the ability to guarantee the cease-fire and its

continuation."[31] Further Iranian commentaries denounced the
Ankara process as an attempt by the United States to establish
"a spying base and spring board to carry out its malicious
schemes in the region,"[32] and "a concerted effort [by] the US and
the Zionist regime . . . to create another Israel in the Kurdish
areas."[33]

The peace monitoring force of some 1,000 local Turkmen
recruited to separate the KDP and PUK forces was denounced by
the PKK as a Turkish attempt "to create another Cyprus in the
region"[34] and a Turkish "occupationist force."[35] In these charac-
terizations the PKK was clearly espousing a position similar to
that held by the Iranians. Despite these developments, however,
the balance between the two warring Iraqi Kurdish factions
returned virtually to the status quo that had existed before the
eruptions of the previous summer. As another temporary cease-
fire settled over Iraqi Kurdistan, the danger of an immediate
Turkish-Iranian involvement receded.

The May 1997 Turkish military intervention into Iraqi Kurdistan in pursuit of the PKK, however, quickly led to a new low in
Turkish-Iranian relations. Against the background of earlier
Turkish allegations concerning Iranian support for domestic
Islamist forces within Turkey itself (analyzed above), the Turkish
military now accused Iran of not only supplying bases, transportation, medicines, hospitals, and uniforms for the PKK, but
also the very S-7 heat-seeking missiles that the PKK, in an
unprecedented action, used to down two Turkish helicopters
over Iraqi Kurdistan.[36] Turkey also claimed that Iran—as well as
Syria and Iraq—was mobilizing its forces along its borders with
Iraqi Kurdistan in response to the Turkish incursion. In addition,
the Kurdish Hizbollah, Kurdistan Conservative Party, and Kurdistan Social Democratic Party—all reputed to have close ties to
Iran—joined the PKK in battle against the Turkish-allied KDP
around Haj Omran near the Iranian border.

Iran quickly denounced the Turkish intervention of May
1997 "as not only a violation of all international laws but the sov-
ereign rights and territorial integrity of the Iraqi Muslim
nation."[37] Turkish accusations of Iranian support for the PKK
were "a joint conspiracy by the Turkish military and Israel"[38] and
fabrications "by Turkey's army against Iran"[39] that constituted
"anti-Islamic performances of the army-led secularist elite" and
"crimes they are committing with their expansionist goals."

Such reactions were clearly intensified by Iran's opposition to Turkey's growing military ties to Israel. Indeed, just prior to Turkey's cross-border incursion in May 1997, Turkish defense minister Turhan Tayan met in Israel with his counterpart, Yitzhak Mordechai (a Jewish Kurd born in Iraq), and they conferred about "common enemies" that were officially identified as "terrorism" and "fundamentalism" but were understood by most as referring to Syria and Iran, respectively. Turkish general Cevik Bir immediately followed Tayan's visit with one of his own to assure the Jewish state of the Turkish military's commitment to their newly established relationship.

In an attempt at damage control, the Iranian deputy foreign minister Alaaddin Brujerdi made a hasty trip to Ankara where he adamantly denied claims that his country was supporting the PKK. However, Brujerdi also conveyed Iran's concern at the presence of Turkish troops in Iraqi Kurdistan, denounced the attempts to sabotage Turkish-Iranian relations, and asked Turkey to take necessary measures against Iranian opposition groups active in Turkey.

In addition to its problems with Iran, relations between the Islamist-led coalition government and the secular-minded military in Turkey had become so bad by this time that the military did not even inform the government that it had invaded Iraqi Kurdistan until the operation was already 12 hours old. The reason given for this lack of coordination was the military's fear: "we were worried about the information we give leaking to the other side."[40] In other words, the Turkish military was afraid that the Turkish government would betray the state. Indeed, once the invasion was on, the military also accused the government of withholding funding for the operation in order to cause it to fail and thus make the military look incompetent before the Turkish public. The Islamist government responded that the Turkish military launched the invasion to try to divert the attention of the Turkish people from domestic problems, a charge supported by Iran.[41] Never before had the institutions of the Turkish state failed to unite fully behind the war against the PKK. Within a month of this confrontation, the military had forced Erbakan's government to resign.

Turkey entered Iraqi Kurdistan not only to curtail the PKK's ability to raid southeastern Turkey from its formidable bases in Iraqi Kurdistan, but also to help Barzani's KDP stabilize its control over its domain in the area. Thus fortified, Barzani would then be able to prevent PKK raids into Turkey. Undoubtedly, a desire to counter Iran's relationship with the PUK in Iraqi Kurdistan also played a role. To explain its support for Turkey's actions, the KDP declared:

> The unjustified PKK presence in Iraqi Kurdistan since 1991 has caused numerous difficulties for the Regional Government and has declared large border areas off bounds for the local authorities, established military zones and have conducted cross-border military activity that has harmed the interests of [the] local population. The PKK has never recognized the legitimate authority of the Kurdistan Regional Government and has behaved as if it is the authority and has intervened in the administrative functions, levied taxes and intimidated the local population. The PKK has behaved as an alternative authority and has denied the KDP the right to exercise its authority in the border areas inside Iraqi Kurdistan. . . . Therefore we would not feel sorry for their removal by whatever force.[42]

In response, Abdullah Ocalan, the leader of the PKK, threatened that the KDP would "be annihilated should you continue with your collaboration. Give up your dirty alliance [with Turkey] at once."[43] He also argued that the Turkish "operation was launched through the cooperation secured between the United States, Israel, and Turkey." Its aim was "not only to hit the PKK, but Iran as well." Semdin (Parmaksiz Zeki) Sakik, one of Ocalan's hard-line field commanders, added that the Turkish incursion was aimed against the Iranian and Arab peoples. Israel was trying to implement its plans to encircle Iran, Iraq, and Syria. The goal of the Turkish state was to overcome its domestic problems through this military operation and establish a buffer zone like the one established by Israel in Lebanon.[44] In a mirror image conspiracy theory, the PKK declared, "the Turkish state has speeded up its occupation and annexation plans to turn south [Iraqi] Kurdistan into Turkish land . . . on behalf of the Turkomans,"[45] while the Turkish deputy prime minister Bulent Ecevit accused the United States and Britain of having secret plans to set up an independent Kurdish state in the aftermath of a new war against Iraq.[46]

For his part, Jalal Talabani, the leader of the PUK, added, "the Ankara negotiations [between the KDP and PUK] were foiled on 14 May [1997] because of the Turkish-Barzani collusion and their agreement to invade Iraqi Kurdistan on the pretext of chasing terrorists."[47] Talabani added that he considered this invasion "a violation of Iraqi sovereignty, Iraqi national stability, and a breach of international law." In taking such action, Turkey had as one of its "foremost aims" the intention of "entrenching the strength and authority of Barzani." Thus, "Turkey has discarded its neutral role and is now an ally of Barzani." However, Talabani concluded, "our ties with Iran are good."

Barzani retorted that the PUK and the PKK "have made an alliance,"[48] while to compound the confusion, the United States reportedly was giving the PUK at least $50,000 a month in covert aid as late as November 1997.[49] The situation in Iraqi Kurdistan was beginning to resemble Hobbes's war of all against all. As Turkish president Demirel explained: "The territory of northern Iraq is a political vacuum; there is no government. . . . And so Turkey has full rights to do this [send in troops] to defend its borders and its population."[50]

CONCLUSION

Following a particularly bloody renewal of the Kurdish civil war in October 1997, which saw overt Turkish support for the KDP against the PUK and the PKK, a precarious cease-fire settled over the region. It seemed likely, however, that the Turkish-Iranian factor in the Iraqi Kurdish civil war would continue its downward slide into increasingly bitter confrontations, if not overt conflict.

Turkey, for example, had been maintaining troops in Iraqi Kurdistan since its intervention of May 1997. In October 1997, Turkish tanks actually approached the outskirts of Irbil and to within 50 miles of Kirkuk, their deepest penetration into Iraqi Kurdistan yet. This action was in support of the KDP in its October 1997 fighting against the PUK and PKK. It clearly showed that Turkey was now actually taking sides in the Kurdish civil war. In reaction, Iran declared, "it was very clear that the smell of Kirkuk's oil has intoxicated the Turkish officials,"[51] and that the incursion constituted "an attempt by the triangle of Washington–

Tel Aviv–Ankara to control the region from the Mediterranean to the Persian Gulf."[52]

For its part, Iran too continued to make incursions into Iraqi Kurdistan in pursuit of the Iranian Kurds and various dissident Iranian groups harboring there. These interventions, however, were carried out on a smaller scale than the Turkish ones. In addition, the multi-billion dollar natural gas deal Turkish prime minister Erbakan had signed with Iran in July 1996 was now moribund. Furthermore, in a dramatic move in December 1997 Turkish president Demirel walked out of a high-profile meeting of the Organization of the Islamic Conference in Tehran, apparently due to the conference's implicit criticism of Turkey's interventions in northern Iraq and its military cooperation with Israel. Problems also beset Turkey's secular-Islamist relationship, which was attenuated by the confrontation with Iran over Iraqi Kurdistan and susceptible to continuing Iranian interest and possible interference. The political vacuum of Iraqi Kurdistan had drawn Turkey and Iran into their sharpest confrontation yet in a relationship heretofore surprisingly amicable despite their bitterly opposed domestic systems and obviously conflicting foreign policies.

However, the longstanding Turkish-Iranian tradition of discreet statecraft and co-existence was unlikely to allow their confrontation to result in outright conflict. Given Turkey's U.S. and now Israeli connections, Iran was unlikely to overtly challenge Turkey in Iraqi Kurdistan. Over the past 20 years, for example, it has been mainly Turkish troops, not Iranian, that have been intervening repeatedly in northern Iraq—by official Turkish account, 57 times since the early 1980s.[53]

6

Prospects

In recent years there has been a remarkable growth of rich and penetrating theoretical analyses of nationalism based on comparative and interdisciplinary methodologies.[1] Although abstract theories can divorce one from the analysis of reality, it would still be useful to apply briefly some of the more apposite theoretical insights to the realities of the contemporary situation in Iraqi Kurdistan.

In the modern world of decolonization and nation-states, the Kurds continue to suffer from a form of internal colonialism that has stunted the full development of their nationalism. Virtually every observer has also noted the negative effect of such primordial divisions as tribe, language, and birthplace on the creation of a Kurdish nation and state.[2] Kurdish nationalism seems stuck in a time warp from which others emerged more than a century ago.

Although there is truth to this view, it glosses over the fact that Turkey, Iran, and the current Arab nation-states themselves were only created in the twentieth century, and in the case of Iraq, Turkey, Iran, and Syria, were created in part on the back of the Kurds whom, one might argue, they continue to hold as an internal colony. Unless this Kurdish bondage ends soon, there is reason to argue that the artificial states that contain the Kurds may assimilate them.

Crawford Young, for example, has analyzed how the artificial states created by the colonial powers in Africa in time came to help mold new senses of ethnic self-definition.[3] Both Ernest Gellner and Benedict Anderson have argued that states, in effect, create nations. "Nationalism is not the awakening of nations to self-consciousness: it invents nations where they do not exist"[4]—or as Anderson puts it, it "imagines"[5] them. Illustrating how the state can be used to create the nation, Massimo d'Azeglio, an Italian nationalist leader during the *Risorgimento,* reputedly exclaimed "We have made Italy, now we have to make Italians"[6] also illustrates how the state can be used to create the nation. All this would suggest that in time the arbitrary state boundaries that include the Kurds may assimilate them, a process that is already occurring in part.

Upon closer analysis, however, it may be unfair to criticize the Kurds for possessing only a halting, stunted sense of nationalism. In his iconoclastic study of the development of the French nation,[7] Eugene Weber documented how most rural and village inhabitants of France did not think of themselves as members of the French nation as late as 1870 or even up to the eve of World War I. As much as 25 percent of the population could not even speak French, while half the people considered it a foreign language. Indeed, even today the *langue d'oc,* one of the two principal groups of medieval French dialects, survives as Provencal with some ten million speakers in southern France. The *langue d'oil* of the northern Paris region gradually developed into modern French. Related dialects of each still persist as patois in some rural areas.[8]

Despite the conventional view that the French were among the oldest nations in Europe, much of her population had yet to be truly integrated well into the nineteenth century. With the partial exception of the areas north and east of Paris, the typical village remained physically, politically, and culturally isolated. To its inhabitants (who remained the majority at the dawn of the twentieth century), the Jacobin model of a centralized, monolingual French nation-state remained a dream. As one nineteenth-century French observer put it: "Every valley is still a little world that differs from the neighboring world as Mercury does from Uranus. Every village is a clan, a sort of state with its own patriotism."[9]

There is no comparable study for any other European nation at the turn of the century. Heuristic insights, however, lie in U.S. immigration data. For the most part they indicate that immigrants from rural areas in southern and eastern Europe

> regularly identified themselves in terms of locale, region, province, and the like. For example . . . Croats described themselves as Dalmatian, Istrian, Slavonian, and the like, but not as Croat. . . . Italians as Neapolitan, Calabrian, and the like, but not as Italian; Poles as Gorali, Kashubi, Silesian, and so on, but not as Polish. . . . [Even] the Netherlander immigrants proved to be a remarkable diverse people whose local identities took precedence over a common identity as Dutch.[10]

The similarity to the current Kurdish situation could not be more apparent. Furthermore, Weber's findings clearly suggest that if the now-prevalent sense of French nationhood had not penetrated into the psyches of the rural masses more than a hundred years after scholars had pronounced it to be in full bloom, then today's fractured Kurdish nationalism may yet develop into a united Kurdish nation-state.

In musing over the meaning of Weber's disclosures, Walker Connor has argued that "nation-formation is a process, not an occurrence."[11] The late formation of the French nation is not unique. "There is ample evidence that Europe's currently recognized nations emerged only very recently, in many cases centuries later than the dates customarily assigned for their emergence."[12]

E. J. Hobsbawm has also documented "how late the ethnic-linguistic criterion for defining a nation actually became dominant."[13] He lists the Irish, Finns, Catalans, Basques, Baltic, and Balkan peoples as examples. To the extent that Connor's and Hobsbawm's conclusions are valid, the Kurds may yet manage to achieve a nation-state out of the present debris of their still divided nationalism. The Kurds are not necessarily guilty of having spawned only a stunted nationalism, as many—including they themselves—have claimed.

Nevertheless, Kurdish nationalism has been slower to develop than those that have achieved statehood in the past century. In partial explanation, Ernest Gellner's argument that "nationalism is, essentially, the general imposition of a high culture on a society where previously low cultures had taken up the lives of the majority"[14] seems relevant. By "high culture" Gellner means one that is "a school-mediated, academy-supervised idiom, codified for the requirements of reasonably precise bureaucratic and technological communication."[15] The Kurdish dialects have obviously not yet met this standard of "high culture."[16]

Karl Deutsch's stress on "nationalism and social communication" adds further insights into the retarded development of Kurdish nationalism:

> Membership in a people essentially consists in wide complementarity of social communication. It consists in the ability to communicate more effectively, and over a wider range of subjects, with members of one large group than with outsiders.[17]

E. J. Hobsbawm has argued the need for state education to transform people into citizens,[18] or, in the case of Kurdistan, tribal communities and local allegiances into a Kurdish nation. Benedict Anderson's insights into what he calls "print-capitalism," or for-profit publishing in the vernacular languages, help explain the rise of the modern Western nation and offer further insights: "The convergence of capitalism and print technology on the fatal diversity of human language created the possibility of a new form of imagined community, which in its basic morphology set the stage for the modern nation."[19]

Paul Brass's instrumentalist view that cultural and religious differences are not necessarily so great as to rule out the creation of a composite national culture is also interesting for those seeking the successful development of a unified Kurdish nationalism out of the different particularisms still prevalent. "It is clear that some primordial attachments are variable. . . . Religious identification too is subject to change. . . . Even one's place of birth and kinship connections may lose their emotional significance for people or be viewed negatively. . . . Many movements create their cultures after-the-fact, as it were."[20]

In analyzing how an underclass emerges as an ethnic group, John Armstrong has argued, "a major sign of emerging ethnic identification, especially in East Central Europe, has been the appearance of an articulate elite among a mass of peasants hitherto distinguished from other social segments in the polity only by . . . linguistic patterns restricted to intimate small-group communication."[21] This has been difficult to accomplish, however, "in sedentary agricultural societies where dominant elites monopolize communication by symbols and supervise the socialization of all members of the polity by inculcation of myths legitimizing the elite's dominance."[22]

Michael Howard has noted how "from the very beginning the principle of nationalism was almost indissolubly linked, both in theory and practice, with the ideas of war."[23] With the possible exception of Norway, it is difficult to think of any nation-state "that came into existence before the middle of the twentieth century, which was not created, and had its boundaries defined, by wars, by internal violence, or by a combination of the two. . . . The concept of the 'nation' became inseparably associated with the wars it had fought."[24]

With telling aptness for the Kurdish predicament, therefore, Howard observed, "it is a chastening exercise to recall the states that have disappeared as the result of unsuccessful wars—or have never succeeded in coming into being."[25] He listed as examples of these "defunct or still-born states" the crusader kingdoms of the Middle East, the Duchy of Burgundy, the great principality of Lithuania, the ethnic blocs of the Ukraine and Armenia, Biafra in Africa, and the Confederate States of America in North America. In the same breath he remarked, "the Kurds struggle still."[26] The fact that since he penned these observations three of his examples of supposedly defunct states (Lithuania, Ukraine, and Armenia) have been resurrected adds further hope to the Kurdish cause.

On an even more positive note, Arend Lijphart has analyzed successful power-sharing in ethnically divided states such as Belgium, Canada, and the Netherlands.[27] His work has spurred policy-oriented research into the conditions of civic (state-building) nationalism in ethnically plural democracies.

In his work Karl Deutsch has pointed out that modernization leads to rapidly increasing social transactions and contacts among diverse social groups. This in turn makes strain and conflict more likely than mutual understanding.[28] "The number of opportunities for possible violent conflict will increase with the volume and range of mutual transactions" because the growing number of transactions "throws a burden upon the institutions for peaceful adjustment or change among the participating populations."[29] Similarly, Walker Connor noted that there was a "point at which a significant number of people perceived that the cumulative impact of the quantitative increases in the intensity of intergroup contacts . . . constituted a threat to their ethnicity."[30]

James Mayall has pointed out that before the collapse of communism the international community had generally been hostile to any redrawing of the map that was not part of the decolonization process. Between Iceland's secession from Denmark in 1944 and the collapse of the Soviet Union in 1991, the only successful secessionary movements were in Singapore (1965), Bangladesh (1971), and Eritrea (1991). Successful waves of state creation (Latin America in the nineteenth century, Europe after World War I, and decolonization after World War II) "have all been associated with the collapse of empires. [But] there are no more empires to collapse and therefore very limited possibilities for further state creation by this route."[31]

Mayall's observations suggest, therefore, that a Kurdish state probably would only emerge if there were a major collapse of the existing state system (Turkey, Iraq, Iran, and Syria, specifically) in the contemporary Middle East. The Kurdish predicament, therefore, is reminiscent of the Polish plight between 1795 and 1919. It took the upheaval of World War I to shake loose a Polish state from the shackles of internal colonialism imposed by Germany (Prussia), Austria, and Russia. Although the Gulf War in 1991 did result in the halting, defective emergence of a rump proto-Kurdish state in northern Iraq, only a total rerolling of the national dice that would follow another world war would be likely to lead to the creation of an independent Kurdistan. And based on the findings of such scholars as Gellner, Anderson, and Young, mentioned above,[32] unless this happens sooner rather than later, many fear for the long-term survival of the Kurdish people themselves as a distinct entity.

Donald Horowitz argues, "whether and when a secessionist movement will emerge is determined mainly by domestic politics, by the relations of groups and regions within the state."[33] His typology of secessionist movements clearly illustrates that backward groups in terms of education and nonagricultural employment who live in poorer regions are far more likely to opt for secession. Interestingly, however, Horowitz also finds that "among the most frequent and precocious secessionists—backward groups in backward regions—economic loss or gain plays the smallest role, ethnic anxiety the largest."[34] Secessionist success, finds Horowitz, "is determined by international politics, by the balance of interests and forces that extend beyond the state."[35]

Turning his attention specifically to the Iraqi Kurds, Horowitz notes that

> even as they fought and died in the 1960s and 1970s [one may also add the 1980s, 1990s, and soon probably the 2000s] they eschewed anything beyond regional autonomy. The reason, presumably, was tactical: had they declared independence as their goal, the Iraqi Kurds would have engendered hostility from neighboring regimes in Iraq, Iran, and Turkey, all of which have Kurdish minorities."[36]

Massoud Barzani seconded this analysis upon returning from a trip to Turkey and Europe early in 1992; he concluded, "the situation in the world today is such that it will not permit any changes in regional borders. Nor will it stand for any partitioning."[37] For the same reasons, Jalal Talabani—Barzani's rival partner—disingenuously added: "We do not want to break away from Iraq; we [only] want a democratic Iraq."[38]

Many have concluded that in the present post-industrial, global era—in which the salience of nationalism can be expected to gradually decline as new, larger economic units such as the European Union form—the Kurds should seek only true democracy within the pre-existing states they presently inhabit. Turkey's fledgling democracy is sometimes said to be the best example.[39] Anthony Richmond, however, has argued that as we continue to move into this new age, denser networks using computer technology and telecommunications are actually encouraging the proliferation of ethnic nationalism.[40] The Kurds constitute a good example. With their host of new sites on the World Wide Web,[41] it has become possible to promote Kurdish nationalism on the cheap.

Based on this brief analysis of recent theoretical writings on nationalism, one may conclude that although the Kurdish predicament will continue, renewed hope is possible. At the dawn of the twenty-first century the Kurdish problem remains. Indeed, it bids to become the single most important issue in the volatile, geostrategically important Middle East if and when the Arab-Israeli dispute is finally settled.

CONCLUSION

One might conclude that it was rather naive to expect a people who lacked any real experience in self-rule to suddenly fashion and maintain a modern democracy. The contemporary experiences of Russia and the various successor states of the former Soviet Union illustrate this point well. Indeed, how have the Kurds been any different in the violence and anarchy they have been experiencing than the people of Afghanistan, Angola, Bosnia, Rwanda, or Somalia, to name just a few? Yet the international community remains pleased to recognize these examples as "states" complete with membership in the United Nations.

The Kurds are not recognized as a state, of course, because their lands are also part of already existing states. To create an independent Kurdistan would threaten the territorial integrity of these pre-existing states. No state on earth will support a doctrine that sanctions its own potential breakup.

It is not all the fault of others, however. The Kurdish people have been the victim of leaders guilty of selfish partisanship and greed. The PUK, for example, points out how the KDP justified Barzani's reasons for not joining the government: "We shall not allow the sacredness and greatness of Leader Barzani to be disgraced" by "the questioning, criticisms, innuendoes and daily abuse" that would be entailed in the parliamentary process.[42] Barzani himself has admitted that in part at least the fighting "has to do . . . with the question of hegemony."[43] As an NGO worker in northern Iraq put it: "Barzani thinks he's the true leader of the Kurds. So does Talabani and they'll fight each other down to their last peshmerga to prove themselves right."[44] Certainly there is a need for less party partisanship and more technical competence in running the Kurdistan Regional Government (KRG).

The 50/50 principle that split power equally between the KDP and the PUK should be cast aside because it paralyzed the initiative of the fledgling Kurdish state established in northern

Iraq following the Gulf War in 1991. Once the situation returns to normal, elections must be held to elect a new parliament. A majority government that respects the rights of the minority may then emerge. The Paris Agreement of July 1994, the Strategic Agreement of November 1994, and the Barzani-Talabani Accord of September 1998, detail the procedures that should be followed. (See chapter 4.)

Finally, when discussing how the Kurds can rebuild their democracy, we must come to grips with the basic problems of (1) primordial loyalties, (2) proliferation of guns and armed militias, and (3) the disastrous economic situation. Each one of these problems is enough to prevent the reinstitution of Kurdish democracy. Together they will make it impossible.

Primordial loyalties include allegiances to families, clans, and tribes. In the Kurdish case these loyalties continue to work against a viable Kurdish nationalism that the people in northern Iraq can share. So far neither Barzani nor Talabani has proven able to make the transition from tribal warlord to true statesman. The Kurds as a nation remain divided, as were the Germans before 1871 and the Italians before 1861. They also lack a Bismarck or Garibaldi.

Unless the Kurds can rise above these primordial allegiances, they will prove correct the claim that "the Kurds, as a group, are ungovernable, even by leaders they themselves have chosen. . . . The Kurdish chiefs today are doing no differently than Kurds have done for centuries i.e., serving foreign interests as mercenaries for pay. They are hired guns; and hired guns do not a movement make."[45]

The proliferation of guns and armed militias must also be contained. Even in the United States guns have challenged some of the very prerequisites upon which democracy rests. And we all know how difficult it is proving to get a handle on this problem in the United States. Clearly in Kurdistan the problem is much worse. Indeed, the situation reminds one of Lebanon during its worst days. How can democracy possibly even begin to work when so many armed men are walking around beyond any effective governmental control?

Finally, the double economic blockade imposed by the United Nations on all of Iraq (with the support of the United States) and by Baghdad on just the Kurds is another major problem that threatens Kurdish democracy.[46] "Ludicrously, the

sanctions cover seed, livestock, farm implements, industrial ma-
chinery—and all the other ingredients of self-sufficiency," one
observer reported.[47]

As a result of the blockade, the KRG has been unable to
revive its economy.[48] Unemployment is running as high as 80 to
90 percent, food prices have surged 200 percent in the past year,
and demonstrations and attempts to gain forced access to
stored food aid have occurred. No well-established Western
democracy could survive under similar circumstances. How can
the Kurds be blamed if they have run into serious difficulties?
Fortunately, the U.N. oil-for-food resolutions have recently
brought some temporary relief to the Kurds, but it remains to be
seen how long this more positive situation will continue.

The creation for the first time of an increasingly influential
and in part highly educated diaspora of some 1 million Kurds in
the West represents another positive factor. Already this new
diaspora is carrying out an important lobbying role both in the
West and in the Kurdish homeland itself. In time it also will
increasingly facilitate the transfer of needed human and technical resources back to the homeland. One may speculate that the
democratically socialized diaspora will also begin to further the
democratization process in Kurdistan. Freed from the state
struggles that divide greater Kurdistan, the next generation of
this new Kurdish diaspora may be expected to become gradually
more pan-Kurdish in outlook.

Clearly, the KDP-PUK fighting presents a serious setback for
democracy in Iraqi Kurdistan, but it does not have to be a disaster. Now that the Gulf War and the resulting U.N. Security Council Resolution 688 have let the Kurdish jinni out of the bottle, it
will be difficult to continue to ignore the Kurdish existence. Even
if Saddam Hussein remains in power, he will not likely become
strong enough or even find it prudent to diminish the role of the
Kurds. Therefore, it still remains possible that the Kurdish people can gain valuable experience from their recent problems and
move forward. If they do, it will only be the result of uncommon
valor and intelligent statesmanship on their part, and generous
international aid and understanding on the part of the international community.

Notes

Introduction

1. Michael M. Gunter, *The Kurds of Iraq: Tragedy and Hope* (New York: St. Martin's Press, 1992).
2. See the reviews of my book in *Middle Eastern Studies* 30 (October 1994), pp. 990–91; *International Affairs* (London) 69 (October 1993), p. 808; *Times Literary Supplement,* Aug. 27, 1993, p. 24; and *Kurdish Studies: An International Journal* 5 (Spring–Fall 1992), pp. 94–95; among others.
3. Edgar T. A. and W. A. Wigram, *The Cradle of Mankind: Life in Eastern Kurdistan,* 2 ed. (London: A. & C. Black, 1922).
4. For a sample see John Hutchinson and Anthony D. Smith, eds., *Nationalism* (Oxford and New York: Oxford University Press, 1994).

Chapter One

1. Edgar T. A. and W. A. Wigram, *The Cradle of Mankind: Life in Eastern Kurdistan,* 2 ed. (London: A. & C. Black, 1922). The following citations from this source are indicated in the text in parentheses.
   Other "classic" studies of the Iraqi Kurds in English include: C. J. Edmonds, *Kurds, Turks, and Arabs: Politics, Travel, and Research in North-Eastern Iraq, 1919–1925* (London and New York: Oxford University Press, 1957); A. M. Hamilton, *Road Through Kurdistan: The Narrative of an Engineer in Iraq* (London: Faber & Faber, 1937); W. R. Hay, *A Soldier in Kurdistan: Rupert Hay's Two Years in Kurdistan* (London: Sidgwick & Jackson, 1921); E. B. Sloane, *To Mesopotamia and Kurdistan in Disguise: With Historical Notices of the Kurdish Tribes and the Chaldeans of Kurdistan* (London: John

Murray, 1926); and Sir Arnold T. Wilson, *Mesopotamia 1917–1920: A Clash of Loyalties* (Oxford: Oxford University Press, 1931).

2. See, for example, David McDowall, *A Modern History of the Kurds* (London: I. B. Tauris, 1996), pp. 89–91.

3. Although population statistics are woefully inadequate in northern Iraq, one estimate indicates that the Turkomans constitute approximately 220,000, or less than 2 percent of the Iraqi population, while the Assyrians number maybe 133,000, or less than 1 percent. See Helen Chapin Metz, ed., *Iraq: A Country Study* (Washington, D.C.: Government Printing Office, 1990), p. 86. The Turks, on the other hand, have claimed as many as 3,000,000 Turkomans in Iraq. ("Turkoman Leader Seeks Turkey's Support on Minority Rights," Istanbul Kanal-7 Television in Turkish, 1800 GMT, Aug. 13, 1996; as cited in *Foreign Broadcast Information Service—West Europe,* Aug. 15, 1996, p. 23.)

4. On the Yezidis, see John Guest, *Survival Among the Kurds: A History of the Yezidis* (London: Kegan Paul International, 1993); and Nelida Fuccaro, *The Other Kurds: Yazidis in Colonial Iraq* (London: I. B. Tauris, 1999).

5. For an analysis of the pre-Islamic religions and their continuing residual influence in the land, see Mehrdad Izady, *The Kurds: A Concise Handbook* (Washington, D.C.: Crane Russak, 1992), pp. 131–66.

6. For a recent analysis, see Vahakn N. Dadrian, *The History of the Armenian Genocide: Ethnic Conflict from the Balkans to Anatolia to the Caucasus* (Providence and Oxford: Berghahn Books, 1995). For more on the role of the Kurds in these events, see pp. 45–48 and 131–34.

7. A third university is now being built in Dohuk.

8. On the Jews of Iraqi Kurdistan, see Erich Brauer, *The Jews of Kurdistan*. Completed and edited by Raphael Patai (Detroit: Wayne State University Press, 1993).

Chapter Two

1. The Kurdish scholar Muhammad Rasool Hawar, however, has written biographies of Sheikh Mahmud Barzinji (the Iraqi Kurd who fought against the British in the 1920s) and Ismail Agha Simko (the Iranian Kurd who also fought during the 1920s).

2. His handing over of Iranian Kurds to the shah's government for execution in order to curry favor with Iran is one example. Korn did, however, produce a useful article covering Mulla Mustafa's last years: David A. Korn, "The Last Years of Mustafa Barzani," *Middle East Quarterly* 1 (June 1994), pp. 12–27. In addition, several other Western authors have given some biographical attention to the elder Barzani within their larger studies. See, for example, Dana

Adams Schmidt, *Journey Among Brave Men* (Boston: Little, Brown, 1964), pp. 93–115; Hassan Arfa, *The Kurds: An Historical and Political Study* (London: Oxford University Press, 1966), pp. 117 ff.; William Eagleton, Jr., *The Kurdish Republic of 1946* (London: Oxford University Press, 1963), pp. 47–54; David McDowall, *A Modern History of the Kurds* (London: I. B. Tauris, 1996), *passim;* and Jonathan C. Randal, *After Such Knowledge What Forgiveness?* (New York: Farrar, Straus and Giroux, 1997), *passim.*

3. The fascinating details given by the Wigrams (see chapter 1) dovetailed nicely with Ayoub's accounts. Edgar T. A. Wigram and W. A. Wigram, *The Cradle of Mankind: Life in Eastern Kurdistan,* 2 ed. (London: A. & C. Black, 1922), pp. 134–57.

4. *Ibid.,* p. 135.

5. See M. M. van Bruinessen, *Agha, Shaikh and State: On the Social and Political Organization of Kurdistan* (Utrecht: University of Utrecht, 1978), pp. 292–93, 329–31, and 346–48; and C. J. Edmonds, "The Kurds and the Revolution in Iraq," *Middle East Journal* 13 (Winter 1959), pp. 5–8.

6. For a discussion, see Mark Sykes, *The Caliph's Last Heritage: A Short History of the Turkish Empire* (London: Macmillan, 1915), pp. 323–25.

7. W. R. Hay, *Two Years in Kurdistan: Experiences of a Political Officer, 1918–1920* (London: Sidgwick & Jackson, 1921), p. 160; and Bruinessen, *Agha, Shaikh and State* (1978), p. 347. Also see Basile Nikitine, "Les Kurds Racontés par Eux-mêmes," *L'Asie Française* no. 230 (March-April 1925), p. 180, who refers to them as "les fous" or the foolish.

8. Bruinessen, *Agha, Shaikh and State* (1978), p. 329. Although some might argue that Bruinessen's characterization of Barzan was an anachronistic exaggeration, it still indicates the unique qualities that set the rather small Barzani tribe apart as a leading force among the Kurds.

9. Wigrams, *Cradle of Mankind,* p. 137.

10. Cited in *ibid.,* pp. 143, 145.

11. Cited in *ibid.,* pp. 141, 143.

12. McDowall, *Modern History of the Kurds,* p. 100.

13. On the events leading up to the execution of Sheikh Abdul Salam II, see Wadie Jwaideh, "The Kurdish Nationalist Movement: Its Origins and Development," Ph.D. dissertation, Syracuse University, Jan. 1960, pp. 315–28. This execution obviously affected the Barzanis' attitude toward the authorities since the executed sheikh was the older brother of the legendary Mulla Mustafa Barzani and thus the uncle of the current Barzani leader, Massoud.

14. Stephen H. Longrigg, *Iraq, 1900 to 1950: A Political, Social, and Economic History* (London: Oxford University Press, 1953), p. 194. Oth-

ers, however, claim that the reputation for eccentricity was simply pinned on the Barzanis by their enemies.

15. For a concise list of the major events in Mulla Mustafa's life, see the World Wide Web site of the KDP at http://www.kdp.pp.se. For further analyses, see the works cited in note 2, above.

16. Cited in Middle East Watch, *Genocide in Iraq: The Anfal Campaign Against the Kurds* (New York: Human Rights Watch, 1993), p. 41.

17. Cited in Edmund Ghareeb, *The Kurdish Question in Iraq* (Syracuse: Syracuse University Press, 1981), p. 155.

18. Massoud has four other sons: Muksi, Mansour, Waysi, and (a new) Mulla Mustafa. He also has three daughters: Monira, Nabila, and Urfa.

19. Randal, *After Such Knowledge,* p. 201.

20. *Ibid.,* p. 299. In rationalizing why the United States and the shah's Iran betrayed Mulla Mustafa, Kissinger argued that "covert action should not be confused with missionary work." Cited in the unauthorized publication of the U.S. House of Representatives Pike Committee Report that investigated the U.S. Central Intelligence Agency in the 1970s, "The CIA Report the President Doesn't Want You to Read," *Village Voice,* Feb. 16, 1976, pp. 85, 87–88.

21. Cited in "Iraq: KDP's Barzani Urges Arab-Kurdish Dialogue," *Al-Majallah* (London), Oct. 5–11, 1997, p. 29; as cited in *Foreign Broadcast Information Service—Near East & South Asia* (97–283), Oct. 10, 1997, p. 2. Hereafter cited as *FBIS-NES.*

22. For further background on the Talabani family, see C. J. Edmonds, *Kurds, Turks and Arabs: Politics, Travel and Research in North-Eastern Iraq, 1919–1925* (London: Oxford University Press, 1957), pp. 267–71; and Martin van Bruinessen, *Agha, Shaikh and State: The Social and Political Structure of Kurdistan* (London: Zed Books, 1992), pp. 221–22.

23. Ghareeb, *Kurdish Question in Iraq,* 183.

24. Sa'ad Jawad, *Iraq and the Kurdish Question, 1958–1970* (London: Ithaca Press, 1981), p. 219n53.

25. Noshirwan Mustafa Amin rose to the number two position in the PUK hierarchy before resigning in frustration in the early 1990s. He currently resides in London where he is writing several books in Kurdish on the Kurdish struggle. Still in his mid-fifties, he may yet return to the political fray in the future.

26. Cited in Suzanne Goldenberg, "Kurds Would Not Fight Iraq," *Guardian,* Nov. 27, 1990.

27. This and the following citations were taken from Najm Abdal al-Karim, "Talabani Tells Al-Majallah: We Would Fight Alongside Arab Forces to Liberate Kuwait!" *Al-Majallah,* Dec. 19–24, 1990; as cited in *FBIS-NES,* Jan. 4, 1991, p. 39.

28. "Kurdish Leader on Significance of Talks in Ankara," Ankara Anato-

lia in English, 1515 GMT, Mar. 14, 1991; as cited in *FBIS-NES,* Mar. 15, 1991, p. 39.

29. "Kurdish Leader Wants 'Democratic Regime,'" Ankara Anatolia in Turkish, 1415 GMT, Mar. 31, 1991; as cited in *Foreign Broadcast Information Service–West Europe,* April 1, 1991, p. 33.

30. "Jalal Talabani Addresses Irbil Masses 29 Aug.," (Clandestine) Voice of the People of Kurdistan in Arabic, 1705 GMT, Sept. 1, 1991; as cited in *FBIS-NES,* Sept. 3, 1991, p. 26.

31. Cited in "Talabani Interviewed on Elections, Unity," Paris Radio Monte Carlo in Arabic, 1725 GMT, May 16, 1992; as cited in *FBIS-NES,* May 18, 1992, p. 19.

32. "PUK Delegation Visits Tehran; Battles in South," Paris Radio Monte Carlo in Arabic, 1700 GMT, Mar. 28, 1992; as cited in *FBIS-NES,* Mar. 30, 1992, p. 22.

33. Jalal Talabani, *Kurdistan wa al-Haraka al-Qawmia al-Kurdia* (Kurdistan and the Kurdish National Movement) (Beirut, 1971), originally written in 1965. Over the years Talabani has written a number of other papers and pamphlets. His first was entitled "Kurdistan Student Union-Iraq, Why?" In 1961, he published a booklet on the requirements for success in the Kurdish nationalist struggle. He followed this with an analysis of the political cadre and the necessity of his being in the party. He also, of course, has written numerous political articles for various Iraqi and Kurdish newspapers and journals.

Chapter Three

1. For chilling analyses, see Samir al-Khalil (Kanan Makiya), *The Republic of Fear: The Politics of Modern Iraq* (Berkeley: University of California Press, 1989); and Derek Hopwood et al., eds., *Iraq: Power and Society* (Reading: Ithaca Press, 1993). Portions of this chapter were originally published as Michael M. Gunter, "The Iraqi National Congress (INC) and the Future of the Iraqi Opposition," *Journal of South Asian and Middle Eastern Studies* 19 (Spring 1996), pp. 1–20.

2. Much of the following description is based on Helen Chapin Metz, ed., *Iraq: A Country Study* (Washington, D.C.: Government Printing Office, 1990), pp. 64–65, 197–99, and 251.

3. See Edmund Ghareeb, *The Kurdish Question in Iraq* (Syracuse: Syracuse University Press, 1981); and Michael M. Gunter, *The Kurds of Iraq: Tragedy and Hope* (New York: St. Martin's Press, 1992).

4. For further analyses, see Michael M. Gunter, "A de facto Kurdish State in Northern Iraq," *Third World Quarterly* 14:2 (1993), pp. 295–319; and Robert Olson, "The Creation of a Kurdish State in the 1990s?" *Journal of South Asian and Middle Eastern Studies* 15 (Summer 1992), pp. 1–25.

5. This and the following citations are taken from a lengthy analysis by Hasan Al-Jalabi, the head of the constitutional committee of INC, "Transformation of Iraqi Opposition into Comprehensive National Entity: Lessons of Uprising and of Beirut Conference up to Vienna Conference," *Al-Hayah* (London), Jan. 23, 24, and 25, 1993; as cited in *Foreign Broadcast Information Service—Near East & South Asia,* Feb. 18, 1993, pp. 29–35; hereafter cited as *FBIS-NES.*

6. The citation came from "Barzani Tells Sa'd Salih Jabr: Kurdish People Made Sacrifices Alone," *Al-Sharq Al-Awsat* (London), May 1, 1991, pp. 1, 4; as cited in *FBIS-NES,* May 10, 1991, p. 17.

7. The following data were taken from "Preparing Committee of Opposition Forces," *Sawt Al-Kuwayt* (London), Jan. 6, 1992, p. 5; as cited in *FBIS-NES,* Jan. 15, 1992, p. 36.

8. This and the following citation were taken from Jalabi, "Transformation of Iraqi Opposition," p. 31. The "material base" was the "75,000 square kms." of Iraqi Kurdistan outside of Saddam's control, while the "human base" consisted of "Iraqi citizens who live in the liberated areas, and in exile and who number no less than 4 million citizens at present." From Jalabi, "Transformations of Iraqi Opposition," p. 31

9. This and the following citation were taken from Jalabi, "Transformations of Iraqi Opposition," p. 31

10. "Al-Da'wah Criticizes Conference," *Beirut Al-Safir,* June 20, 1992, p. 12; as cited in *FBIS-NES,* June 22, 1992, p. 27.

11. This and the following citations were taken from Jalabi, "Transformation of Iraqi Opposition," p. 31.

12. This and the following citation were taken from a document of INC entitled simply "The Iraqi National Congress," n.d.

13. The following data were obtained largely from Abd-al-Mun'im al-A'sam, "Sawt Al-Kuwayt Exclusively Publishes Names of 26 Executive Committee Members. Iraqi Opposition to Keep Its Main Offices in Liberated Territories," *Sawt Al-Kuwayt* (London), Nov. 5, 1992, pp. 1, 7; as cited in *FBIS-NES,* Nov. 9, 1992, p. 27; and "Iraqi National Council," n.d.

14. Trevor House, 100 Brompton Road, London SW3 1ER. Tel.: 4471-582-3205; Fax: 4471-581-3218.

15. Tel.: 873-1514503, Fax: 873-1514504.

16. Cited in "Temporary Government Planned," Ankara Anatolia in Turkish, 1630 GMT, Oct. 28, 1992; as cited in *FBIS-NES,* Oct. 29, 1992, p. 28.

17. This and the following citation were taken from Jalabi, "Transformation of Iraqi Opposition," pp. 32–34.

18. The following analysis and citations are based on or taken from INC documents entitled "The Iraqi National Congress: Democratic Renewal, Reconstruction, and Reconciliation," n.d.; "Iraqi National

Congress: Executive Council News Conference, 13 January 1993,"
n.d.; "The Iraqi National Congress," n.d.; and "Report of the Meeting
of the Presidential Council and Executive Council of the Iraqi
National Council Salahuddin, Iraq 22–24 February, 1993," n.d.

19. Cited in Zaki Shihab, "Interview with Major General Hasan al-
Naqib. . . ," *Al-Wasat* (London), April 12, 1993, pp. 34–36; as cited in
FBIS-NES, April 20, 1993, p. 23.

20. The following data and citations are taken from Abdallah al-Dardari,
"Interview with Muhammad Baqir al-Hakim . . . ," *Al-Hayah* (London), June 15, 1993, p. 3; as cited in *FBIS-NES*, June 17, 1993, p. 30.

21. The following discussion and citations are taken from "INC Reportedly Readying Army for Saddam's Fall," Paris AFP in English, 0426
GMT, Sept. 18, 1994; as cited in *FBIS-NES*, Sept. 19, 1994, pp. 36–37.

22. This and the following citations were taken from Amberin Zaman,
"Iraqi Deserters Defy Surgeon's Saw," *Daily Telegraph* (London),
Nov. 1, 1994, p. 21; as cited in *FBIS-NES*, Nov. 3, 1994, pp. 34–35.

23. This and the following citation were taken from "Opposition Leader:
Only Army Can Topple Saddam," Paris AFP in English, 1541 GMT,
Oct. 12, 1994; as cited in *FBIS-NES*, Oct. 13, 1994, p. 45.

24. This and the following citations were taken from David Hirst, "Saddam's Foes Left High and Dry as West Fears Revolt," *Guardian* (London), Nov. 11, 1994, p. 16; as cited in *FBIS-NES*, Nov. 14, 1994, p. 36.

25. Salim Badawi, "Telephone Interview with Staff Major Wafiq al-
Samarra'i," Paris Radio Monte Carlo in Arabic, 1815 GMT, March 17,
1995; as cited in *FBIS-NES*, March 20, 1995, p. 17.

26. See, for example, Jane Arraf, "Only Whispers of Iraqi Opposition in
Baghdad," Reuters, Dec. 30, 1993; as cited in *The Kurds: Recent Wire
Reports,* Dec. 30, 1993, which also refers to "extensive Saudi funding
for Iraqi exiles" and "the well-funded Iraqi opposition abroad";
"Major Changes in Iraqi Opposition Movements' Ranks Abroad," *Al-
Quds Al-Arabi* (London), Nov. 27–28, 1993, p. 3; as cited in *FBIS-NES*,
Dec. 1, 1993, p. 22, which adds: "However, it [the U.S.] did not spec-
ify which quarter received this sum [$40 million]"; and Zaki Shihab,
"Interview with Muhammad Bahr-al-Ulum," *Al-Wasat* (London), May
24–30, 1993, pp. 34–35; as cited in *FBIS-NES*, May 28, 1993, p. 18.

27. This and the following citation were taken from Shihab, "Interview
with Bahr-al-Ulum."

28. This information and the following citations were taken from Shihab, "Interview . . ."

29. "Opposition Leader Talabani on U.S. Pledge of Support," Kuwait
KUNA in Arabic, 0755 GMT, June 19, 1993; as cited in *FBIS-NES*, June
21, 1993, p. 40.

30. Cited in Zuhayr Qusaybati, "Interview with Jalal Talabani," *Al-Hayah*
(London), Dec. 16, 1993, p. 7; as cited in *FBIS-NES*, Dec. 21, 1993, p.

      34. Talabani apparently was referring to the same U.S. money that al-Ulum cryptically mentioned above.

31. This and the following citation were taken from Shihab, "Interview with al-Naqib."

32. This and the following were cited in Zaki Shihab, "Report on Interview with INC Secretary Dr. Abd-al-Husayn Sha'ban," *Al-Wasat* (London), Dec. 13, 1993, pp. 32–36; as cited in *FBIS-NES,* Dec. 16, 1993, p. 28.

33. Cited in "Major Changes in Iraqi Opposition Movements' Ranks Abroad." See note 24 for the full citation to this source.

34. "UNIC's al-Jalabi Speaks on Opposition Activities," *Al-Quds Al-Arabi* (London), Aug. 8, 1994, p. 4; as cited in *FBIS-NES,* Aug. 11, 1994, p. 27.

35. Elaine Sciolino, "C.I.A. Asks Congress for $19 Million to Undermine Iraq's Rulers and Rein in Iran," *New York Times,* April 12, 1995, p. A4. The following data were taken from this source.

36. Cited in "Al-Jalabi on UINC Role in Kurdistan," *Al-Hayah* (London), Aug. 8, 1994, p. 4; as cited in *FBIS-NES,* Aug. 10, 1994, p. 35. Illustrative of how ephemeral and small many of the 70 odd opposition groups were, another report stated that only 19 parties were reported members of INC in 1993, while 7 had withdrawn or frozen their memberships as of the summer of 1995. Leslie Plommer and Karen Dabrawski, "Opposition Collapsing amid Internal Rivalries," *Guardian* (London), July 1, 1995, p. 1.

37. This and the following citations were taken from "SAIRI Spokesman Explains," (Clandestine) Voice of Iraqi Islamic Revolution in Arabic, 1430 GMT, Nov. 1, 1992; as cited in *FBIS-NES,* Nov. 2, 1992, p. 25.

38. This and the following citation were taken from "'First Successful' Opposition Meeting Concludes," Ankara Anatolia in Turkish, 1500 GMT, Oct. 31, 1992; as cited in *FBIS-NES,* Nov. 2, 1992, p. 24.

39. These points and the following citation were taken from Kamran Qurrah Daghi et al., "Damascus Attacks Opposition," *Al-Hayah* (London), Oct. 28, 1992, pp. 1, 4; as cited in *FBIS-NES,* Oct. 30, 1992, p. 18.

40. Sciolino, "C.I.A. Asks Congress for $19 Million," p. A4.

41. Cited in Zuhayr Qusaybati, "Al-Naqib: I Cooperate with Barzani to Change the Regime," *Al-Hayah* (London), Aug. 7, 1995, p. 6; as cited in *FBIS-NES,* Aug. 9, 1995, p. 33.

42. Cited in Ibrahim Humaydi and Zuhayr Qusaybati, "Al-Naqib Tells Al-Hayah: The Congress is Finished and I Shall Not Return to Northern Iraq," *Al-Hayah* (London), Aug. 4, 1995, pp. 1, 6; as cited in *FBIS-NES,* Aug. 8, 1995, p. 43.

43. Cited in *ibid.*

44. Zuhayr Qusaybati and Kamran Qurrah Daghi, "Iraqi Kurdish Oppositionists Continue Polemics," *Al-Hayah* (London), Aug. 5, 1995, pp. 1, 6; as cited in *FBIS-NES,* Aug. 9, 1995, pp. 29–30.

45. This and the following citation were taken from Ibrahim Hamaydi, "Al-Samarra'i Accuses al-Hakim of Racism . . . ," *Al-Hayah* (London), Aug. 6, 1995, pp. 1, 6; as cited in *FBIS-NES,* Aug. 9, 1995, p. 31.
46. This and the following citations were taken from "Opposition Leader Calls for Overthrow of Regime," Kuwait KUNA in Arabic, 0704 GMT, July 11, 1995; as cited in *FBIS-NES,* July 11, 1995, p. 56.
47. Cited in "SAIRI Leader: Conditions Conducive for Change," Tehran Voice of the Islamic Republic of Iran in English, 1230 GMT, July 26, 1995; as cited in *FBIS-NES,* July 27, 1995, p. 29. Indeed, by early November 1995, al-Hakim reportedly had deployed some 5,000 members of his Badar force south of Sulaymaniya in agreement with Talabani. Further deployments were projected. Barzani, however, disassociated himself from the project. See Ihsan Dorthardes, "Iran Will Hit Saddam Through Saddam's Frontline," *Hurriyet* (Turkey), Nov. 3, 1995, p. 20; as cited in *FBIS-NES,* Nov. 8, 1995, p. 29.
48. The following citations and data were taken from "London: Iraqi Opposition Meeting Calls for Tightening the Noose of Isolation Around the Regime," *Al-Hayah* (London), Sept. 1, 1995, p. 7; as cited in *FBIS-NES,* Sept. 5, 1995, pp. 46–47.
49. This and the following citations were taken from *ibid.*
50. The following discussion is based on "Husayn Kamil Forming New Political Party," *Al-Mashriq* (Amman), Nov. 27, 1995, p. 1; as cited in *FBIS-NES,* Nov. 28, 1995, p. 39; and "Husayn Kamil on Opposition Groups, Other Issues," *Al-Watan Al'Arabi* (Paris), Nov. 27, 1995, pp. 16–19; as cited in *FBIS-NES,* Nov. 20, 1995, pp. 38–39.
51. "Monarchist Movement Leader Explains Aims, Policies," *Al-Hadath* (Amman), Oct. 18, 1995, p. 7; as cited in *FBIS-NES,* Oct. 20, 1995, p. 32.
52. "Opposition Figure on Reinstating Hashemite Kingdom," *Al-Bilad* (Amman), Nov. 8, 1995, p. 5; as cited in *FBIS-NES,* Nov. 8, 1995, p. 30.
53. "King Husayn Said Seeking to Base Iraqi Opposition in Amman," Riyadh SPA in Arabic, 1832 GMT, Nov. 23, 1995; as cited in *FBIS-NES,* Nov. 24, 1995, p. 23; and "Iraqi Group and Figures Criticize Federation Plan," *Al-Sharq Al-Awsat* (London), Dec. 6, 1995, p. 4; as cited in *FBIS-NES,* Dec. 7, 1995, p. 41.
54. "Oppositionist Comments on King Husayn's Plan," Tehran Voice of the Islamic Republic of Iran in Arabic, 1730 GMT, Nov. 22, 1995; as cited in *FBIS-NES,* Nov. 30, 1995, p. 33.
55. Tim Weiner, "Iraqi Offensive into Kurdish Zone Disrupts U.S. Plot to Oust Hussein," *New York Times,* Sept. 7, 1996, pp. 1, 4; and Jonathan C. Randal, "Iraqi Opposition Describes Mass Execution Near Irbil," *Washington Post,* Sept. 2, 1996, p. A20.
56. Cited in Weiner, "Iraqi Offensive into Kurdish Zone Disrupts U.S. Plot," p. 4.
57. Kevin Fedarko, "Saddam's Coup," *Time,* Sept. 23, 1996, p. 44.

58. John Lancaster and David B. Ottaway, "With CIA's Help, Group in Jordan Targets Saddam," *Washington Post,* June 23, 1996, accessed over the Internet.

59. The following analysis is based on R. Jeffrey Smith and David B. Ottaway, "Anti-Saddam Operation Cost CIA $100 Million," *Washington Post,* Sept. 15, 1996, pp. A1, A29–A30; Jim Hoagland, "CIA's 'Zipless Coup' in Iraq Is a Matchless Flop," *International Herald Tribune,* May 9, 1997; Jim Hoagland, "How CIA's Secret War on Saddam Collapsed," *Washington Post,* June 26, 1997, pp. A21, A28–A29; Walter Pincus, "Justice Asked to Investigate Leaks by CIA Ex-Officials," *Washington Post,* July 19, 1997, p. A16; James Risen, "CIA Failure, Under Clinton, to Overthrow Saddam," *Los Angeles Times,* Feb. 15, 1998, accessed over the Internet. Also interviews with Ahmad Chalabi, London, Dec. 16, 1997; Wafiq al-Samarra'i, London, Dec. 15, 1997; and Latif Rashid, London, Dec. 14, 1997.

60. Cited in Hoagland, "How CIA's Secret War on Saddam Collapsed," p. A29.

61. This and the following quote are cited in the unauthorized publication of the U.S. House of Representatives Pike Committee Report, which investigated the CIA in the mid-1970s and was published as "The CIA Report the President Doesn't Want You to Read," *Village Voice,* Feb. 16, 1976, pp. 70–92.

62. Cited in Smith and Ottaway, "Anti-Saddam Operation Cost CIA $100 Million," p. A29.

63. Cited in Hoagland, "How CIA's Secret War on Saddam Collapsed," p. A28.

64. Cited in Smith and Ottaway, "Anti-Saddam Operation Cost CIA $100 Million," p. A29.

65. Cited in Hoagland, "How CIA's Secret War on Saddam Collapsed," p. A29.

66. "Talabani Interviewed on Situation in Northern Iraq," *Sabah* (Istanbul), Oct. 20, 1996, p. 5; as cited in *Foreign Broadcast Information Service—West Europe* (96-205), Oct. 20, 1996, p. 1.

67. "Iraq: TV Carries Confessions of CIA 'Agents,'" Baghdad Iraq Television Network in Arabic, 1900 GMT, Dec. 20, 1996; as cited in *FBIS-NES* (96-248), Dec. 20, 1996, p. 7.

68. The following discussion is largely based on Pary Karadaghi, "Kurdish Evacuees from Iraqi Kurdistan," *Kurdistan Times* 2 (November 1997), pp. 139–45; and Eric Lipton, "New Life, New Struggles Confront Kurdish Exiles," *Washington Post,* Dec. 30, 1996, accessed over the Internet.

69. James Risen, "Evidence to Deny 6 Iraqis Asylum May Be Weak, Files Show," *New York Times,* Oct. 13, 1998, accessed over the Internet. See also Tim Weiner, "Ex-CIA Chief Offers Aid to Iraqis Facing

Deportation," *New York Times,* Mar. 21, 1998, accessed over the Internet.

70. This and the following citation were taken from John Burgess and David B. Ottaway, "Iraqi Opposition Unable to Mount Viable Challenge," *Washington Post,* Feb. 12, 1998, accessed over the Internet. See also Rend Rahim Francke, "The Opposition," in *Iraq Since the Gulf War: Prospects for Democracy,* Fran Hazelton, ed. (London and New Jersey: Zed Books, 1994), pp. 153–77.

71. Initiative recommended by the Committee for Peace and Security in the Gulf, Washington, D.C., Feb. 22, 1998, accessed over the Internet.

72. The following discussion and citation are taken from Tim Weiner, "C.I.A. Drafts Covert Plan to Topple Saddam," *New York Times,* Feb. 26, 1998, accessed over the Internet.

73. "Iraqi Opposition Leader Presses for U.S. Support," Reuters, Feb. 26, 1998, accessed over the Internet.

74. The following data and citation were taken from INC Press Release, "INC Welcomes [U.S.] Congress Support," May 1, 1998, accessed over the Internet.

75. The following data were taken from Jon Kyl, "Erosion of Resolve on Iraq," Washington Times, Aug. 27, 1998, accessed over the Internet.

76. Cited in the INC Press Release, "INC Welcome's [U.S.] Congress Support," May 1, 1998, accessed over the Internet.

77. Cited in Thomas W. Lippman, "U.S. Aims to Unify Foes of Saddam: War Crimes Case is Considered," *Washington Post,* Aug. 2, 1998, accessed over the Internet. Jon Kyl, "Erosion of Resolve on Iraq," *Washington Times,* Aug. 27, 1998, accessed over the Internet.

78. The following discussion is largely based on David Rogers, "Clinton Seeking Support for Plan Against Saddam: Congress Is Asked to Give Broad New Authority for Covert Operations," *Wall Street Journal,* July 17, 1998; and Daniel Pearl, "U.S. Approaches Groups in Iran Opposing Iraq Head," *Wall Street Journal,* July 31, 1998, both accessed over the Internet.

79. Carol Giacomo, "U.S. Plans New Effort To Boost Iraqi Opposition," Reuters, June 17, 1998, accessed over the Internet.

80. "State Dept List of Iraqi Opposition Groups Memo," June 10, 1998, accessed over the Internet.

81. "Iraq: Iraqi Opposition Urges Kurds to Rejoin Anti-Saddam Camp," Paris AFP (North European Service) in English, 0755 GMT, Sept. 8, 1998; as cited in *FBIS-NES* (98-251), Sept. 8, 1998, p. 1.

82. Cited in the text translation of Barzani's interview in *Al-Hayat,* Sept. 15, 1998, as accessed over the Internet. Elsewhere Barzani added: "Neither the Iraqi regime nor any other regime can be toppled with $5 million. It seems that the Americans are not familiar with the situation in Iraq. The regime cannot be toppled so easily." Cited in the

interview with Barzani by Muhammad Sadiq in *Al-Sharq Al-Awsat* (London), Sept. 19, 1998; as cited in *FBIS-NES* (98-262), Sept. 19, 1998, p. 2.

83. Cited in the interview with Talabani by Salah Awwad, *Al-Quds Al-Arabi* (London), Sept. 22, 1998; as cited in *FBIS-NES* (98-266), Sept. 23, 1998, p. 3.

84. For details, see Vernon Loeb, "Congress Stokes Visions of War to Oust Saddam: White House Fears Fiasco in Aid to Rebels," *Washington Post,* Oct. 20, 1998, p. A1, accessed over the Internet.

Chapter Four

1. The Kurdish question in Iraq up to the 1970s and the fall of Mulla Mustafa Barzani in 1975 has been well covered by Edmund Ghareeb, *The Kurdish Question in Iraq* (Syracuse, NY: Syracuse University Press, 1981). Also see Edgar O'Ballance, *The Kurdish Revolt, 1961–1970* (Hamden, CT: Archon Books, 1973); Sa'ad Jawad, *Iraq and the Kurdish Question, 1958–1970* (London: Ithaca Press, 1981); and Ismet Sheriff Vanly, "Kurdistan in Iraq," in *People without a Country: The Kurds and Kurdistan,* ed. by Gerard Chaliand (London: Zed Press, 1980), pp. 153–210. For more recent events, see Michael M. Gunter, *The Kurds of Iraq: Tragedy and Hope* (New York: St. Martin's Press, 1992); Human Rights Watch/Middle East, *Iraq's Crime of Genocide: The Anfal Campaign Against the Kurds* (New York: Human Rights Watch/Middle East, 1995); and David McDowall, *A Modern History of the Kurds* (London: I. B. Tauris, 1996), pp. 343–91.

    The archives of the Human Rights Initiative of the University of Colorado at Boulder now contain the captured Iraqi secret police files spanning the period from the 1960s to 1991. These materials include documents concerning Saddam's Anfal campaign of genocide against the Kurds in the late 1980s; information on government policies, directives, and decrees; military operations and troop movements including the use of chemical weapons during the Iran-Iraq War and against the Kurds; elimination of villages; disappearances; collaborators; pro-government Kurdish militias; the Arabization campaign for Kurdish areas; and the political and human rights situation during the crisis over Kuwait. Portions of this chapter were earlier published as Michael M. Gunter, "The KDP-PUK Conflict in Northern Iraq," *Middle East Journal* 50 (Spring 1996), pp. 225–41.

2. For analyses, see Michael M. Gunter, "A de facto Kurdish State in Northern Iraq," *Third World Quarterly* 14:2 (1993), pp. 295–319; Robert Olson, "The Creation of a Kurdish State in the 1990s?" *Journal of South Asian and Middle Eastern Studies* 15 (Summer 1992), pp. 1–25; and

Robert Olson, "The Kurdish Question and Geopolitic and Geostrategic Changes in the Middle East after the Gulf War," *Journal of South
Asian and Middle Eastern Studies* 17 (Summer 1994), p. 44–67.

3. "Barzani, Talabani Declare Trend toward Unity," Al-Hayah (London),
Dec. 11, 1992, pp. 1, 6; as cited in *Foreign Broadcast Information Ser-
vice—Near East & South Asia,* Nov. 16, 1992, p. 33. Hereafter cited as
FBIS-NES.

4. *Ibid.*

5. The best source on the Mahabad Republic is William Eagleton, Jr.,
The Kurdish Republic of 1946 (London: Oxford University Press,
1963). Also see the useful Archie Roosevelt, Jr., "The Kurdish
Republic of Mahabad," *The Middle East Journal* 1 (July 1947), pp.
247–69; and the special issue entitled "The Republic of Kurdistan:
Fifty Years Later," *International Journal of Kurdish Studies* 11:1 & 2
(1997).

6. Most of the specific dates and facts reported here were taken from
a brief KDP document I obtained while attending the party's
eleventh congress in Irbil in August 1993 entitled "Kurdistan Democratic Party (KDP) Congresses 1946–1993."

7. Jawad, *Iraq and the Kurdish Question,* p. 20.

8. Dana Adams Schmidt, *Journey Among Brave Men* (Boston: Little,
Brown, 1964), p. 123.

9. The following data concerning Talabani come largely from documents supplied to me by the PUK entitled *Overview: Developments
in Iraqi Kurdistan,* April 1994.

10. Martin van Bruinessen, "The Kurds Between Iran and Iraq," *Middle
East Report,* no. 141 (July–August 1986), pp. 16. For enlightening
analyses of the diversity in Kurdish languages, see Amir Hassanpour, *Nationalism and Language in Kurdistan, 1918–1985* (San Francisco: Mellen Research University Press, 1992); Mehrdad Izady, *The
Kurds: A Concise Handbook* (Washington: Taylor & Francis, 1992),
pp. 167–75; and Philip G. Kreyenbroek, "On the Kurdish Language,"
in *The Kurds: A Contemporary Overview,* ed. by Philip G. Kreyenbroek and Stefan Sperl (London: Routledge, 1992), pp. 68–83.

11. It is important to remember, however, that although they are Muslims, most Kurds are not overly religious. Indeed, an old Kurdish saying has it that compared to an unbeliever, a Kurd is a good Muslim.

12. Cited in Schmidt, *Journey Among Brave Men,* p. 204.

13. Cited in Bruinessen, "The Kurds Between Iran and Iraq," p. 22.

14. Cited in Ghareeb, *Kurdish Question in Iraq,* p. 183. Similarly, Mulla
Mustafa's son Massoud reportedly declared during the recent fighting:
"I prefer Arabs to Talabani, because they are fighting for Arab nation-
alism but Talabani is fighting to betray his own people." Cited in Hayri

Birler, "PUK Gaining Iran's Support by Suppressing IKDP," *Turkish Daily News,* April 19, 1995, p. A2; as cited in *FBIS-NES,* April 26, 1995, p. 28.

15. Cited in *Tercuman* (Turkey), Oct. 10, 1986, p. 7.
16. Omar Sheikmous, "The Current Situation of the Kurds in Iraq," unpublished paper, June 1988, p. 3.
17. Cited in "Address by Madame Danielle Mitterrand," *Kurdistan Review,* April 1994, p. 10. Mrs. Mitterrand's remarks were made in a speech to the Royal Institute of International Affairs, Chatham House, London, Jan. 14, 1994.
18. Cited in Kurdistan Democratic Party Research Department, "What Happened in Iraqi Kurdistan? May 1994," June 1994, p. 7.
19. The IMK received only 5.1 percent of the vote for parliament in the May 1992 elections and thus failed to meet the 7 percent required to receive any representation. Its leader Sheikh Osman Abdul Aziz also ran a very distant third to Barzani and Talabani for the position of supreme leader (president).

     Aziz accused the PUK "of 30 years of corruption, deviation and fratricide in northern Iraq" and of helping "Westerners spread HIV viruses in Iraq's Kurdistan." Cited in "Kurdish Spokesman: West Behind Clashes in Kurdistan," Tehran IRNA in English, 2000 GMT, Dec. 29, 1993; as cited in *FBIS-NES,* Dec. 30, 1993, p. 29. In another interview Aziz declared: "Our aim is to establish an Islamic state in northern Iraq similar to the one in Iran. . . . Once we take the Kurds in Turkey into an independent Kurdistan we will establish a great Islamic state." "Islamic Leader Sees Goal as Islamic Kurdistan," London Kanal-6 Television in Turkish, GMT 94 [*sic*]; as cited in *FBIS-NES,* Jan. 14, 1994, p. 33.

     The PUK charged, "Iran directly and through proxy radical Islamic groups and elements within the KDP, has been engaged in sustaining and escalating the conflict." Patriotic Union of Kurdistan, Foreign Relations Committee, "On the Recent Events in Iraqi Kurdistan," May 29, 1994, p. 2. Since the Iraqi Kurdish Islamists are divided into some eight different groups—one of which, the Revolutionary Hizballah, is headed by Sheikh Adham Barzani—Aziz's goals are not likely to be obtained in the near future. Recently Sheikh Osman Abdul Aziz was succeeded by his brother Mulla Ali Abdul Aziz as leader of the IMK.
20. See "Barzani Message Blames Both Sides for Fighting," (Clandestine) Voice of Iraqi Kurdistan in Arabic, 1740 GMT, Dec. 27, 1993; as cited in *FBIS-NES,* Dec. 28, 1993, p. 26. Eventually the KDP and IMK became de facto allies against the PUK.
21. Cited in "Unscheduled Announcement," (Clandestine) Voice of Iraqi Kurdistan in Arabic," 1610 GMT, Dec. 26, 1993; as cited in *FBIS-NES,* Dec. 28, 1993, p. 25.

22. Kendal Nezan is a Turkish Kurdish physicist who fled from Turkey in 1971 and has since become a major critic of the Turkish government's policies. Over the years Dr. Nezan has developed close ties with the French government, in particular, with Danielle Mitterrand, the wife of the former socialist president (served 1981–1995). Najmaldin O. Karim was born in Iraqi Kurdistan, served while a young man as the personal physician of the elderly Mulla Mustafa Barzani, and later became an American neurosurgeon living in Washington, D. C. Because of his great knowledge of and connections with both the KDP and the PUK, as well as contacts made with U.S. officials in Washington, Dr. Karim has played an important, behind-the-scenes role in current Iraqi Kurdish politics. (See below in text.)

23. The following citations and data about the Paris Agreement are taken from the copy printed in Patriotic Union of Kurdistan, Foreign Relations Committee, "Iraqi Kurdistan: A Situation Report on Recent Events: The Context and Specifics of the Infighting in Iraqi Kurdistan," Feb. 1995, pp. 53–61.

24. In response to a letter from the U.S. State Department that said the intra-Kurdish fighting must stop because it harms the Kurdish people and that the United States, along with other states, would withdraw its support if the clashes continued, Barzani and Talabani held another inconclusive meeting in the parliament in Irbil on August 29, 1994. Adnan Husayn, "Kurdish Leaderships in Northern Iraq Pledge to Withdraw Armed Militias from Cities," *Al-Sharq Al-Awsat* (London), Sept. 1, 1994, p. 5; as cited in *FBIS-NES,* Sept. 2, 1994, pp. 28–29; and "Iraqi Kurds End Fighting Due to U.S. Letter," *Ozgur Ulke* (Istanbul), Sept. 6, 1994, p. 4; as cited in *Foreign Broadcast Information Service—West Europe,* Sept. 15, 1994, pp. 56–57; hereafter cited as *FBIS-WEU.*

25. Cited in PUK Foreign Relations Committee, "Context and Specifics of the Infighting in Iraqi Kurdistan," p. 62. See note 23 above for the full citation to this source.

26. Adnan Husayn, "Renewal of Armed Confrontations between Iraqi Kurds: Accusations Aimed at Non-Kurdish Parties," *Al-Sharq Al-Awsat* (London), Jan. 8, 1995, p. 2; as cited in *FBIS-NES,* Jan. 10, 1995, p. 30. For a brief analysis of how smaller armed groups switching sides further fueled the KDP-PUK civil war, see David McDowall, "Iraq and Turkey: Dealing with the Kurds," *Middle East International,* no. 537 (Nov. 8, 1996), p. 16.

27. "17 Kurdistan Parties Condemn Fighting," (Clandestine) Voice of the People of Kurdistan in Arabic, 1600 GMT, Jan. 5, 1995; as cited in *FBIS-NES,* Jan. 10, 1995, p. 28.

28. Cited in PUK Foreign Relations Committee, "The Context and Specifics of the Infighting in Iraqi Kurdistan," p. 18.

29. "New Inter-Kurdish Fighting, Casualties Reported," (Clandestine) Voice of the People of Kurdistan in Arabic, 1530 GMT, Feb. 8, 1995; as cited in *FBIS-NES*, Feb. 9, 1995, p. 33.
30. "Barzani Berated for 'Collusion' with Turkish Army," (Clandestine) Voice of the People of Kurdistan in Arabic, 1525 GMT, Mar. 24, 1995; as cited in *FBIS-NES*, Mar. 28, 1995, p. 38.
31. "PUK's Talabani on Kurdish Infighting," *Al-Hayah* (London), Jan. 11, 1995, p. 6; as cited in *FBIS-NES*, Jan. 13, 1995, p. 23.
32. "KDP Forces Reportedly 'Purge' Areas," (Clandestine) Voice of Iraqi Kurdistan in Arabic, 1630 GMT, Jan. 7, 1995; as cited in *FBIS-NES*, Jan. 10, 1995, p. 30.
33. "Futile Attack Thwarted," (Clandestine) Voice of Iraqi Kurdistan in Arabic, 1715 GMT, Mar. 27, 1995; as cited in *FBIS-NES*, Mar. 28, 1995, p. 39. *Josh* (little donkey or jackass) is a derogatory word the Kurds use for Kurds who support Baghdad.
34. Amnesty International, *Iraq: Human Rights Abuses in Iraqi Kurdistan since 1991* (New York: Amnesty International, 1995).
35. Cited in *Ibid.*
36. Cited in Selim Caglayan, "Clinton Reprimands Barzani and Talabani," *Hurriyet* (Istanbul), Jan. 28, 1995, p. 18; as cited in *FBIS-WEU*, Feb. 1, 1995, p. 27. The British sent the Kurds a similar note warning them that "British public opinion would find it hard to understand continued Western guarantees ... when the Kurds were using such violence against each other." Cited in David Hirst and Karen Dabrowska, "Britain Tells Kurds Battles Must End," *Guardian*, Jan. 23, 1995.
37. Cited in Kurdish National Congress of North America, "The Washington Declaration Regarding Peace, Reconciliation and Democracy in Iraqi Kurdistan," Mar. 1995; hereafter cited as "KNC Proposals."
38. *Ibid.*
39. Cited in *ibid.*
40. Cited in Amberin Zaman, "Kurds Turn Iraqi Safe Zone into Killing Fields," *Daily Telegraph* (London), April 5, 1995, p. 15; as cited in *FBIS-NES*, April 7, 1995, p. 28.
41. Ergun Balci, "Northern Iraq," *Cumhuriyet* (Istanbul), July 31, 1995, p. 9; as cited in *FBIS-WEU*, Aug. 9, 1995, p. 43.
42. Patriotic Union of Kurdistan, Committee on Foreign Relations, "On the Status of Iraqi Kurdistan: An Open Letter to the Friends of the Kurdish People," July 2, 1995.
43. Adnan Husayn, "Interview with Mas'ud Barzani," *Al-Sharq al-Awsat* (London), Aug. 9, 1995, p. 3; as cited in *FBIS-NES*, Aug. 10, 1995, p. 27.
44. This and the following are based on Kurdistan Democratic Party press release "KDP and PUK Meet Under U.S. Auspices," Aug. 12, 1995.

45. Cited in "Kurd Leader Gives Interview on Plans, Issues," London BBC World Service in Arabic, 0510 GMT, Sept. 27, 1995; as cited in *FBIS-NES,* Sept. 28, 1995, p. 44.
46. Cited in Ilnur Cevik, "Exclusive Telephone Interview," Turkish Daily News, Sept. 20, 1995, pp. 1, A7; as cited in *FBIS-WEU,* Sept. 26, 1995, p. 28.
47. Cited in Ilnur Cevik, "Officials Say Syria Holds PUK, PKK Cards," *Turkish Daily News,* Sept. 28, 1995, pp. 1, A8; as cited in *FBIS-WEU,* Oct. 4, 1995, p. 29.
48. Cited in "SAIRI Chief Interviewed on Internecine Strife," *Tehran Times,* Oct. 11, 1995, p. 2; as cited in *FBIS-NES,* Oct. 26, 1995, p. 46.
49. "Kurdish Parties Agree to Bury Their Differences," Tehran IRNA in English, 2240 GMT, Oct. 11, 1995; as cited in *FBIS-NES,* Oct. 13, 1995, p. 36.
50. Kevin McKierman, "The Kurdish Question and U.S. Policy," *Independent* (Santa Barbara, Calif.), Sept. 19, 1996, p. 16. For further criticism of the U.S. lack of support for the Iraqi Kurds, see Katherine A. Williams, "How We Lost the Kurdish Game," *Washington Post,* Sept. 15, 1996, p. C1.
51. "Barzani on Security Strip, Turkish Visit," (Clandestine) Voice of Iraqi Kurdistan, 1820 GMT, Sept. 23, 1996; as cited in *FBIS-NES,* Sept. 23, 1996.
52. "Talabani Hits Barzani Stance," *Al-Wasat* (London), Sept. 9–15, 1996; as cited in *FBIS-NES,* Sept. 15, 1996.
53. Cited in "Barzani on Security Strip, Turkish Visit," (Clandestine) Voice of Kurdistan, 1820 GMT, Sept. 23, 1996; as cited in *FBIS-NES,* Sept. 23, 1996.
54. Jonathan C. Randal, "Iraqi Opposition Describes Mass Execution Near Irbil," *Washington Post,* Sept. 2, 1996, p. A20; and Jeffrey Smith, "CIA Operation Fell with Iraqi City," *Washington Post,* Sept. 8, 1996, p. A28.
55. Barham Salih, PUK representative in the United States, telephone interview, Sept. 13, 1996.
56. Cited in Patrick Cockburn, "Kurds' Peace and Unity Takes Saddam by Surprise," *Independent* (London), Sept. 17, 1996, p. 10; as cited in *FBIS-NES,* Sept. 17, 1996.
57. "New Government Announced in Kurdistan Region," (Clandestine) Voice of Iraqi Kurdistan, 1830 GMT, Sept. 26, 1996; as cited in *FBIS-NES,* Sept. 26, 1996.
58. "Sources Claim PUK Peshmergas Advancing on Irbil," *Corriere Della Sera* (Milan), Oct. 15, 1996, p. 10; as cited in *FBIS-WEU,* Oct. 15, 1995.
59. "PUK Official Interviewed on 'Collapse' of KDP Forces," Tehran Voice of the Islamic Republic of Iran in Arabic, Oct. 13, 1996; as cited in *FBIS-NES,* Oct. 13, 1996.

60. The following analysis and citation were taken from Kate Clark, "Iraqi Kurdistan: A Bleak and Uncertain Future," *Dialogue* (London), April 1997, p. 3. For further background, see Akram Jaff, "The Fractured Economy of Kurdistan," March 1998, available over the Internet at the Web site of the Washington Kurdish Institute, http://www.kurd.org/kurd.

61. *Ittihad* (PUK), May 31, 1997; as cited in "Iraq: Talabani Interviewed on Turkish Operation, Other Issues," *FBIS-NES* (97-152), June 1, 1997, p. 2.

62. The following details are largely based on Institut Kurde de Paris, "Fresh Kurdish Factional Clashes in Iraq," *Information and Liaison Bulletin*, September–October 1997, p. 3; and "Talabani's Party: We Started the Fighting to Impose a Settlement," *Al-Sharq al-Awsat* (London), Oct. 15, 1997, p. 1; as cited in *FBIS-NES* (97-288), Oct. 15, 1997, p. 1.

63. This and the following citation were taken from "PUK-KDP Truce Ends, Turkish Jets Raid Region," *Turkish Daily News,* Oct. 25, 1997, accessed over the Internet.

64. Saadet Oruc, "Abdurrahman: This Is a Turning Point in N. Iraq," *Turkish Daily News,* Oct. 17, 1997, accessed over the Internet; and KDP press release, "Peace Monitoring Force . . . Reaffirms PUK Responsibility of the Cease-Fire Violation," July 23, 1997.

65. Adnan Husayn, "Talabani Requests Arms from Baghdad," *Al-Sharq al-Awsat* (London), Nov. 2, 1997, p. 1; as cited in *FBIS-NES,* (97-307), Nov. 3, 1997, p. 1.

66. Talabani's and Barzani's letters were published in "Talabani-Barzani Peace Proposals," *Kurdistan Review* (Kurdish National Congress of North America), December 1997, pp. 3, 5–6.

67. The following points were taken from "Kurdish Groups Attempt Unity but Remain Pawns," *Briefing* (Ankara), Feb. 16, 1998, p. 10.

68. "Talabani's Meeting with Iraqi Intelligence Director," *Al-Wasat* (London), Jan. 26–Feb. 1, 1998, pp. 4–5; as cited in *FBIS-NES* (98-027), Jan. 27, 1998, pp. 1–2.

69. Ilnur Cevik, "Massoud Barzani: In the End Our Problem Will Be Solved in Baghdad," *Turkish Daily News,* Dec. 12, 1997, accessed over the Internet. Also see "Iraq: KDP's Barzani Urges Arab-Kurdish Dialogue," *Al-Majallah* (London), Oct. 5–11, 1997, p. 29; as cited in *FBIS-NES* (97-283), Oct. 10, 1997, p. 1; and Saadet Oruc, "Kurds Continue Flirting with Baghdad," *Turkish Daily News,* May 13, 1998, accessed over the Internet.

70. This and the following citation were taken from Huda al-Husayni, "Barzani Warns That Others Will Fill U.S. Vacuum in Northern Iraq," *Al-Sharq al-Awsat* (London), April 25, 1998, p. 2; as cited in *FBIS-NES* (98-118), April 28, 1998, pp. 2–3.

71. "Russian Ambassador Meets Talabani and Barzani," *Kurdistan Observer,* April 18, 1998, accessed over the Internet.

72. Saadet Oruc, "Iraq Allows PKK Bases in Mosul, Kirkuk," *Turkish Daily News,* July 17, 1998, accessed over the Internet.
73. This and the following citation were taken from Bretislav Turecek, "Our Democracy Is Unique," *Tyden* (Prague), April 28, 1998, p. 102; as cited in *FBIS-NES* (98-120), April 30, 1998, pp. 1–2.
74. The following information and data were taken from Ilnur Cevik, "Turkey Will Have to Live with the Realities in Northern Iraq," *Turkish Daily News,* Aug. 10, 1998; Saadet Oruc, "Another Facet of Iraqi Kurds," *Turkish Probe,* Aug. 9, 1998; and Dominic Evans, "Kurds Nervous over Iraqi Campaign to End Sanctions," Reuters, July 4, 1998, all accessed over the Internet.
75. "No Agreement Between PUK and KDP Yet," *Kurdistan Observer,* May 1, 1998, accessed over the Internet.
76. Interview with Aziz Muhammed, *Al-Sharq al-Awsat* (London), May 23, 1998, accessed over the Internet.
77. Barham Salih, telephone interview with the author, Mar. 26, 1998. On a more positive note, however, Salih added that the Kurdish administration in northern Iraq was acquiring an air of "normalcy and permanency." School curricula and office communications were now in Kurdish.
78. "Interview with KNC President, Dr. Najmaldin Karim," *Kurdistan Observer,* May 20, 1998, accessed over the Internet.
79. Cited in Saadet Oruc, "Diplomatic Maneuvers in Iraqi Kurdistan," *Turkish Probe,* July 26, 1998, accessed over the Internet.
80. This copy of the Barzani-Talabani or Washington Accord was supplied to the author by Barham Salih, the representative of the PUK in the United States. For further details concerning the accord, see Harun Kazaz, "What Was Signed Between the KDP and the PUK in Washington, and Where Is It Leading?" *Turkish Daily News,* Oct. 5, 1998, accessed over the Internet.
81. Cited in Harun Kazaz, "Ambiguity Surrounds N. Iraq Kurdish Agreement," *Turkish Probe,* Oct. 11, 1998, accessed over the Internet.
82. These U.S. guarantees concerning the military protection of the Iraqi Kurds were described to the author in interviews in Washington, D.C. with Barham Salih of the PUK on October 5, 1998; and Farhad Barzani, the representative of the KDP in the United States, on October 6, 1998. Massoud Barzani himself explained after signing the accord with Talabani that U.S. Secretary of State Madeleine Albright "assured us that the United States would continue to care for and protect the Kurdish people." Cited in Muhammad Sadiq, "Interview with Mas'ud Barzani," *Al-Sharq al-Awsat* (London), Sept. 19, 1998; as cited in *FBIS-NES* (98-262), Sept. 19, 1998.
83. Despite these Turkish concerns, the Barzani-Talabani accord specifically declared "that Iraq be reformed on a federative basis that

would maintain the nation's unity and territorial integrity," and that protecting Iraq's borders meant that the Iraqi Kurds "will prevent the PKK from destabilizing and undermining the peace or from violating the Turkish border."

84. Cited in Salah Awwad, "Interview with Jalal Talabani," *Al-Quds al-Arabi,* Sept. 22, 1998, p. 3; as cited in *FBIS-NES* (98–266), Sept. 23, 1998.

Chapter Five

1. The PKK—headed by Abdullah (Apo) Ocalan—is a Kurdish party from Turkey that has been carrying on an insurgency against the Turkish government since 1984. For background, see Michael M. Gunter, *The Kurds and the Future of Turkey* (New York: St. Martin's Press, 1997); Kemal Kirisci and Gareth M. Wynrow, *The Kurdish Question and Turkey: An Example of a Trans-state Ethnic Conflict* (London: Frank Cass, 1997); Henri J. Barkey and Graham E. Fuller, *Turkey's Kurdish Question* (New York: Rowman & Littlefield, 1998); and Ismet G. Imset, *The PKK: A Report on Separatist Violence in Turkey (1973–1992)* (Istanbul: Turkish Daily News Publications, 1992). Portions of this chapter were originally published as Michael M. Gunter, "Turkey and Iran Face Off in Kurdistan," *Middle East Quarterly* 5 (March 1998), pp. 33–40.

2. Cited in "SAIRI Chief Interviewed on Internecine Strife," *Tehran Times,* Oct. 11, 1995, p. 2; as cited in *Foreign Broadcast Information Service—Near East & South Asia,* Oct. 26, 1995, p. 46. Hereafter cited as *FBIS-NES.*

3. "Kurdish Parties Agree to Bury Their Differences," Tehran IRNA in English, Oct. 11, 1995; as cited in *FBIS-NES,* Oct. 13, 1995, p. 36.

4. *Tehran Times,* Sept. 3, 1996, p. 2; as cited in *FBIS-NES,* Sept. 3, 1996, p. 1.

5. "Common Objectives and Strategy of Turkey and the Zionist Regime to Occupy Northern Regions of Iraq," *Jomhuri-ye Eslami* (Tehran), Dec. 18, 1997, p. 11; as cited in *FBIS-NES* (98-012), Jan. 12, 1998, p. 5. Israel, though, saw its Turkish connection in northern Iraq as an opportunity to balance how Iran had gotten close to the Israeli border through Hizballah in southern Lebanon. For a background assessment of the new Turkish-Israeli links, see Amikam Nachmani, "The Remarkable Turkish-Israeli Tie," *Middle East Quarterly* 5 (June 1998), pp. 19–29.

6. Robert D. Kaplan, *The Ends of the Earth: A Journey to the Frontiers of Anarchy* (New York: Vintage Books, 1997), p. 239.

7. Atila Eralp, "Facing the Challenge: Post-Revolutionary Relations with Iran," in *Reluctant Neighbor: Turkey's Role in the Middle East,* Henri J. Barkey, ed. (Washington, D.C.: United States Institute of

Peace Press, 1996), pp. 93–112; and Suha Bolukbasi, "Turkey Copes with Revolutionary Iran," *Journal of South Asian and Middle Eastern Studies* 13 (Fall/Winter 1989), pp. 94–109.

8. Article 118 of the current (1982) Turkish Constitution states that the civilian "Council of Ministers shall give priority consideration to the decisions of the National Security Council concerning the measures that it deems necessary for the preservation of the existence and independence of the State, the integrity and indivisibility of the country, and the peace and security of society." "Constitution of the Turkish Republic," as cited in *Turkey: Yearbook 1983* (Ankara: Prime Ministry Directorate General of Press and Information, 1983), p. 629.

9. This and the following citations were taken from "The Fire in Northern Iraq Will Engulf the Aggressors," *Jomhuri-Ye Eslami* (Tehran), Jan. 5, 1997, p. 16; as cited in *FBIS-NES*, Jan. 5, 1997, p. 2.

10. This and the following citation were taken from "Rafsanjani: I Am Concerned About Northern Iraq," *Turkish Daily News*, Dec. 18, 1996.

11. Cited in "ATC Gathering Reveals Growing Division in Turkey, Fails to Impress Americans," *Briefing* (Ankara), Feb. 24, 1997, p. 13. Also see Stephen Kinzer, "To Turkish General, East Is East but West Is Best," *New York Times*, Mar. 16, 1997, accessed over the Internet.

12. Cited in "Bir Clarifies Military's Duties . . . And Opinions," *Briefing* (Ankara), April 14, 1997, p. 7.

13. "Recommendations of the State Security Council Meeting and Comment," *Briefing* (Ankara), Mar. 10, 1997, p. 4. These anti-Iranian revelations are reminiscent of the earlier accusations that pro-Iranian terrorists had been behind the car-bombing assassination of the prominent Turkish secularist journalist Ugur Mumcu in February 1993, a murder that has never been solved. They also failed to consider the revelations made in the Susurluk scandal that broke in November 1996 concerning right-wing government-sponsored hit men murdering government opponents in recent years in return for the government turning a blind eye to their drug trafficking and other criminal activities.

14. The following data were taken from "Back to That Familiar Fork in the Road," *Briefing* (Ankara) Mar. 17, 1997, p. 9.

15. Cited in "Turkey: General on Need for Force Against Countries Backing Kurds," Paris AFP in English, 1152 GMT, April 29, 1997; as cited in *FBIS-NES*, April 29, 1997, p. 1.

16. This and the following were taken from "Back to That Familiar Fork."

17. Hamid Mowlana, "Gradual US Defeat and Iran's Victory," *Keyhan* (Tehran), April 24, 1997, pp. 14, 16; as cited in *FBIS-NES*, April 24, 1997, p. 2.

18. Kelly Couturier, "Anti-Secularism Eclipses Kurdish Insurgency as Turkish Army's No. 1 Concern," *Washington Post*, April 5, 1997, p. A22.
19. Cited in "Threats from Within," *Briefing* (Ankara), May 5, 1997, p. 5.
20. See Daniel Pipes, "Hot Spot: Turkey, Iraq, and Mosul," *Middle East Quarterly* 2 (Sept. 1995), pp. 65–68. For background, see C. J. Edmonds, *Kurds, Turks and Arabs: Politics, Travel and Research in North-Eastern Iraq, 1919–1925* (London: Oxford University Press, 1957); and Peter J. Beck, "A Tedious and Perilous Controversy: Britain and the Settlement of the Mosul Dispute, 1918–1926," *Middle Eastern Studies* 17 (April 1981), pp. 256–76.
21. Barcin Yinanc, "Iran's Assurance on the Badar Forces," *Milliyet* (Istanbul), Dec. 24, 1995, p. 10; as cited in *Foreign Broadcast Information Service—West Europe*, Dec. 26, 1995, p. 28. Hereafter cited as *FBIS-WEU*.
22. Cited in "Iraq: Kurdish Radio Says Iranian Planes Bomb Sites Near Irbil," (Clandestine) Voice of Iraqi Kurdistan in Arabic, 1800 GMT, July 29, 1996; as cited in *FBIS-NES*, July 30, 1996, p. 27.
23. "Confidential Documents of PUK Leader Jalal Talabani Seized by KDP on Sep 1, 1996 at Talabani's HQ and Office in Erbil City." (Translated and released by the KDP in October 1996.)
24. "Turkey's Security Zone Plan to Undermine Regional Peace," *Tehran Times*, Sept. 7, 1996, p. 2; as cited in *FBIS-NES*, Sept. 7, 1996, p. 1.
25. "Ankara—From Verbiage to Practice," *Jomhuri-Ye Eslami*, Sept. 12, 1996, p. 16; as cited in *FBIS-NES*, Sept. 12, 1996, p. 1.
26. "Text" of "exclusive" interview with Jalal Talabani, *Milliyet* (Istanbul), Sept. 22, 1996, p. 16; as cited in *FBIS-WEU*, Sept. 22, 1996, p. 1.
27. KDP press release "Iran Has Stepped Up Its Intervention in Iraqi Kurdistan to Kill US Peace Initiative," Oct. 23, 1996. The KDP claimed that Iran had committed Revolutionary Guards Corps troops, as well as the Badar Forces mentioned above.
28. Cited in Namo Aziz, "The Enemy Is Called Iran," *Die Zeit* (Hamburg), Oct. 25, 1996, p. 16; as cited in *FBIS-NES*, Oct. 25, 1996, p. 2.
29. "Turkey: KDP Calls On Turkey to Adopt 'Open Diplomatic Support,'" Ankara Anatolia in Turkish, 1529 GMT, Oct. 14, 1996; as cited in *FBIS-WEU*, Oct. 14, 1996, p. 1.
30. "Kurdish Groups Should Be Self-Reliant," *Tehran Times*, Oct. 22, 1996, p. 2; as cited in *FBIS-NES*, Oct. 22, 1996, pp. 1–2.
31. "Iran: United States Said 'Not a Reliable Mediator' in Kurdistan," Tehran Voice of the Islamic Republic First Program Network in Persian, 1100 GMT, Oct. 24, 1996; as cited in *FBIS-NES*, Oct. 24, 1996, pp. 1–2.
32. Hasan Alsalih, "US Intervention Will Only Aggravate Conflict," *Kayhan International* (Iran), Mar. 13, 1997, p. 8; as cited in *FBIS-NES*, Mar. 14, 1997, p. 1.

33. "Iraqi Kurds Must Be Cautious About US Plots," *Tehran Times*, Mar. 1, 1997, p. 2; as cited in *FBIS-NES*, Mar. 4, 1997, p. 1.
34. "Turkey: Ocalan Says PKK Establishing Itself in Southern Kurdistan," London MED TV Television in Turkish, 1715 GMT, April 14, 1997; as cited in *FBIS-TOT*, April 14, 1997, p. 1.
35. "MED TV on Turkish Army Preparations, 'Secret' KDP-YNK [PUK] Deal," London MED TV Television in Turkish, 1815 GMT, Mar. 18, 1997; as cited in *FBIS-WEU*, Mar. 19, 1997, p. 1.
36. "New Alignments Begin to Settle In," *Briefing* (Ankara), June 16, 1997, p. 14; and "Turkey: Military Forces Seize Katyusha Rockets, Flour from Iran," *Sabah* (Istanbul), May 30, 1997, p. 17; as cited in *FBIS-WEU*, June 2, 1997, p. 1. Illustrative of how difficult it was to prove who really was supplying weapons to the PKK, other reports accused Syria, Greece, Armenia, and Russia. See Kelly Couturier, "Army Contends Cross-Border Offensive Has Already Caused Severe Kurdish Loses," *Washington Post*, June 12, 1997, accessed via the Internet; and Bill Gertz, "Russian Smuggling Ring Arms Kurdish Rebels in Turkey," *Washington Times*, June 23, 1997, accessed over the Internet.
37. H. Jaferzadeh, "Turkish Troops Should Be Out of Iraq," *Kayhan International* (Iran), May 27, 1997, p. 2; as cited in *FBIS-NES*, June 2, 1997, p. 1.
38. Amberin Zaman, "Turkish Premier and Army Clash over Links with Iran," *London Daily Telegraph*, June 11, 1997.
39. This and the following citations were taken from "Turkey's Army Fabricate Accusations Against Iran," Tehran Voice of the Islamic Republic of Iran in English; as cited in *FBIS-NES*, June 1, 1997, p. 1.
40. Cited in "Military Moves Resolutely in N. Iraq," *Briefing* (Ankara), May 26, 1997, p. 11.
41. "Turkey Invades Iraq for Second Time," *Tehran Times*, May 15, 1997, p. 2; as cited in *FBIS-NES*, May 15, 1997, p. 1.
42. KDP Political Bureau, "A Clarification from KDP Politburo on Turkish Army Incursion into Iraqi Kurdistan Against PKK Elements," May 14, 1997.
43. This and the following citation were taken from "Turkey: Ocalan Warns KDP, Says Operation Aims to Hit Iran Too," London MED TV Television in Turkish, 1715 GMT, May 17, 1997; as cited in *FBIS-TOT*, May 17, 1997, p. 1.
44. Cited in "Turkey: ARGK Commander Urges Kurds Everywhere To 'Respond in Kind,'" London MED TV Television in Turkish, 1715 GMT, May 23, 1997; as cited in *FBIS-TOT*, May 24, 1997, p. 1. Adding a further element to the equation, Sakik himself defected to the KDP in March 1998 and was then captured in Iraqi Kurdistan by Turkish commandos operating out of helicopters the following month.

160   THE KURDISH PREDICAMENT IN IRAQ

45. "Turkey: PKK Warns Against Establishment of Turkoman State in Iraq," London MED TV Television in Turkish, 1730 GMT, April 12, 1998; as cited in *FBIS-TOT* (98-104), April 14, 1998, p. 1.
46. "Foreign Plots and a Little Paranoia," *Briefing* (Ankara), Feb. 15, 1998, p. 12.
47. This and the following citations were taken from "Iraq: Talabani Interviewed on Turkish Operation, Other Issues," (Clandestine) Voice of the People of Kurdistan, published by the PUK newspaper *al-Ittihad,* May 31, 1997; as cited in *FBIS-NES,* June 1, 1997, pp. 1–2.
48. Ilnur Cevik, "Massoud Barzani: In the End Our Problem Will Be Solved in Baghdad," *Turkish Daily News,* Dec. 12, 1997, accessed over the Internet.
49. Jim Hoagland, "Before Turkey Joins Europe," *Washington Post,* Nov. 2, 1997, p. C7.
50. Cited in Ferit Demir, "Turkish Artillery Shells Kurdish Rebels in Iraq," Reuters, May 21, 1998, accessed over the Internet.
51. "The Changing Nature of the Crisis in Northern Iraq!" *Jomhuri-ye Eslami* (Tehran), Oct. 12, 1997, pp. 1, 13; as cited in *FBIS-NES* (97-293), Oct. 20, 1997, p. 1.
52. "Turkey Is Playing with Fire," *Tehran Times,* Oct. 16, 1997, p. 4; as cited in *FBIS-NES,* Oct. 24, 1997, p. 1.
53. "A Plethora of Reports Rattles Nerves," *Briefing* (Ankara), June 8, 1998, p. 7.

Chapter 6

1. For an excellent introduction, see John Hutchinson and Anthony D. Smith, eds., *Nationalism* (Oxford and New York: Oxford University Press, 1994).
2. See, for example, Martin van Bruinessen, *Agha, Shaikh and State: The Social and Political Structures of Kurdistan* (London: Zed Books, 1992).
3. Crawford Young, "Ethnicity and the Colonial and Post-Colonial State in Africa," in Paul Brass, ed., *Ethnic Groups and the State* (London: Croom Helm, 1985), pp. 73–81.
4. Ernest Gellner, *Thought and Change* (London: Weidenfeld and Nicholson, 1964), p. 168.
5. Benedict Anderson, *Imagined Communities: Reflections on the Origin and Spread of Nationalism* (London: Verso, 1991).
6. Cited in Benyamin Neuberger, "State and Nation in African Thought," *Journal of African Studies* 4:2 (1977), p. 202.
7. Eugene Weber, *Peasants into Frenchmen: The Modernization of Rural France, 1870–1914* (Stanford: Stanford University Press, 1976).
8. Although the former is recognized as standard German, two principal divisions of the German language still persist as *Hochdeutsch*

(High German) and *Plattdeutsch* (Low German). There also are two official forms of Norwegian, *bokmal* (book language)—also called *riksmal* (national language)—and *nynorsk* (new Norwegian)—also known as *landsmal* (country language). Modern Greek, too, has two different versions, a demotic or popular literary style and a reformed classical style. In other words, the persisting profusion of separate Kurdish dialects—Kurmanji, Sorani, Dimili (Zaza), and Gurani, among others—that is often blamed for divisions within the Kurdish nation is not unique. What would help further develop Kurdish nationalism, of course, would be for one of these dialects to emerge as the standard Kurdish language.

 9. Weber, *Peasants into Frenchmen,* p. 47.
10. Walker Connor, *Ethnonationalism: The Quest for Understanding* (Princeton: Princeton University Press, 1994), pp. 221, 222.
11. Walker Connor, "When Is a Nation?" *Ethnic and Racial Studies* 13:1 (1990), p. 100.
12. *Ibid.*
13. E. J. Hobsbawm, *Nations and Nationalism Since 1780: Programme, Myth, Reality,* 2 ed. (Cambridge: Cambridge University Press, 1990), p. 102.
14. Ernest Gellner, *Nations and Nationalism* (Oxford: Blackwell, 1983), p. 57.
15. *Ibid.*
16. On the development and prospects for the Kurdish language, see Amir Hassanpour, *Nationalism and Language in Kurdistan, 1918–1985* (San Francisco: Mellen Research University Press, 1992).
17. Karl W. Deutsch, *Nationalism and Social Communication: An Inquiry into the Foundations of Nationality* (Cambridge: MIT Press, 1953), p. 71.
18. Eric Hobsbawm and Terence Ranger, eds., *The Invention of Tradition* (Cambridge: Cambridge University Press, 1983).
19. Anderson, *Imagined Communities,* p. 46.
20. Paul G. Brass, "Elite Groups, Symbol Manipulation and Ethnic Identity among the Muslims of South Asia," in David Taylor and Malcolm Yapp, eds., *Political Identity in South Asia* (London: Curzon Press, 1979), pp. 36, 38.
21. John A. Armstrong, *Nations before Nationalism* (Chapel Hill: University of North Carolina Press, 1982), p. 7.
22. *Ibid.,* pp. 6–7.
23. Michael Howard, *The Lessons of History* (New Haven and London: Yale University Press, 1991), p. 39.
24. *Ibid.,* p. 40.
25. *Ibid.*
26. *Ibid.*

27. Arend Lijphart, *Democracy in Plural Societies* (New Haven and London: Yale University Press, 1977).
28. Deutsch, *Nationalism and Social Communication,* pp. 99–100.
29. Karl W. Deutsch, *Political Community at the International Level: Problems of Definition and Measurement* (Garden City: Doubleday, 1954), p. 39.
30. Walker Connor, "Nation-Building or Nation-Destroying?" *World Politics* 24 (April 1972), pp. 330–31.
31. James Mayall, *Nationalism and International Society* (Cambridge: Cambridge University Press, 1990), p. 64.
32. See notes 3, 4, and 5 above.
33. Donald L. Horowitz, *Ethnic Groups in Conflict* (Berkeley: University of California Press, 1985), p. 230.
34. *Ibid.,* p. 259.
35. *Ibid.,* p. 230.
36. *Ibid.,* pp. 231–32.
37. "Kurds' Barzani Discusses Peace Efforts, Autonomy," (Clandestine) Kurdistan Voice of Iraqi Kurdistan in Arabic, 1653 GMT, Apr. 13, 1992; as cited in *Foreign Broadcast Information Service—Near East & South Asia,* Apr. 15, 1992, p. 41. Hereafter cited as *FBIS-NES.* As recently as May 1998, Barzani repeated this position: "We are realists and are fully aware that it would not be practical to secede from Iraq and to establish an independent government. The neighboring states in the region reject this, and will not hesitate to resort to military action if we take any steps towards secession and toward establishing an independent state. The Iraqi Government cannot accept this and the international situation does not allow it." Salah Qallab, "Barzani: The Arabs' Doors Are Closed to Us," *Al-Sharq al-Awsat* (London), May 11, 1998, p. 2; as cited in *FBIS-NES* (98-131), May 11, 1998, pp. 1–2.
38. PUK Leader Talabani Interviewed," *2000 Ikibin'e Dogru* (Istanbul), May 31, 1992, pp. 10–12; as cited in *FBIS-NES,* June 1992, p. 27. Elsewhere Talabani declared: "We must be realistic. At present it is impossible to modify the borders between all the countries in the area. The unity of all the Kurds does remain the final objective, because a divided nation cannot give up its dream to be united. It remains inside us, but it is a dream, and a responsible political leadership cannot act on the basis of dreams." Gabriel Bertinetto, "If Saddam Falls, I Will Give Up the Kurdish Dream," *L'Unita* (Rome), May 10, 1994, p. 17; as cited in *FBIS-NES,* May 11, 1994, p. 59.
39. See, for example, David McDowall, *A Modern History of the Kurds* (London and New York: I. B. Tauris, 1996), p. 446. According to the knowledgeable British journalist Hazhir Teimourian, Jalal Talabani too feels this way. Personal interview with the author, London, Dec. 15, 1997.

40. Anthony H. Richmond, "Ethnic Nationalism and Postindustrialism," *Ethnic and Racial Studies* 7:1 (1984), pp. 5–16.

41. The PUK site on the World Wide Web is http://www.puk.org and the KDP site is http://www.kdp.pp.se. The Washington Kurdish Institute has a very useful site at http://www.kurd.org/kurd. For other addresses, see the bibliography. On the other hand, Patrick Ball of the Science and Human Rights Program at the American Association for the Advancement of Science recently concluded, "the Internet is grossly overplayed as a force for change in the Third World [where] . . . very few people have access to online communications." Cited in Ashley Craddock, "Organizer Doubts Net's Role in Pushing Human Rights," Reuters, June 15, 1998, accessed over the Internet.

42. Statement made by Francois Hariri, KDP politburo member, in the Sept. 29, 1994, issue of the KDP newspapers *Golan* and *Khebat*; as cited in PUK Foreign Relations Committee, "Context and Specifics of the Infighting in Iraqi Kurdistan," p. 11.

43. Zuhayr Qusaybati, "Interview with . . . Mas'ud Barzani," *Al-Hayah* (London), June 5, 1994, pp. 1, 4; as cited in *FBIS-NES*, June 8, 1994, p. 36. Barzani also attributed the fighting to "ways of tackling problems and resolving a political matter" and "the mobilization and education of cadres." *Ibid.*

44. Cited in Amberin Zaman, "Kurds Turn Iraqi Safe Zone into Killing Fields," *Daily Telegraph* (London), April 5, 1995, p. 15; as cited in *FBIS-NES*, April 7, 1995, p. 28.

45. Stephen C. Pelletiere, *The Kurds and Their Agas: An Assessment of the Situation in Northern Iraq* (Carlisle Barracks, PA: Strategic Studies Institute, 1991), pp. 1, 25. For an equally pessimistic evaluation, see Chris Hedges, "Quarrels of Kurdish Leaders Sour Dreams of a Homeland," *New York Times*, June 28, 1994, pp. A1, A5.

46. In addition, the neighboring states of Iran, Turkey, and Syria maintain their own economic blockades to various degrees because of their hostility to any idea of a Kurdish state. Finally and rather pathetically, since the internal fighting between the KDP and the PUK broke out in May 1994, each faction has established a de facto blockade against the territory controlled by the other. For a recent analysis of the economic situation in Iraqi Kurdistan, see Akram Jaff, "The Fractured Economy of Kurdistan," available on the World Wide Web site of the Washington Kurdish Institute, http://www.kurd.org/kurd. Click "Akram Jaff" on the Advisory Board page.

47. Susan Kinsley, "Kurdistranded," *Washington Post*, June 6, 1993, p. C4.

48. The following data are largely taken from Caryle Murphy, "Economy Tests Kurds' Self-Rule," *Washington Post*, May 10, 1994, p. A10.

Selected Bibliography

Since this book is a sequel to my earlier study, *The Kurds of Iraq: Tragedy and Hope,* 1992, most of the entries in this bibliography come after that date. For works before that date, see the bibliography in my earlier book. Also for numerous additional references to specific articles in newspapers, weeklies, or those that appeared in translation or news service clippings, see the notes.

INTERVIEWS AND CORRESPONDENCE

Abdurrahman, Sami. KDP politburo member. Salahuddin, Iraqi Kurdistan, Aug. 13, 1993.

Ahmad, Galawez. Wife of Ibrahim Ahmad. London, Dec. 14, 1997.

Ahmad, Ibrahim. Secretary general of the KDP 1953–64. London, Dec. 20, 1997.

Amin, Noshirwan Mustafa. Former PUK politburo member. London, Dec. 21, 1997.

Avebury, Eric. Member of British House of Lords and authority on the Kurds. London, Dec. 18, 1997.

Baker, Frank. Foreign Office British Government. London, Dec. 18, 1997.

Barzani, Ayoub. Unofficial Barzani family chronicler. Salahuddin, Iraqi Kurdistan, Aug. 18, 1993.

Barzani, Farhad. KDP representative in the United States and nephew of Massoud Barzani. Washington, D.C., July 30, 1998.

Barzani, Masrour. Eldest son of Massoud Barzani. Princeton University, N.J., Mar. 20, 1998.

———. Correspondence, May 25, 1998.

Barzani, Massoud. KDP president. Salahuddin, Iraqi Kurdistan, Aug. 13, 1993.

Barzani, Nechirvan. KDP politburo member. Salahuddin, Iraqi Kurdistan, Aug. 19, 1993.

Bauer, Dana. U.S. Dept. of State official. Vienna, Austria, July 3, 1998.

Benna, Siamend. KDP official in London. London, Dec. 22, 1997.

Chalabi, Ahmad. President of the executive council of INC. Irbil, Iraqi Kurdistan, Aug. 14, 1993.

———. London, Dec. 16, 1997.

Costello, Patrick. Foreign policy advisor to the Parliamentary Group of the Party of European Socialists. Vienna, Austria, July 2, 1998.

Davenport, Frank. U.S. Dept. of State official. Washington, D.C., April 4, 1997.

Deutsch, Robert. U.S. Dept. of State official. Washington, D.C., Aug. 9, 1997.

Dizeyee, Homer. U. S. Voice of America broadcaster and longtime friend of Jalal Talabani. Washington, D.C., Aug. 9, 1997.

Ergil, Dogu. Turkish academic. Vienna, Austria, July 4, 1998.

Fatah, Omar. PUK politburo member. Irbil, Iraqi Kurdistan, Aug. 19, 1993.

Galbraith, Peter. Former U.S. ambassador. Washington, D.C., July 28, 1998.

Gaugl, Susanne. Deputy international secretary of the Parliamentary Group of the Party of European Socialists. Vienna, Austria, July 1, 1998.

Ghareeb, Edmund. Academic authority on the Iraqi Kurds. Washington, D.C., July 17, 1997.

Ghasi, Ali Homam. Son of Qazi Muhammad, president of the Republic of Kurdistan at Mahabad. Damascus. Syria, Mar. 13–14, 1998.

Hale, William. Academic authority on Turkey. London, Mar. 10, 1998.

Hasan, Akif. European representative of the National Liberation Front of Kurdistan (ERNK/PKK). Vienna, Austria, July 2, 1998.

Hawar, Muhammad Rasool. Kurdish academic. London, Dec. 21, 1997.

Izady, Mehrdad. Kurdish academic. New York City, Mar. 21, 1998.

Karadaghi, Kamran. Senior political correspondent of *Al-Hayat*. London, Mar. 9, 1998.

Karadaghi, Pary. Executive director of Kurdish Human Rights Watch, Inc. Washington, D.C., Nov. 10, 1997.

Karim, Habib Muhammad. Former secretary general of the KDP. Irbil, Iraqi Kurdistan, Aug. 19, 1993.

Karim, Najmaldin O. President of the Kurdish National Congress of North America. Numerous interviews 1993–1998.

Kutschera, Chris. French authority on the Kurds. Vienna, Austria, July 3, 1998.

Laizer, Sheri. Journalist and expert on the Kurds. London, Mar. 7, 1998.

McDowall, David. British writer and expert on the Kurds. Vienna, Austria, July 3, 1998.

Mamand, Rasul. Former PUK politburo member. Irbil, Iraqi Kurdistan, Aug. 19, 1993.

Mango, Andrew. British academic expert on Turkey. London, Mar. 11, 1998.

Masum, Fuad. Former prime minister of the Kurdistan Regional Government. Irbil, Iraqi Kurdistan, Aug. 19, 1993.

Miran, Dilshad. KDP representative in London. London, Dec. 22, 1997.

Morrison, Andrew. U.S. Dept. of State official. Washington, D.C., Nov. 10, 1997.

Nezan, Kendal. Director, Institut Kurde de Paris. Washington, D.C., Aug. 9, 1997.

Ocalan, Abdullah (Apo). President of the Kurdistan Workers Party (PKK). Damascus, Syria, Mar. 13–14, 1998.

Othman (Osman, Uthman), Mahmud. Former secretary general of the KDP. London, Dec. 18, 1997.

Pickart, George. U. S. Senate Foreign Relations Committee staff. Irbil, Iraqi Kurdistan, Aug. 16, 1993.

Pond, Suzanne. U.S. Dept. of State official. Washington, D. C., April 4, 1997.

Randal, Jonathan. Senior foreign correspondent, *Washington Post*. Washington, D.C., Aug. 9, 1997.

Rashid, Latif. Vice president of the executive council of INC and brother-in-law of Jalal Talabani. London, numerous interviews Dec. 14–23, 1997.

Rashid, Shanaz. Daughter of Ibrahim Ahmad and sister-in-law of Jalal Talabani. London, Dec. 22, 1997.

Rasul, Kosrat. Prime minister of the Kurdistan Regional Government. Irbil, Iraqi Kurdistan, Aug. 14, 1993.

Sabir, Mohammed Ismail. PUK representative in France. Vienna, Austria, July 2, 1998.

Sabir, Sabah. Brother-in-law of Jalal Talabani. London, Dec. 20, 1997.

Sakellariou, Jannis. Member of the European Parliament. Vienna, Austria, July 4, 1998.

Salih, Barham. PUK representative in the United States. Numerous interviews, 1993–1998.

Saliky, Atia (Talabany). Wife of Nuri Talabany. London, Dec. 19, 1997.

Salim, Jawar Namiq. Speaker of the Kurdistan Regional Government Parliament. Irbil, Iraqi Kurdistan, Aug. 12, 1993.

Samarra'i, Wafiq. Former chief of Iraqi military intelligence. London, Dec. 15, 1997.

Sheikhmous, Omar. Former PUK politburo member. Washington, D.C., July 28, 1998.

Shorish, Sami. Kurdish journalist. London, U.K., Dec. 17, 1997.

Smothers Bruni, Mary Ann. U.S. writer who has traveled in Iraqi Kurdistan extensively. Providence, R.I., Nov. 23, 1996.

Sreebny, Dan. U.S. Dept. of State official. Washington, D.C., April 4, 1997.

Steinbach, Udo. German academic and editor. Vienna, Austria, July 2, 1998.

Talabani, Hero. Wife of Jalal Talabani. Irbil, Iraqi Kurdistan, Aug. 16, 1993.

Talabani, Jalal. PUK secretary general. Irbil, Iraqi Kurdistan, Aug. 16, 1993.

Talabani, (Sheikh) Jengi. Brother of Jalal Talabani. London, Dec. 15, 1997.

Talabani, Qubad. Son of Jalal Talabani. London, Dec. 23, 1997.

Talabany, Nuri. Kurdish academic and distant cousin of Jalal Talabani. London, Dec. 19, 1997.

Teimourian, Hazhir. Kurdish journalist. London, Dec. 16, 1997.

Vanly, Ismet Cherif. Kurdish academic. Irbil, Iraqi Kurdistan, Aug. 18, 1993.

Zebari, Hoshyar. KDP politburo member responsible for international relations. Princeton University, N.J., Mar. 20, 1998.

TRANSLATIONS AND NEWS CLIPPINGS SERVICES

American Kurdish Information Network. *Kurdish News* (Washington, D.C.).

Foreign Broadcast Information Service—Near East & South Asia (referred to as *FBIS-NES*); and *Foreign Broadcast Information Service—West Europe* (referred to as *FBIS-WEU*). Received over the Internet for a fee via http://wnc.fedworld.gov.

Institut Kurde de Paris. *Information and Liaison Bulletin* (Paris).

Kurdish National Congress of North America. *Kurdistan Review* (Lake Forest, Calif.).

Kurdistan Information Centre. *Kurdistan Information Bulletin; Kurdistan Human Rights Bulletin;* and *Kurdish News Bulletin* (London).

Turkish Radio Hour. Daily news items. Haywood, Calif. Received over e-mail for a fee via trh@netcom.com.

Washington Kurdish Institute. Daily news articles. Washington, D.C. Received over e-mail via wki@kurd.org.

NEWSPAPERS, WEEKLIES, ETC.

Briefing (Ankara)
Christian Science Monitor
Economist (London)
International Herald Tribune
Namah (Badlisy Center for Kurdish Studies, Inc. Tallahassee, Fla.)
New York Times
Time
Turkish Daily News
Wall Street Journal
Washington Post

WORLD WIDE WEB SITES

One may readily sample the Internet's offerings concerning the Kurds or Kurdistan by using any one of the following search engines (http: //www.): (1) yahoo.com, (2) altavista.digital.com, and (3) lycos.com. The following are some selected World Wide Web sites of interest (http://www.):

akaKurdistan (continuing archive for Susan Meiselas, *Kurdistan: In the Shadow of History*). akaKURDISTAN.com

American Kurdish Information Network (USA). kurdistan.org

Arm the Spirit (Canada). burn.ucsd.edu/~ats/

Center for Kurdish Political Studies (USA). This center has created Web sites with information on the Kurdistan Workers Party (PKK) and three of its affiliates: (1) Free Women's Union of Kurdistan (YAJK) yajk.org; (2) Kurdistan Workers Party (PKK) pkk.org; (3) National Liberation Front of Kurdistan (ERNK) ernk.org; and (4) People's Liberation Army of Kurdistan (ARGK) argk.org

Christian Science Monitor. csmonitor.com

Initiative on Conflict Resolution and Ethnicity (UK). incore.ulstc.uk/cds/ countries/kurdistan.html

Iraq Foundation (USA). iraqfoundation.org/

Iraqi National Congress (UK). inc.org.uk/

Kurdish Human Rights Project (London). khrp.org

Kurdish Human Rights Watch, Inc. (USA). khrw.com

Kurdish Library and Documentation Centre (Sweden). marebalti-cum.se/kurd/index.htm

Kurdistan Democratic Party (KDP). kdp.pp.se

Kurdistan Information Centre (UK). burn.ucsd.edu/~kurdistan/

Kurdistan Observer (UK). mnsi.net/~mergan95/ruzvon.htm

Kurdistan Save the Children/Kurdistan Children's Fund (UK). netcom-uk.co.uk/~kcf/

Kurdistan Web (Kurdish news, information, and documentation, multi-lingual database). Humanrights.de/~kurdweb/

MED TV. med-tv.be/med/

New York Times. nytimes.com

Patriotic Union of Kurdistan (PUK). puk.org

Press Agency Ozgurluk. ozgurluk.org

Turkish Daily News. turkishdailynews.com

Ultimate Collection of News Links. Links to over 5000 newspapers and other news sites. pppp.net/links/news/

Wall Street Journal. wsj.com (note: omit initial www.)

Washington Kurdish Institute (USA). kurd.org/kurd

Washington Post. washingtonpost.com

ARTICLES, REPORTS, MONOGRAPHS, AND BOOKS

"Address by Madame Danielle Mitterrand." *Kurdistan Review* (KNC), April 1994, p. 10.

Amnesty International. *Iraq: Human Rights Abuses in Iraqi Kurdistan Since 1991.* New York: Amnesty International, 1995.

Anderson, Benedict. *Imagined Communities: Reflections on the Origin and Spread of Nationalism.* London: Verso, 1991.

Arfa, Hassan. *The Kurds: An Historical and Political Study.* London: Oxford University Press, 1966.

Armstrong, John. *Nations before Nationalism.* Chapel Hill: University of North Carolina Press, 1982.

Aykan, Mahmut Bali. "Turkey's Policy in Northern Iraq, 1991–95." *Middle Eastern Studies* 32 (October 1996), pp. 343–66.

Baram, Amatzia. "Between Impediment and Advantage: Saddam's Iraq." special report. United States Institute of Peace, June 1998.

——— and Barry Rubin, eds. *Iraq's Road to War.* New York: St. Martin's Press, 1993.

Barkey, Henri J. and Graham E. Fuller. *Turkey's Kurdish Question.* New York: Rowman & Littlefield, 1998.

Beck, Peter J. "A Tedious and Perilous Controversy: Britain and the Settlement of the Mosul Dispute, 1918–1926." *Middle Eastern Studies* 17 (April 1981), pp. 256–76.

Bengio, Ofra, ed. *Saddam Speaks on the Gulf Crisis: A Collection of Documents.* Tel Aviv: Tel Aviv University, 1992.

Bolukbasi, Suha. "Turkey Copes with Revolutionary Iran." *Journal of South Asian and Middle Eastern Studies* 13 (Fall/Winter 1989), pp. 94–109.

Brass, Paul G. "Elite Groups, Symbol Manipulation and Ethnic Identity Among the Muslims of South Asia," in David Taylor and Malcolm Yapp, eds., *Political Identity in South Asia.* London: Curzon Press, 1979, pp. 35–43.

Brauer, Erich. *The Jews of Kurdistan.* Completed and edited by Raphael Patai. Detroit: Wayne State University Press, 1993.

Bruinessen, Martin van. *Agha, Shaikh and State: The Social and Political Structures of Kurdistan.* London: Zed Books, 1992.

———. *Agha, Shaikh and State: On the Social and Political Organization of Kurdistan.* Utrecht: University of Utrecht, 1978.

———. "The Kurds Between Iran and Iraq." *Middle East Report,* no. 141 (July-August 1986), pp. 14–27.

Bruni, Mary Ann Smothers. *Journey Through Kurdistan.* Austin: University of Texas at Austin, 1995.

Chaliand, Gerard, ed. *A People without a Country: The Kurds and Kurdistan.* New York: Olive Branch Press, 1993.

"The CIA Report the President Doesn't Want You to Read" (Pike Committee Report). *Village Voice,* Feb. 16, 1976, pp. 70–92.

Connor, Walker. *Ethnonationalism: The Quest for Understanding.* Princeton: Princeton University Press, 1994.

———. "Nation-Building or Nation-Destroying?" *World Politics* 24 (April 1972), pp. 319–55.

———. "When Is a Nation?" *Ethnic and Racial Studies* 13:1 (1990), pp. 92–100.

Deutsch, Karl W. *Nationalism and Social Communication: An Inquiry into the Foundations of Nationality.* Cambridge: MIT Press, 1953.

———. *Political Community at the International Level: Problems of Definition and Measurement.* Garden City: Doubleday, 1954.

Dunn, Michael Collins. "The Kurdish 'Question': Is There an Answer?" *Middle East Policy* 4 (Sept. 1995), pp. 72–86.

Eagleton, William, Jr. *The Kurdish Republic of 1964.* London: Oxford University Press, 1963.

Edmonds, C. J. *Kurds, Turks and Arabs: Politics, Travel and Research in North-Eastern Iraq, 1919–1925.* London: Oxford University Press, 1957.

———. "The Kurds and the Revolution in Iraq." *Middle East Journal* 13 (Winter 1959), pp. 1–10.

Entessar, Nader. "Kurdish Conflict in a Regional Perspective," in M. E. Ahari, ed., *Change and Continuity in the Middle East: Conflict Resolution and Prospects for Peace.* New York: St. Martin's Press, 1996, pp. 47–73.

Eralp, Atila. "Facing the Challenge: Post-Revolutionary Relations with Iran," in Henri J. Barkey, ed., *Reluctant Neighbor: Turkey's Role in the Middle East*. Washington, D.C.: United States Institute of Peace, 1996.

Francke, Rend Rahim. "The Opposition," in Fran Hazelton, ed., *Iraq Since the Gulf War: Prospects for Democracy*. London: Zed Books, 1994, pp. 153–77.

Freij, Hanna Yousif. "Tribal Identity and Alliance Behaviour Among Factions of the Kurdish National Movement in Iraq." *Nationalism & Ethnic Politics* 3 (Autumn 1997), pp. 86–110.

Frelick, Bill. "Operation Provide Comfort: False Promises to the Kurds," in Gerard Chaliand, ed., *A People without a Country: The Kurds and Kurdistan*. New York: Olive Branch Press, 1993, pp. 231–37.

Fuccaro, Nelida. *The Other Kurds: Yazidis in Colonial Iraq*. London: I. B. Tauris, 1999.

Fuller, Graham E. *Iraq in the Next Decade: Will Iraq Survive Until 2002?*. (A Rand note—N-3591) Santa Monica, Calif.: Rand, 1993.

Gellner, Ernest. *Thought and Change*. London: Weidenfeld and Nicholson, 1964.

———. *Nations and Nationalism*. Oxford: Blackwell, 1983.

Ghareeb, Edmund. *The Kurdish Question in Iraq*. Syracuse: Syracuse University Press, 1981.

Guest, John S. *Survival Among the Kurds: A History of the Yezidis*. London: Kegan Paul International, 1993.

Gunter, Michael M. *The Kurds in Turkey: A Political Dilemma*. Boulder: Westview Press, 1990.

———. *The Kurds of Iraq: Tragedy and Hope*. New York: St. Martin's Press, 1992.

———. *The Kurds and the Future of Turkey*. New York: St. Martin's Press, 1997.

———. "A De Facto Kurdish State in Northern Iraq." *Third World Quarterly* 14:2 (1993), pp. 295–319.

———. "The Iraqi National Congress (INC) and the Future of the Iraqi Opposition." *Journal of South Asian and Middle Eastern Studies* 19 (Spring 1996), pp. 1–20.

———. "The KDP-PUK Conflict in Northern Iraq." *Middle East Journal* 50 (Spring 1996), pp. 225–41.

———. "Turkey and Iran Face Off in Kurdistan." *Middle East Quarterly* 5 (March 1998), pp. 33–40.

Hamilton, A. M. *Road through Kurdistan: The Narrative of an Engineer in Iraq*. London: Faber and Faber, 1937.

Hassanpour, Amir. *Nationalism and Language in Kurdistan, 1918–1985*. San Francisco: Mellen Research University Press, 1992.

Hay, W. R. *Two Years in Kurdistan: Experiences of a Political Officer, 1918–1920.* London: Sidgwick & Jackson, 1921.

Hazelton, Fran, ed. *Iraq Since the Gulf War: Prospects for Democracy.* London: Zed Books, 1994.

Hoagland, Jim. "How CIA's Secret War on Saddam Collapsed." *Washington Post,* June 26, 1997, pp. A21, A28–A29.

Hobsbawm, E. J. *Nations and Nationalism Since 1780: Programme, Myth, Reality.* 2 ed. Cambridge: Cambridge University Press, 1990.

——— and Terence Ranger, eds. *The Invention of Tradition.* Cambridge: Cambridge University Press, 1983.

Hopwood, Derek, Habib Ishow, and Thomas Koszinowski, eds. *Iraq: Power and Society.* Reading: Ithaca Press, 1993.

Horowitz, Donald L. *Ethnic Groups in Conflict.* Berkeley: University of California Press, 1985.

Howard, Michael. *The Lessons of History.* New Haven and London: Yale University Press, 1991.

Human Rights Watch/Middle East. *Iraq's Crime of Genocide: The Anfal Campaign Against the Kurds.* New Haven: Yale University Press, 1995.

Hutchinson, John and Anthony D. Smith, eds. *Nationalism.* Oxford and New York: Oxford University Press, 1994.

Ignatieff, Michael. *Blood & Belonging: Journeys into the New Nationalism.* Toronto: Viking, 1993.

Imset, Ismet G. *The PKK: A Report on Separatist Violence in Turkey (1973–1992).* Istanbul: Turkish Daily News Publications, 1992.

Iraqi National Congress (INC). "The Iraqi National Congress: Democratic Renewal, Reconstruction, and Reconciliation." n.d.

Izady, Mehrdad. *The Kurds: A Concise Handbook.* Washington: Crane Russak, 1992.

Jalabi, Hasan Al-. "Transformation of Iraqi Opposition into Comprehensive National Entity: Lessons of Uprising and of Beirut Conference up to Vienna Conference." *Al-Hayah* (London), Jan. 23, 24, and 25, 1993; as cited in *FBIS-NES,* Feb. 18, 1993, pp. 29–35.

Jawad, Sa'ad. *Iraq and the Kurdish Question, 1958–1970.* London: Ithaca Press, 1981.

Jentleson, Bruce W. *With Friends Like These: Reagan, Bush, and Saddam, 1982–1990.* New York: W. W. Norton & Company, 1994.

Jwaideh, Wadie. "The Kurdish Nationalist Movement: Its Origins and Development." Ph.D. dissertation, Syracuse University, 1960.

Kaplan, Robert D. *The Ends of the Earth: A Journey to the Frontiers of Anarchy.* New York: Vintage Books, 1997.

Karadaghi, Pary. "Kurdish Evacuees from Iraqi Kurdistan." *Kurdistan Times* 2 (November 1997), pp. 139–45.

Kashi, Ed. *When the Borders Bleed: The Struggle of the Kurds.* New York: Pantheon Books, 1994.

Kelly, Michael. *Martyrs' Day: Chronicle of a Small War.* New York: Vintage Books, 1994.

Khadduri, Majid and Edmund Ghareeb. *War in the Gulf, 1990–91: The Iraq-Kuwait Conflict and Its Implications.* New York: Oxford University Press, 1997.

Khalil, Samir al- (Kanan Makiya). *The Republic of Fear: The Politics of Modern Iraq.* Berkeley: University of California Press, 1989.

Kirisci, Kemal. "Turkey and the Kurdish Safe-Haven in Northern Iraq." *Journal of South Asian and Middle Eastern Studies* 19 (Spring 1996), pp. 21–39.

——— and Gareth M. Winrow. *The Kurdish Question and Turkey: An Example of a Trans-state Ethnic Conflict.* London: Frank Cass, 1997.

Korn, David A. "The Last Years of Mustafa Barzani." *Middle East Quarterly* 1 (June 1994), pp. 12–27.

Kreyenbroek, Philip G. and Stefan Sperl, eds. *The Kurds: A Contemporary Overview.* London: Routledge, 1992.

Kreyenbroek, Philip G. and Christine Allison, eds. *Kurdish Culture and Identity.* London: Zed Books, 1996.

Kurdish National Congress of North America. "The Washington Declaration Regarding Peace, Reconciliation and Democracy in Iraqi Kurdistan." March 1995.

Kurdistan Democratic Party. "Kurdistan Democratic Party (KDP) Congresses 1946–1993." [c.1993].

———. "What Happened in Iraqi Kurdistan May 1994." June 1994.

Laizer, Sheri. *Martyrs, Traitors and Patriots: Kurdistan after the Gulf War.* London: Zed Books, 1996.

Lijphart, Arend. *Democracy in Plural Societies.* New Haven and London: Yale University Press, 1977.

Longrigg, Stephen H. *Iraq, 1900 to 1950: A Political, Social, and Economic History.* London: Oxford University Press, 1953.

Lukitz, Liora. *Iraq: The Search for National Identity.* London: Frank Cass, 1995.

McDowall, David. *A Modern History of the Kurds.* London: I. B. Tauris, 1996.

———. *The Kurds.* No. 96/4. London: Minority Rights Group, 1996.

———. "Iraq and Turkey: Dealing with the Kurds." *Middle East International,* no. 537 (Nov. 8, 1996), pp. 16–17.

Makiya, Kanan. *Cruelty and Silence: War, Tyranny, Uprising and the Arab World.* New York: W. W. Norton & Company, 1993.

Mayall, James. *Nationalism and International Society.* Cambridge: Cambridge University Press, 1990.

Meho, Lokman I., com. *The Kurds and Kurdistan: A Selective and Anno-tated Bibliography.* Westport Conn.: Greenwood Press, 1997.

Meiselas, Susan. *Kurdistan: In the Shadow of History.* New York: Random House, 1997.

Metz, Helen Chapin, ed. *Iraq: A Country Study.* Washington, D.C.: Government Printing Office, 1990.

Middle East Watch. *Genocide in Iraq: The Anfal Campaign Against the Kurds.* New York: Human Rights Watch, 1993.

Moynihan, Daniel Patrick. *Pandaemonium: Ethnicity in International Politics.* Oxford: Oxford University Press, 1993.

Nachmani, Amikam. "The Remarkable Turkish-Israeli Tie." *Middle East Quarterly* 5 (June 1998), pp. 19–29.

National Foreign Assessment Center (U.S. Central Intelligence Agency). *The Kurdish Problem in Perspective.* Aug. 1979.

Neuberger, Benyamin. "State and Nation in African Thought." *Journal of African Studies* 4:2 (1977), pp. 199–205.

Nikitine, Basile. "Les Kurds Racontes par Eux-memes." *L'Asie Francaise,* no. 230 (March–April 1925).

O'Ballance, Edgar. *The Kurdish Struggle, 1920–94.* New York: St. Martin's Press, 1996.

Olson, Robert. *The Kurdish Question and Turkish-Iranian Relations: From World War I to 1998.* Costa Mesa, Calif.: Mazda Publishers, 1998.

———. "The Creation of a Kurdish State in the 1990s?" *Journal of South Asian and Middle Eastern Studies* 15 (Summer 1992), pp. 1–25.

———. "The Kurdish Question and Geopolitic and Geostrategic Changes in the Middle East after the Gulf War." *Journal of South Asian and Middle Eastern Studies* 17 (Summer 1994), pp. 44–67.

Operation Provide Comfort. "Fact Sheet." May 6, 1993.

Patriotic Union of Kurdistan. "Overview: Developments in Iraqi Kurdi-stan." April 1994.

———. "Iraqi Kurdistan: A Situation Report on Recent Events: The Context and Specifics of the Infighting in Iraqi Kurdistan." Feb. 1995.

———. "On the Status of Iraqi Kurdistan: An Open Letter to the Friends of the Kurdish People." July 2, 1995.

Pelletiere, Stephen. *The Kurds and Their Agas: An Assessment of the Situation in Northern Iraq.* Carlisle Barracks, Penn.: Strategic Studies Institute, 1991.

———. "America and the Emerging Power Vacuum in Northern Iraq." Draft paper, U.S. Army War College, 1996.

Pipes, Daniel. *The Hidden Hand: Middle East Fears of Conspiracy.* New York: St. Martin's Press, 1996.

————. "Hot Spot: Turkey, Iraq, and Mosul." *Middle East Quarterly* 2 (Sept. 1995), pp. 65–68.

Randal, Jonathan C. *After Such Knowledge What Forgiveness? My Encounters with Kurdistan.* New York: Farrar, Straus and Giroux, 1997.

Richmond, Anthony H. "Ethnic Nationalism and Postindustrialism." *Ethnic and Racial Studies* 7:1 (1984), pp. 5–16.

Schmidt, Dana Adams. *Journey Among Brave Men.* Boston: Little, Brown, 1964.

Sheikmous, Omar. "The Current Situation of the Kurds in Iraq." Unpublished paper, June 1988.

Simons, Geoff. *Iraq: From Sumer to Saddam.* New York: St. Martin's Press, 1994.

Sloane, E. B. *To Mesopotamia and Kurdistan in Disguise: With Historical Notices of the Kurdish Tribes and the Chaldeans of Kurdistan.* London: John Murray, 1926.

Smith, R. Jeffrey and David B. Ottaway. "Anti-Saddam Operation Cost CIA $100 Million." *Washington Post,* Sept. 15, 1996, pp. A1, A29–A30.

Sykes, Mark. *The Caliph's Last Heritage: A Short History of the Turkish Empire.* London: Macmillan, 1915.

"Talabani-Barzani Peace Proposals." *Kurdistan Review* (KNC), Dec. 1997, pp. 3, 5–6.

Talabany, Nouri. *Attempts to Change the Ethnic-National Composition of the Kirkuk Region.* London, 1997. Pamphlet in the author's possession.

Thornhill, Teresa. *Sweet Tea with Cardamom: A Journey through Iraqi Kurdistan.* London: Pandora, 1997.

Turkey: Yearbook 1983. Ankara: Prime Ministry Directorate General of Press and Information, 1983.

Weber, Eugene. *Peasants into Frenchmen: The Modernization of Rural France, 1870–1914.* Stanford, Calif.: Stanford University Press, 1976.

Wigram, Edgar T. A. and W. A. Wigram. *The Cradle of Mankind: Life in Eastern Kurdistan.* 2 ed. London: A. & C. Black, Ltd., 1922.

Wilson, Sir Arnold T. *Mesopotamia 1917–1920: A Clash of Loyalties.* Oxford: Oxford University Press, 1931.

Young, Crawford. "Ethnicity and the Colonial and Post-Colonial State in Africa," in Paul Brass, ed., *Ethnic Groups and the State.* London: Croom Helm, 1985, pp. 73–81.

Index

Index

181

Susurluk (Turkish political scandal), 157n13
Syria, x, 72, 76, 78, 84, 86, 109, 111, 113, 114, 115, 119, 122, 123, 127, 132, 163n46; Iraqi opposition and, 33, 34, 38, 46, 47, 48, 50; tripartite conferences with Iran and Turkey, 78, 111, 113

Taha, Sheikh Seyyid of Nehri, 14
Talabani, Hero, 13, 19, 23
Talabani, Jalal, ix–x, 6, 11, 13, 19, 20, 21, 22–32, 68, 69–70, 71, 72, 74, 75, 76, 78, 79, 80, 85, 86, 89, 97, 98, 100, 120, 133, 134, 135, 141n33, 162n38; Barzani, Massoud, relations with, viii, 28, 29, 35, 76–77, 80, 83, 84, 90ff, 101, 107; Iraqi opposition and, 29, 33, 36, 38, 39, 41, 44, 64–65; Turkey, relations with, 28, 30–31, 84, 88, 98, 109, 121, 125; United States, relations with, 20, 30, 31; see also Iraqi Kurds, civil war (1994–98); PUK
Talabani, Jengi (Sheikh), 13, 22
Talabani, Mukarram, 23
Talabanis, 22–23
Talabany, Nouri (Dr.), 13, 48
Tayan, Turhan, 123
Tenet, George, 62
Tikrit, Rafi Dahham al-, 97
Tikriti, Salah Omar Ali, 53
Turkey, 21, 27, 28, 29, 30, 58, 67, 72, 76, 80, 83, 86, 99, 101, 106, 108, 127, 132, 133, 163n46; Iran, confrontations with over northern Iraq, x, 111–26; Iraqi Kurdistan, military incursions into, x, 78, 85, 87, 88, 98, 109, 118–19, 122–26; Islamists-secularists conflict in, 114, 116–18, 121, 123, 126; Israel, relations with, 112–13, 115, 117, 122, 123, 126; KDP, support for, 4, 80, 84, 88, 89, 111, 112, 115, 119, 123–24, 125; Kurds, fear of, 54, 78, 90, 109, 111; PUK, opposition to, 31, 84, 88, 89, 119; tripartite conferences with Iran and Syria, 78, 111, 113
Turkomen (minority in Iraqi Kurdistan), 40, 42, 46, 48, 74, 86, 87, 101, 105, 124, 138n3

Ubaydi, Mahdi al-, 46, 47
Ukraine, 131
Ulum, Muhammad Bahr al-, 37, 39, 44, 46, 47, 48
United Kingdom; see Britain
United Nations, 27, 30, 42, 61, 99, 106, 112, 116, 134, 135
United Nations Security Council Resolution 688 (April 5, 1991), 36, 41, 67, 102, 105, 108, 136
United Nations Security Council Resolution 986 (April 14, 1995), 95, 97, 99, 136; see also UNSC Resolution 1153
United Nations Security Council Resolution 1153 (February 20, 1998), 99, 136; see also UNSC 986
United States, 5, 18, 27, 111, 135; Iran, relations with, 84, 85, 112, 113, 114, 115; Iraq, relations with, 86, 90, 114; Iraqi Kurds, relations with, ix, 20, 29, 80, 81, 82, 84, 85, 87, 88, 100–109, 112, 125, 155n82; Iraqi opposition, relations with, 29, 44, 49, 50, 51–58, 60–68; Kurdish population in, 5, 27; Turkey, relations with, 54, 113, 114

Velayeti, Ali Akbar, 117

Weber, Eugene (scholar), 128–29
Welch, David, 100
Wigram, Edgar T. A. (Wigrams), 1ff, 14, 15; see also Cradle of Mankind
Woolsey, R. James Jr., 60

Yelda, Albert (Arbart), 40
Yezidis, 2, 7
Young, Crawford (scholar), 128, 132

Zaleh (PKK camp), 114
Zangana, Abdul Khaleq, 76
"Zap republic" (PKK), 118
Zaza, 161n76; see also Dimili
Zebari, Hoshyar, ix, 12, 19, 39, 43
Zebaris (Kurdish tribe), 14, 18
Ziad Aghaz (Sheikh), 68